Weight Watchers™

COOKBOOK

WENDY VEALE

TED SMART

First published in Great Britain by Simon and Schuster, 1998
A Viacom Company

This edition produced for The Book People Ltd, Hall Wood Avenue,
Haydock, St Helens WA11 9UL

Simon and Schuster Ltd
West Garden Place
Kendal Street
London W2 2AQ

Design: Jane Humphrey
Typesetting: Stylize Digital Artwork
Photography: Steve Baxter
Styling: Marian Price
Food preparation: Jane Stevenson

A CIP catalogue record is available from the British Library

ISBN 0 68482 144 3

Printed and bound in Italy

Pictured on the front cover: *(clockwise from top left)* Chicken Noodle Soup, page 11;
*Baked Peaches with Ricotta and Almonds, page 170; Grilled Vegetable Kebabs with a
Hot Tomato Glaze, page 77; Roast Rack of Lamb with Flageolet Beans and Rosemary,
page 115; Chocolate Fondue with Fresh Fruit Dippers, page 167; Avocado and Orange
Salad with Tomato and Tarragon Dressing, page 30*
Pictured on the back cover: *Sausage, Red Onion and Apple Casserole, page 104; Black
Forest Sundae, page 182*

Recipe notes:
Egg size is medium, unless otherwise stated.
Vegetables are medium-sized, unless otherwise stated.
It is important to use proper measuring spoons, not cutlery, for spoon measures.
1 tablespoon = 15 ml; 1 teaspoon = 5 ml.
Dried herbs can be substituted for fresh ones, but the flavour may not always be as
good. Halve the fresh-herb quantity stated in the recipe.
Ⓥ shows the recipe is suitable for vegetarians

Contents

Introduction

Obviously whoever said, 'too much of good thing is bad for you' had yet to discover the Weight Watchers Programme *1,2,3 Success Plus™*! And here is the latest Programme cookbook: The *1,2,3 Success Plus Cookbook,* packed with over 300 delicious recipes and something for every occasion.

1,2,3, Success Plus™!

Nothing could be simpler than *1,2,3 Success Plus™*. It allows you to enjoy all your favourite foods and treats. There's no need to look longingly at other people's platefuls; and there's no need to worry when faced with preparing the family's packed lunches or entertaining friends. Instead you can enjoy sharing delicious meals with friends and family.

When you join Weight Watchers, your Leader will tell you how many Points you have to 'spend' each day. Every food has a Points value, from a high-Point mini pork pie to a low-Point Lemon Soufflé Omelette (page 166). Points are allocated to foods according to how many Calories and how much saturated fat they contain. You'll soon find that you are naturally avoiding foods that are high in saturated fat because they use up a lot of your Points!

Your Leader will give you tips on how best to use your Points and suggest ways of adapting your favourite recipes to save Points and lose weight. To help you, we've included in the *1,2,3 Success Plus Cookbook* some delicious, low-Point versions of traditional family favourites, guaranteed to satisfy the liveliest of appetites (try our Shepherd's Pie with Parsnip and Potato Topping, page 114). If you have a special occasion coming up at the weekend, you could keep your mid-week meals low in Points so you can carry over the saved Points to a great weekend. *1,2,3 Success Plus™* fits in with every sort of lifestyle, making it easy to get to your Goal Weight and stay there. You couldn't ask for a more flexible diet.

About this book . . .

Every chapter is packed with hints and tips on cooking techniques that give you tasty, low-fat results. If you are cooking just for yourself or for more than the recipe serves, most recipes can be divided or multiplied easily. Suggestions and variations are given, so you can extend your repertoire; boredom need never set in! Advice on ingredients and their uses will help you plan ahead.

Each recipe is clearly labelled with total Points per dish and Points per serving. Do remember, however, that the Points will only include what is listed as an ingredient of the recipe and not any additional serving suggestion. Many of the recipes and photographs suggest accompaniments, so do calculate the Points for additional salads, vegetables, breads, rice or pasta and so on. As no foods are forbidden on **1,2,3 Success Plus™** you can enjoy all your favourite foods – as long as you count the Points.

Weight Watchers – a name you can trust

With **1,2,3 Success Plus™** you have the reassurance of knowing that your diet has a name behind it which has helped millions of Weight Watchers Members lose weight and maintain that weight loss. So start turning the pages of the *1,2,3 Success Plus Cookbook* and choose the recipes that will get you on the road to looking and feeling great and help you stay at Goal Weight.

For more details about the **1,2,3 Success Plus™** Programme and Weight Watchers Meetings phone 0345 123 000.

Soups

Soup is one of the most satisfying meals: soups are enjoyed by all the family, are easy to make and, with such a vast selection of good, fresh ingredients to hand, the combinations are endless. At the end of this chapter, you will find some tasty accompaniments to serve with soup, as well as a list of breads and other delicious finishing touches.

◆   Vegetable-based soups are low in Points, delicious, and healthy, packed full of vitamins and high in fibre, as long as the ingredients you select are as fresh and flavoursome as possible.

◆   To freeze soup, cool it quickly and then divide it between individual containers or put in one large container, leaving some space for the liquid to expand as it freezes. For best results, freeze for no more than 2–3 months.

◆   Keep a selection of Weight Watchers from Heinz or other low-calorie soups in the cupboard, or at the office.

◆   Invest in a good-quality Thermos flask, with a wide pouring mouth, so you can transport and enjoy hot, nourishing and chunky soups to keep you going on the coldest of days. Soup is a real comforter.

◆   Experiment with different vegetables (check your Points list first) and herbs. The variations are endless, so there is no excuse for boredom!

◆   Light, low-in-Points soups are ideal as a first course when entertaining. Always enjoyable and easy to prepare (in advance, to help ease last-minute panics!) soups suit all occasions.

◆   Add a finishing touch with a swirl of low-fat plain yogurt or some tasty croûtons, to show that ***1,2,3 Success Plus*** is a delicious way to shed unwanted pounds.

◆   Chilled soups are delicious and so refreshing in the heat of summer. Try Cream of Leek and Potato Soup with Shredded Chicken (page 16) or Iced Tomato and Basil Soup (page 21).Don't forget to chill the serving bowls and add a cube or two of ice to each bowl, before ladling in the soup.

Scotch Broth

This is a soup to warm you on the coldest of days and is substantial enough for a light lunch. Serve with crusty white bread.

115 g (4 oz) lean minced lamb
25 g (1 oz) pearl barley
1 large onion, chopped finely
2 carrots, chopped
2 small turnips, chopped
2 leeks, sliced thinly
salt and freshly ground black
*   pepper*
4 tablespoons chopped fresh
*   parsley, to serve*

1. Dry-fry the mince in a large saucepan for 5 minutes, stirring frequently to separate and lightly brown it. Pour on 1.2 litres (2 pints) of cold water. Bring to the boil and then use a large, shallow spoon to remove any scum that forms on the surface.

2. Reduce the heat, add the pearl barley and prepared vegetables and season with salt and pepper. Cover and leave to simmer gently for 50–60 minutes.

3. Adjust the seasoning to taste. Stir in the parsley, ladle into warm soup bowls and serve immediately.

Cook's note

Replace the pearl barley with a 'Broth Mix' of assorted dried pulses. Remember that these may require soaking overnight, and somewhat longer cooking.

Big Boston Baked Bean and Ham Soup

Based on the American hot-pot, this easy variation makes a delicious and filling soup. For a perfect end to your meal, round it off with some fresh fruit or a Melon and Grape Salad with Ginger, Honey and Lime Dressing (see page 34).

1 small onion, chopped finely
420 g can of Weight Watchers
*   from Heinz baked beans*
425 g (15 oz) canned chopped
*   plum tomatoes*
115 g (4 oz) lean cooked ham,
*   diced small*
2 teaspoons brown sugar
2 teaspoons tomato purée
2 teaspoons wine vinegar
salt and freshly ground black
*   pepper*

1. Place the onion and 5 tablespoons of water in a medium-sized saucepan. Bring the water to a gentle simmer and then cover and cook for 5 minutes or until the onion has softened.

2. Add the baked beans, tomatoes and 350 ml (12 fl oz) of cold water. Bring to the boil and then add the ham, sugar, tomato purée and vinegar. Reduce the heat and leave to simmer, uncovered, for 10 minutes.

3. Season to taste, with salt and pepper. Serve in warmed bowls.

Cook's note

A dash of Tabasco or Worcestershire sauce adds a kick to this soup!

Three Bean and Parsley Potage

Points per serving: 2
Total Points per recipe: 8

Serves: 4
Preparation time: 20 minutes
Cooking time: 25 minutes
Freezing: recommended
Calories per serving: 155

1 onion, chopped
2 garlic cloves, crushed
2 teaspoons sunflower or
    olive oil
100 g (3¹/₂ oz) potato, peeled
    and chopped
600 ml (1 pint) vegetable stock
300 ml (¹/₂ pint) skimmed milk
115 g (4 oz) fresh green beans,
    chopped
115 g (4 oz) canned cannellini
    beans, drained and rinsed
115 g (4 oz) canned borlotti or
    red kidney beans, drained
    and rinsed
salt and freshly ground black
    pepper
3 tablespoons chopped fresh
    parsley, to serve

1. Mix the onion and garlic with the oil. Heat a saucepan until hot, then stir in the onion and garlic mix. Cook for 5 minutes, until golden brown.
2. Stir in the potato and cook for a further 2 minutes.
3. Add the stock, milk and green beans. Season to taste, bring to the boil and then cover, reduce the heat and leave to simmer for 15 minutes.
4. Stir in the canned beans and simmer for a further 10 minutes. Mix in the parsley and check the seasoning. Serve hot.

Weight Watchers note

By mixing together the onion, garlic and a very small quantity of oil before frying, you can ensure that the onion is well coated and is less likely to 'catch' in the pan.

Spicy Mexican Bean Soup

Points per serving: 3
Total Points per recipe: 6

Serves: 2
Preparation time: 10 minutes
Cooking time: 15 minutes
Freezing: recommended
Calories per serving: 170

This spicy soup is an ideal, warming dish on a chilly day. Serve with crusty bread.

1 small onion, chopped
1 garlic clove, crushed
1 teaspoon sunflower or olive oil
1 teaspoon ground coriander
¹/₂ teaspoon ground cumin
200 g (7 oz) canned, chopped
    tomatoes
300 ml (¹/₂ pint) vegetable stock
    or water
200 g (7 oz) canned red kidney
    beans, drained and rinsed
¹/₂ teaspoon dried oregano
2 tablespoons low-fat plain
    fromage frais, to serve
salt and freshly ground black
    pepper
paprika

1. Mix together the onion, garlic and oil. Heat a saucepan until hot and then stir in the onion mixture. Cook until lightly browned, for about 5 minutes.
2. Stir in the coriander and cumin and cook for a further minute.
3. Add the tomatoes, stock or water, kidney beans and oregano. Season to taste and bring to the boil.
4. Cover and leave to simmer gently for 15 minutes, stirring occasionally.
5. Ladle into warmed bowls and serve hot, topped with the fromage frais and a dusting of paprika.

Weight Watchers note

As a treat, enjoy a small (50 g/1³/₄ oz) bag of tortilla chips, to accompany the soup (this will add 4 Points to your meal).

Thai-Style Sweetcorn and Chicken Soup

This spicy, Thai-style soup depends on a well-flavoured chicken stock (see page 205). It is a simply flavoured soup, to which you can add peas or chopped red peppers or carrots.

425 ml (³/₄ pint) Basic Chicken
    Stock (see also page 205)
115 g (4 oz) cooked boneless,
    skinless chicken breast,
    shredded
100 g (3¹/₂ oz) sweetcorn kernels
¹/₂ teaspoon chilli paste or 1 small
    fresh green chilli, de-seeded
    and finely chopped
40 g (1¹/₂ oz) thread egg-noodles
salt and coarsely ground black
    pepper

1. Heat the stock in a saucepan. Stir in the chicken, sweetcorn and chilli paste or chilli. Bring to the boil and then reduce the heat and leave to simmer for 5 minutes.
2. Lightly crush the noodles in your hand as you add them to the soup. Simmer for a further 5 minutes, until the noodles are soft. Season with salt and pepper. Ladle into two large bowls and serve at once.

Cook's note

Ready-prepared chilli paste is a real convenience, particularly as chillies require such careful handling to avoid getting their juice in your eyes. A teaspoon of paste is roughly equivalent to 1 fresh chilli, de-seeded.

Provençal Tuna Soup

Despite the ever-increasing availability of delicious new food products, canned tuna fish and tomatoes still remain loyal friends to anyone on a diet! Here's a delicious, sustaining soup to prove the 'point'.

2 teaspoons vegetable oil
1 onion, chopped finely
1 carrot, chopped finely
1 celery stick, sliced finely
1 garlic clove, crushed
1 courgette, sliced thinly
425 g (15 oz) canned chopped
    tomatoes
2 tablespoons tomato purée
850 ml (1¹/₂ pints) vegetable
    stock
2 teaspoons dried herbes
    de Provence or dried
    mixed herbs
425 g (15 oz) canned tuna
    in brine
400 g (14 oz) canned butter
    beans or cannellini beans,
    drained
Tabasco sauce (optional)
salt and freshly ground black
    pepper

1. Heat the oil in a large saucepan and gently sauté the onion, carrot, celery and garlic for 5 minutes or until softened but not browned.
2. Add the courgette, chopped tomatoes, tomato purée, stock and herbs. Cover and leave to simmer for 15 minutes.
3. Add the tuna, with its brine, and beans. Season to taste with a dash of Tabasco, if you like, and salt and pepper. Leave to simmer gently for a further 10 minutes. Serve in warm soup bowls.

Variation

A few chopped green beans or broccoli florets can replace the courgette. Kidney beans work well instead of cannellini beans, too.

Weight Watchers note

If you have enough Points to spare, take a look at the tempting soup accompaniments (pages 25–28). Garlic Croûtes (page 26) will taste delicious with this.

Chicken Noodle Soup

Points per serving: 2½
Total Points per recipe: 10

Serves: 4
Preparation time: 5 minutes
Cooking time: 10 minutes
Freezing: not recommended
Calories per serving: 185

Simplicity itself – but do use a good, fresh stock, now widely available at supermarkets.

1.2 litres (2 pints) Basic Chicken Stock (see page 205)
225 g (8 oz) skinless, boneless chicken breast, sliced finely
100 g (3½ oz) thread egg-noodles
4 spring onions, chopped
1 small red pepper, de-seeded and chopped
2 tablespoons light soy sauce
1 tablespoon chopped fresh coriander
salt and freshly ground black pepper

1. Bring the stock to a steady simmer. Add the chicken and cook for 5 minutes.
2. Add the noodles, spring onions and red pepper and simmer for a further 5 minutes.
3. Stir in the soy sauce and coriander. Season with salt and pepper, to taste. Serve in warm soup bowls.

Variation

If you are more adventurous, experiment by adding grated fresh root ginger, de-seeded fresh red chillies or chopped garlic. Bamboo shoots and bean sprouts can be added, too.

Cook's note

Coriander is bursting with flavour in its stems as well as the leaf, so always chop the whole herb. Scissors are handy for this job.

Spiced Lamb and Chick-pea Soup

Points per serving: 4
Total Points per recipe: 16

Serves: 4
Preparation time: 15 minutes
Cooking time: 30 minutes
Freezing: recommended
Calories per serving: 230

A blend of mystical spices and wholesome ingredients makes this Middle-Eastern soup ideal for a warming lunch or supper. Serve with pitta bread.

175 g (6 oz) lean minced lamb
2 onions, chopped finely
2 garlic cloves, crushed
1 teaspoon ground cumin
1 teaspoon ground coriander
1 teaspoon mild chilli powder
½ teaspoon ground cinnamon
a pinch of crushed dried chillies (optional)
400 g (14 oz) canned chopped tomatoes
4 tablespoons tomato purée
700 ml (1¼ pints) vegetable stock or water
1 tablespoon mint jelly
400 g (14 oz) canned chick-peas, drained
salt and freshly ground black pepper

1. Dry-fry the minced lamb in a large, non-stick pan, until browned. Add the onions and garlic and sauté for 5 minutes, stirring frequently.
2. Reduce the heat, stir in the spices and cook for a minute. Add the canned tomatoes, tomato purée and stock or water. Cover and leave to simmer for 20 minutes.
3. Stir in the mint jelly, add the chick-peas and leave to simmer, uncovered, for a further 10 minutes.
4. Season with salt and pepper. Serve piping hot, in warm soup bowls.

Cook's note

You can substitute 2 teaspoons of sugar and 1 teaspoon of dried mint for the mint jelly, without increasing the Points.

Smoked Cod Bisque

Points per serving: 3
Total Points per recipe: 12
Serves: 4
Preparation time: 10 minutes
Cooking time: 30 minutes
Freezing: recommended
Calories per serving: 270

A nutritious and economical dish for the whole family but special enough for entertaining, too.

225 g (8 oz) potato, cubed
1 small onion, chopped
1 small carrot, chopped
1 small turnip, chopped
    (optional)
850 ml (1½ pints) skimmed
    milk
a pinch of grated nutmeg
450 g (1 lb) smoked cod or
    haddock fillet
50 g (1¾ oz) frozen peas
115 g (4 oz) peeled, cooked
    prawns, chopped
1 tablespoon chopped fresh
    parsley
salt and freshly ground black
    pepper

1. Place the potato, onion, carrot, turnip, if using, and milk in a saucepan, with the nutmeg. Cover, bring to a simmer and cook for 15 minutes or until the vegetables are just tender.
2. Lay the fish on top of the vegetables and continue to simmer, covered, for about 5 minutes or until the fish is opaque and flakes easily.
3. Remove the fish, discarding any skin and bones, and transfer half the fish, with the vegetables and milk, to a liquidiser or food processor. Blend for 20 seconds or until smooth.
4. Pour the soup back into the saucepan, add the peas, peeled prawns and parsley and simmer for 5 minutes. Add the remaining fish, broken into flakes and heat through for a further minute. Season to taste with salt and pepper and ladle into warm bowls.

Variation

For a splash of luxury, stir in 4 tablespoons of half-fat cream just before serving; add ½ Point per serving.

Cook's note

If you choose to use unsmoked white fish, add a couple of strands of saffron at step 1. The delicate spice will enhance the bisque in both flavour and colour.

Irish Potato, Cabbage and Bacon Soup

Points per serving: 3
Total Points per recipe: 12
Serves: 4
Preparation time: 20 minutes
Cooking time: 20 minutes
Freezing: recommended
Calories per serving: 250

4 rashers of rindless smoked
    streaky bacon, chopped
2 leeks, sliced thinly
1 carrot, chopped
350 g (12 oz) potatoes, peeled
    and cubed
175 g (6 oz) green cabbage,
    cored and shredded
2 tablespoons chopped fresh
    parsley or chives
850 ml (1½ pints) vegetable
    stock
150 ml (¼ pint) skimmed milk
salt and freshly ground black
    pepper

1. Gently dry-fry the bacon in a non-stick pan until the fat begins to run. Add the leeks and carrot, cover and gently cook for a further 5 minutes, until softened.
2. Add the potatoes, cabbage, half the parsley or chives and stock. Bring to the boil, cover and reduce the heat. Simmer gently for 20 minutes, or until the vegetables are tender.
3. Add the milk and gently reheat. Season to taste with salt and pepper.
4. Serve piping hot in warm soup bowls, sprinkled with the remaining parsley or chives.

Variations

Omit the bacon, which reduces the Points to 1 per serving.

Add ½ teaspoon of caraway seeds for extra flavour.

🅥 if you omit bacon (see variation)

Hungarian Goulash Soup

Serves: 4
Preparation time: 10 minutes
Cooking time: 25 minutes
Freezing: recommended
Calories per serving: 195

Minced pork or turkey will be equally as delicious as the traditional beef in this spicy, rich soup. It is particularly good garnished with a swirl of low-fat plain yogurt, but watch those Points!

175 g (6 oz) extra-lean minced beef
2 onions, chopped finely
1 celery stick, chopped
1 small red or green pepper, de-seeded and chopped
2 teaspoons paprika
1 teaspoon ground cumin
690 g jar of chunky passata
600 ml (1 pint) vegetable stock
1 teaspoon sugar
40 g (1½ oz) small pasta shapes for soup e.g. farfalle or shells
1 tablespoon chopped fresh parsley
salt and freshly ground black pepper

1. Dry-fry the minced beef in a large non-stick pan, until browned. Add the onions, celery and pepper and sauté for 5 minutes, stirring frequently.
2. Reduce the heat, mix in the paprika and cumin and cook for a minute. Add the passata, stock, sugar and pasta. Cover and leave to simmer for 25 minutes. Stir occasionally.
3. Stir in the chopped parsley and season to taste with salt and pepper. Serve, piping hot, ladled into warm soup bowls.

Variation
Just before serving, swirl a tablespoon of low-fat plain yogurt into each bowl, which doesn't add any Points.

Cook's note
If you do not have tiny pasta shapes in your storecupboard, use spaghetti, broken into short lengths.

Look out for chunky or sieved passata – a thick tomato sauce now available in most supermarkets.

Tomato and Lentil Soup

Serves: 4
Preparation time: 5 minutes
Cooking time: 30 minutes
Freezing: recommended
Calories per serving: 170

Not only are lentils packed with goodness; the Romans considered them conducive to a calm temperament. A good reason to keep a pack handy!

1 tablespoon vegetable oil
2 onions, chopped finely
2 celery sticks, sliced
1 carrot, chopped finely
1 garlic clove, crushed
100 g (3½ oz) split red lentils, washed and drained
800 g (1 lb 12 oz) canned chopped tomatoes
1 tablespoon tomato purée
700 ml (1¼ pints) vegetable or chicken stock
½ teaspoon dried thyme or ground cumin
salt and freshly ground black pepper

1. Heat the oil in a large saucepan, stir in the onions, celery, carrot and garlic and sauté gently for 5 minutes.
2. Add the lentils, canned tomatoes, tomato purée, stock and thyme or cumin. Bring to the boil, cover and leave to simmer gently for 25–30 minutes.
3. Season to taste with salt and pepper and serve piping hot, in warm soup bowls.

Variation
Replace the lentils with 50 g (1¾ oz) of brown rice.

Weight Watchers note
Turkey rashers (see page 27) would be delicious crumbled over the soup. Allow ½ Point for each rasher.

Ⓥ if using vegetable stock

Cream of Leek and Potato Soup with Shredded Chicken

Points per serving: 2
Total Points per recipe: 8

Serves: 4
Preparation time: 10 minutes
Cooking time: 20 minutes
Freezing: recommended
Calories per serving: 135

Whilst this is a warming soup for the winter months, you can also serve it on a balmy hot day really well chilled, as 'Vichyssoise'.

2 teaspoons half-fat butter or low-fat spread
2 leeks, sliced finely
2 × 100 g (3¹/₂ oz) potatoes, peeled and cubed
1 onion, chopped finely
¹/₄ teaspoon dried rosemary or thyme
600 ml (1 pint) boiling vegetable stock or water
175 g (6 oz) boneless, skinless chicken breast
300 ml (¹/₂ pint) skimmed milk
salt and freshly ground black pepper
2 teaspoons snipped fresh chives, to garnish

1. Melt the butter or spread in a large saucepan and gently sauté the leeks, potatoes and onion for 10 minutes or until softened.
2. Add the herbs, stock or water and chicken breast. Cover and leave to simmer for 15 minutes.
3. Remove the chicken and wrap it in foil. Transfer the soup to a liquidiser or food processor and blend for about 20 seconds, or until smooth. Return to the saucepan, stir in the milk and gently heat through, until piping hot. Season to taste, with salt and pepper.
4. Finely shred the chicken and divide between four warm soup bowls. Ladle the soup over the chicken and sprinkle with the chives.

Variation

225 g (8 oz) of celeriac would be a tasty alternative to potatoes and would reduce your Points per serving to 1¹/₂.

Spicy Fish Soup with Potato

Points per serving: 4
Total Points per recipe: 16

Serves: 4
Preparation time: 15 minutes
Cooking time: 20 minutes
Freezing: recommended
Calories per serving: 280

A substantial soup, similar to an American chowder but with the heat of the Deep South!

4 × 125 g (4¹/₂ oz) cod steaks
1 tablespoon lemon juice
4 teaspoons vegetable oil
2 onions, chopped finely
1 carrot, chopped
1 garlic clove, crushed
1 red or yellow pepper, de-seeded and sliced finely
1 fresh red or green chilli, de-seeded and chopped finely
450 g (1 lb) baby new potatoes, sliced thinly
¹/₂ teaspoon dried oregano
1.2 litres (2 pints) fish or vegetable stock
a few saffron strands or a pinch of ground turmeric
salt and freshly ground black pepper

1. Season the cod steaks with salt and pepper and sprinkle over the lemon juice.
2. Meanwhile, heat the vegetable oil in a large saucepan and gently cook the onions, carrot, garlic, red or yellow pepper and chilli for 5 minutes, or until softened.
3. Lay the cod steaks on top, add the potatoes, oregano, stock and saffron or turmeric. Cover, and bring to a gentle simmer; cook for 20 minutes or until the potatoes are tender.
4. Check the seasoning. Serve in large, warm bowls.

Variation

Replace the fresh chilli with ¹/₂ teaspoon dried chilli flakes or a teaspoon of chilli paste.

Cook's note

Wash your hands thoroughly after handling fresh chillies, to help prevent the chilli juice from stinging your eyes.

Creamy Parsnip and Orange Soup

Points per serving: 2½
Total Points per recipe: 10
Serves: 4
Preparation time: 10 minutes
Cooking time: 30 minutes
Freezing: recommended
Calories per serving: 130

2 teaspoons vegetable oil

1 onion, chopped finely

450 g (1 lb) parsnips, chopped

700 ml (1¼ pints) vegetable stock

½ teaspoon ground coriander

½ teaspoon sugar

150 ml (¼ pint) freshly squeezed orange juice

salt and freshly ground black pepper

4 tablespoons half-fat crème fraîche or half-fat cream, to serve

1 tablespoon chopped fresh coriander or parsley, to garnish

1. Heat the vegetable oil in a large non-stick saucepan, add the onion and parsnips, cover and cook gently for 5 minutes, or until softened but not browned.

2. Add the stock, ground coriander and sugar. Bring to the boil and then reduce the heat and leave to simmer, covered, for 20 minutes or until the parsnips are cooked.

3. Transfer the soup to a liquidiser or food processor and blend for 20 seconds or until smooth. Add the orange juice.

4. Return to the saucepan and reheat gently for 3–4 minutes. Season to taste with salt and pepper.

5. Divide between four warmed soup bowls. Swirl a tablespoon of cream into each bowl and garnish with the chopped herbs. Serve immediately.

Variation

Replace the parsnips with carrots. This will reduce your Points per serving to 1½.

Cook's note

One fresh orange will yield about 4 tablespoons (60 ml) of orange juice. It's easier to use the chilled, freshly squeezed orange juice on sale in supermarkets, though!

Mediterranean Roasted Vegetable Soup

Points per serving: ½
Total Points per recipe: 2
Serves: 4
Preparation time: 10 minutes
Cooking time: 30 minutes
Freezing: not recommended
Calories per serving: 75

This soup captures the rich flavour and colours of the Mediterranean. Serve it with crusty bread.

1 large carrot, halved lengthways

1 onion, sliced thickly

1 green pepper, de-seeded and quartered

1 red pepper, de-seeded and quartered

2 teaspoons sunflower or olive oil

4 tablespoons dry white wine

4 medium-size tomatoes, skinned and chopped

700 ml (1¼ pints) vegetable stock

½ teaspoon dried mixed herbs

salt and freshly ground black pepper

fresh parsley sprigs, to garnish

1. Preheat the oven to Gas Mark 7/220°C/425°F.

2. Pop the vegetables into a plastic food bag, with the oil, and shake well to coat. Tip on to a baking tray and roast for 10–15 minutes, turning the vegetables once or twice.

3. Remove the vegetables, peel any blackened skin from the peppers and then chop all the vegetables quite finely.

4. Place in a saucepan, with the wine and cook, uncovered, until all the wine evaporates.

5. Add the tomatoes, stock and herbs. Season well and bring to the boil. Then reduce the heat and leave to simmer for 10 minutes.

6. Check the seasoning, ladle into hot serving bowls and garnish with sprigs of parsley.

Cook's note

Roasting or grilling vegetables really intensifies their flavour and aids the digestive system, too!

Minty Lettuce and Spring Onion Soup

Points per serving: ½
Total Points per recipe: 2
Serves: 4
Preparation time: 5 minutes
Cooking time: 30 minutes
Freezing: recommended
Calories per serving: 50

A refreshing soup that is ideal for dealing with the glut of home-grown lettuces that seems to crop up every summer! Do use fresh mint in this instance.

1 small onion, chopped
600 ml (1 pint) chicken or
*   vegetable stock*
4 spring onions, chopped
450 g (1 lb) green lettuce leaves,
*   e.g. iceberg or Webb's,*
*   chopped roughly*
2 teaspoons cornflour
150 ml (¼ pint) semi-skimmed
*   milk*
1–2 teaspoons lemon juice
3 tablespoons chopped fresh
*   mint*
salt and freshly ground black
*   pepper*
4 fresh mint sprigs, to garnish

1. Put the onion and stock in a large saucepan. Cover and bring to the boil, reduce the heat and simmer for 10 minutes.
2. Add the spring onions and lettuce. Cover and leave to simmer for 15 minutes.
3. Transfer to a liquidiser or food processor and blend until smooth. Return to the saucepan.
4. Blend the cornflour with the milk and stir into the soup. Bring back to the boil, stirring, until slightly thickened.
5. Season to taste, with salt and pepper and a little lemon juice and stir in the chopped mint. Serve in four warmed bowls, garnishing each with a sprig of mint.

Variation
Swirl a tablespoon of half-fat cream or low-fat plain yogurt into each portion just before serving. A tablespoon of half cream will add ½ Point per serving.

Cook's note
A food processor makes light work of shredding, chopping and puréeing – you could consider investing in one to save time.

Cream of Celeriac, Potato and Chive Soup

Points per serving: ½
Total Points per recipe: 2
Serves: 4
Preparation time: 10 minutes
Cooking time: 30 minutes
Freezing: recommended
Calories per serving: 75

If you enjoy celery and have not yet discovered celeriac, then try this thick soup. Celeriac has the flavour of celery but the texture of potato – you can mash it, purée it or even roast it!

225 g (8 oz) celeriac, peeled and
*   cut into 2.5 cm (1-inch)*
*   cubes*
150 g (5½ oz) potato, peeled
*   and cut into 2.5 cm*
*   (1-inch) cubes*
1 onion, chopped
1 bay leaf
300 ml (½ pint) hot vegetable
*   stock*
300 ml (½ pint) skimmed milk
2 tablespoons snipped fresh
*   chives*
salt and freshly ground black
*   pepper*
grated nutmeg, to garnish

1. Put the celeriac, potato, onion, bay leaf and stock in a large saucepan. Cover, bring to the boil and then reduce the heat and leave to simmer for 15–20 minutes or until the vegetables are tender.
2. Remove the bay leaf. Transfer the soup to a liquidiser or food processor and blend until smooth. Return to the saucepan.
3. Stir in the milk and chives. Season well with nutmeg, salt and pepper to taste. Gently reheat the soup.
4. Serve in four warm soup bowls, garnished with an extra sprinkling of freshly grated nutmeg.

Variation
For a spicy soup, add a teaspoon of curry paste at step 1.

Weight Watchers note
This would taste delicious with a garnish of crisp turkey rashers (see page 27) but don't forget to calculate those Points!

Cook's note
Celeriac tends to discolour, so try to eat this soup on the same day that you make it. A dash of lemon juice will help maintain the colour but compromises a little on the flavour.

V if using vegetable stock

V

Spicy Tomato Soup

> **Points per serving: ¹/₂**
> **Total Points per recipe: 2**
>
> Serves: 4
> Preparation time: 10 minutes
> Cooking time: 25 minutes
> Freezing: recommended
> Calories per serving: 50

A real tomato soup and not a can in sight! This fragrant soup uses fresh tomatoes, flavoured with 'the Queen of Spices': cardamom.

*450 g (1 lb) fresh tomatoes,
    skinned and chopped*
1 large onion, chopped finely
2 teaspoons plain flour
1 tablespoon tomato purée
5 green cardamoms
*2.5 cm (1-inch) piece of
    cinnamon stick or
    ¹/₄ teaspoon ground
    cinnamon*
*salt and freshly ground black
    pepper*
*4 tablespoons low-fat plain
    Bio-yogurt, to garnish*
*1 spring onion, chopped finely,
    to garnish*

1. Place the tomatoes, onion and 1.2 litres (2 pints) of water in a large saucepan. Bring to the boil, reduce the heat and simmer, uncovered, for 10 minutes.
2. Blend the flour with the tomato purée and 2 tablespoons of water, to a smooth paste. Whisk into the tomato mixture.
3. Lightly crush the cardamom pods and the cinnamon stick (this releases the aromatic oils). Add to the soup. Season with a little salt and pepper. Simmer, uncovered, for a further 15 minutes.
4. Strain the soup though a metal sieve, pressing the mixture with the back of a wooden spoon.
5. Return the soup to the saucepan and reheat. Pour into warm soup bowls and swirl a tablespoon of yogurt and some spring onion into each portion.

Cook's note

To use cardamom, either crush the pod lightly and discard after cooking, or open the pod and remove the seeds, which can then be used whole (or ground, if specified).

French Onion Soup with Cheese Croûtes

> **Points per serving: 2**
> **Total Points per recipe: 8**
>
> Serves: 4
> Preparation time: 15 minutes
> Cooking time: 50 minutes
> Freezing: recommended
> Calories per serving: 175

The secret behind a dark French onion soup is simply slow cooking, which allows the onions to caramelise and the colour to develop. Do not be tempted to cut corners!

25 g (1 oz) half-fat butter
*450 g (1 lb) onions, sliced
    thinly*
1 tablespoon plain flour
284 ml tub of fresh beef stock
*4 × 2.5 cm (1-inch) slices of
    French bread*
*25 g (1 oz) Edam cheese, grated
    finely*

1. Melt the butter in a large saucepan. Add the onions, cover and cook over a low heat for 15 minutes or until the onions are very soft.
2. Remove the lid and continue to cook them gently for a further 15 minutes or until they turn golden brown.
3. Sprinkle in the flour and cook, stirring for 1 minute.
4. Make the stock up to 600 ml (1 pint), with boiling water. Gradually blend this into the onions. Bring to the boil, cover, reduce the heat and leave to simmer for 20 minutes.
5. Meanwhile, preheat the grill to its highest setting. Toast the French bread slices on both sides, sprinkle the cheese over each slice and pop back under the grill for 2 minutes or until the cheese has melted.
6. Place a toasted cheese slice in each warm soup bowl. Ladle the soup over and serve immediately.

Cook's note

If you cannot buy fresh chilled stock or make your own, resort to a stock cube!

Ⓥ if using vegetable stock and vegetarian cheese

Ⓥ

Indonesian Hot and Sour Soup

Points per serving: 1
Total Points per recipe: 4

Serves: 4
Preparation time: 20 minutes
Cooking time: 20 minutes
Freezing: not recommended
Calories per serving: 65

There is no substitute for the lively flavours of the fresh ingredients in this recipe; it's a stunning soup to tantalise the taste buds!

1 lemon-grass stalk
1 fresh red chilli, sliced (with seeds)
2 garlic cloves, sliced thinly
2.5 cm (1-inch) piece of fresh root ginger, sliced thinly
a tied bundle of fresh coriander
1.2 litres (2 pints) Basic Chicken Stock (see page 205)
125 g (4¹/₂ oz) boneless, skinless chicken breast fillet, sliced finely
50 g (1³/₄ oz) baby button mushrooms, sliced finely
50 g (1³/₄ oz) canned water chestnuts, drained and sliced
2 tablespoons lime juice
2 tablespoons light soy sauce
4 spring onions, shredded, to garnish
¹/₂ small red pepper, de-seeded and shredded, to garnish

1. Crush the lemon grass, using a rolling pin. Place in a large saucepan, with the chilli, garlic, ginger, coriander and stock. Cover and bring to the boil.
2. Reduce the heat, add the chicken and mushrooms and simmer, covered, for 15 minutes.
3. Add the water chestnuts, lime juice and soy sauce. Discard the coriander bundle. Taste: if extra salt is required, add a dash of soy sauce. Heat for a further 5 minutes.
4. Divide the soup between hot bowls and garnish with the spring onions and red pepper shreds.

Variation

Replace the chicken stock and chicken with fish stock and chopped cooked prawns, adding the prawns at step 3.

Cook's note

Look out for the convenient fresh selection packs of Thai herbs and spices, which generally include lemon grass, chillies and coriander.

Cream of Cauliflower and Broccoli Soup

Points per serving: ¹/₂
Total Points per recipe: 2

Serves: 4
Preparation and cooking time:
25 minutes
Freezing: not recommended
Calories per serving: 70

A perfect soup to use up florets of cauliflower, broccoli or even the odd brussels sprout! It's light and delicious – with variations to transform it into a main-meal soup.

350 g (12 oz) cauliflower and broccoli florets, chopped
1 small onion, chopped
1 teaspoon chopped fresh thyme
600 ml (1 pint) vegetable stock
2 teaspoons cornflour
300 ml (¹/₂ pint) skimmed milk
a pinch of freshly grated nutmeg
2 tablespoons half-fat crème fraîche
salt and freshly ground black pepper

1. Gently simmer the cauliflower, broccoli, onion, thyme and stock, in a covered saucepan, for 15 minutes or until tender.
2. Blend the cornflour to a smooth paste with 2–3 tablespoons of the milk and the nutmeg and add the paste, with the remaining milk. Bring to a gentle boil, stirring constantly, until the soup thickens slightly.
3. Transfer the soup to a liquidiser or food processor and blend with the crème fraîche until smooth.
4. Season to taste. Return the soup to the saucepan and reheat gently for 3–4 minutes. Serve in warm soup bowls.

Variation

Accompany with Creamy Cheese and Herb Croûtons (see page 26); add 1¹/₂ Points per serving. For a more substantial, chunky soup, add 50 g (1³/₄ oz) of soup pasta at step 1. Do not blend at step 3. Add ¹/₂ Point per serving.

For a cauliflower and broccoli cheese soup, add 100 g (3¹/₂ oz) grated half-fat Cheddar cheese at step 4. Add 1¹/₂ Points per serving.

Mushroom Soup with Dijon Mustard

2 teaspoons half-fat butter or
    low-fat spread
1 small onion, chopped
1 garlic clove, crushed
1 tablespoon chopped fresh
    thyme or 1 teaspoon dried
    thyme
450 g (1 lb) brown (chestnut)
    or open-cap mushrooms,
    chopped
850 ml (1½ pints) vegetable
    stock
1 tablespoon Dijon mustard
4 tablespoons half-fat crème
    fraîche
2 tablespoons dry sherry
1 tablespoon cornflour
salt and freshly ground black
    pepper

1. Melt the butter or spread in a large saucepan. Add the onion, garlic and thyme and sauté gently for 5 minutes or until soft but not browned.
2. Add the mushrooms and stir-fry for 2–3 minutes. Add the stock, bring to the boil, then reduce the heat, cover and leave to simmer for 20 minutes.
3. Transfer the soup to a liquidiser or food processor and blend with the mustard and crème fraîche for 30 seconds, or until very smooth.
4. Return the soup to the saucepan. Blend the sherry and cornflour together and add to the soup, stirring. Heat gently until the soup thickens. Season to taste with salt and pepper. Serve piping hot, in warmed soup bowls.

Cook's note
Look out for brown (chestnut) mushrooms, which are more flavoursome than button or open-cap mushrooms and now widely available at supermarkets.

   Mustard tends to lose its heat once re-heated so, if you freeze this recipe, you may need to add a little extra mustard before serving.

Iced Tomato and Basil Soup

No need to get hot and bothered over this soup! There is no cooking required – just allow plenty of time to chill this delicious summer starter thoroughly.

450 g (1 lb) ripe tomatoes
1 small onion or shallot
1 tablespoon tomato purée
1 tablespoon chopped fresh
    basil, plus extra to garnish
600 ml (1 pint) vegetable stock
½ teaspoon white sugar
salt and freshly ground black
    pepper

1. Roughly chop the tomatoes and onion or shallot. Place in a liquidiser or food processor, with the tomato purée, basil, stock and sugar. Blend for about 30 seconds, until smooth. Sieve.
2. Season with salt and freshly ground pepper. Chill for at least 2 hours.
3. Serve in chilled soup bowls or glass dishes, garnished with extra chopped basil.

Variation
Just before serving, swirl a tablespoon of half-fat crème fraîche into each portion, adding ½ Point per serving.

Cook's note
When seasonal, home-grown tomatoes are not in abundance, look out, instead, for the varieties sold on their vine. They are bursting with flavour and have a brilliant red colour too.

French Onion Soup with Cheese Croûtes *(page 19)*
Curried Apple and Leek Soup *(opposite)*

Creamy Cheese, Watercress and Mushroom Soup

Points per serving: 1
Total Points per recipe: 4
Serves: 4
Preparation time: 20 minutes
Cooking time: 20 minutes
Freezing: recommended, before adding cream cheese
Calories per serving: 95

2 onions, chopped finely
1 garlic clove, crushed
350 g (12 oz) button
mushrooms, wiped and
sliced
600 ml (1 pint) vegetable stock
a bunch or bag of fresh
watercress, trimmed
300 ml (1/2 pint) skimmed milk
a pinch of grated nutmeg
125 g (41/2 oz) low-fat soft
cheese
salt and freshly ground black
pepper

1. Gently simmer the onions, garlic, mushrooms and stock together in a covered pan for 20 minutes. At this stage, reserve a few slices of mushroom for garnish.
2. Add the watercress, milk and a good pinch of nutmeg, cover and simmer for a further 5 minutes.
3. Transfer to a liquidiser or food processor and blend with the cream cheese, until smooth. Season to taste with salt and pepper.
4. Return the soup to the saucepan and reheat gently for 3–4 minutes. It is very important that you do no allow it to boil.
5. Serve in warmed soup bowls, garnished with the reserved mushroom slices.

Variation
Replace the watercress with spinach.
If you wish, omit the low-fat soft cheese and deduct 1/2 Point per serving.

Weight Watchers note
Remember that many low-fat dairy products (e.g. yogurt or soft cheese) will curdle if over-heated, so take care to reheat the soup gently.

Curried Apple and Leek Soup

Points per serving: 1
Total Points per recipe: 4
Serves: 4
Preparation time: 10 minutes
Cooking time: 35 minutes
Freezing: recommended
Calories per serving: 105

2 teaspoons sunflower spread
or margarine
1–2 teaspoons mild curry
powder, to taste
3 leeks, chopped
100 g (31/2 oz) potato, cubed
2 tart apples, e.g. Granny
Smiths, peeled, cored and
chopped
700 ml (11/4 pints) vegetable
stock
4 tablespoons low-fat plain
yogurt
salt and freshly ground black
pepper
snipped fresh chives or paprika,
to garnish (optional)

1. Melt the margarine in a large saucepan. Add the curry powder and cook for a minute. Add the leeks, potato and apples and sauté gently for 5 minutes.
2. Add the stock, cover and leave to simmer for 20 minutes.
3. Transfer the soup to a food processor or liquidiser and blend for 20 seconds or until very smooth.
4. Return to the saucepan, season to taste, reheat and ladle into warmed soup bowls. Swirl a tablespoon of plain yogurt into each bowl and garnish with a sprinkling of chives or paprika.

Cook's note
This soup is also delicious served chilled.

23

Ⓥ if using vegetarian soft cheese

Ⓥ if using vegetarian margarine

Golden Vegetable Soup

A vibrant purée of root vegetables, with the warmth of spices, makes for a welcoming, velvety winter soup.

350 g (12 oz) carrots, chopped
225 g (8 oz) swede, chopped
1 small onion, chopped
150 g (5½ oz) parsnip or
    potato, chopped
1 litre (1¾ pints) vegetable
    stock
1 teaspoon ground cumin
1 teaspoon ground coriander
6 tablespoons low-fat plain
    yogurt
salt and freshly ground black
    pepper
chopped fresh parsley or
    coriander, to garnish

1. Place the carrots, swede, onion and parsnip or potato in a large saucepan, with the stock. Bring to the boil, cover, reduce the heat to a simmer and cook for 15–20 minutes or until the vegetables are tender.
2. Transfer the soup to a liquidiser or food processor and blend to a smooth purée. Return to the saucepan.
3. Stir in the cumin and coriander and season to taste, with salt and pepper. Reheat gently, for 3–4 minutes.
4. Just before ladling into warmed soup bowls, stir in the plain yogurt. Garnish with fresh herbs.

Variation

Pumpkin is a delicious, golden vegetable which will work extremely well in place of the carrots or swede.

Replace the spices with a teaspoon of grated orange zest and 2 tablespoons of orange juice.

Cook's note

See page 205 for a quick, home-made vegetable stock; it's not quite as convenient as a handy stock cube but far superior in taste.

Farmhouse Vegetable Soup

A real comforter and an ideal recipe for using up odd vegetables, this is delicious served with Creamy Cheese and Herb Croûtons (see page 26).

2 leeks, sliced finely
2 carrots, grated coarsely
1 large parsnip, grated coarsely
50 g (1¾ oz) pearl barley
425 g (15 oz) canned chopped
    tomatoes
1 teaspoon dried mixed herbs
1.2 litres (2 pints) vegetable
    stock
salt and freshly ground pepper

1. Place all the ingredients in a large saucepan.
2. Bring to the boil, reduce the heat, cover and leave to simmer gently for 40 minutes.
3. Season to taste with salt and pepper. Serve in warm soup bowls.

Variation

Chop and change the choice of vegetables – try grated celeriac, shredded cabbage or finely chopped broccoli; and replace the pearl barley with split red lentils.

Carrot and Apple Soup

<table>
<tr><td>Points per serving: 1</td></tr>
<tr><td>Total Points per recipe: 4</td></tr>
</table>

Serves: 4

Preparation time: 15 minutes

Cooking time: 25 minutes

Freezing: recommended

Calories per serving: 75

So many fruit and vegetables make surprise appearances together – and here's another good partnership. It's bursting with health and vitality!

2 teaspoons vegetable oil
1 onion, chopped finely
350 g (12 oz) carrots, chopped
225 g (8 oz) Bramley apple,
    peeled, cored and chopped
1/2 teaspoon ground ginger
    (optional)
850 ml (1 1/2 pints) water or
    vegetable stock
2 teaspoons cornflour
salt and freshly ground black
    pepper

1. Heat the oil in a large saucepan. Add the onion, carrots, apple and ginger. Cover and cook gently, shaking the pan occasionally, for 10 minutes.
2. Blend a couple of tablespoons of stock with the cornflour. Add the remaining stock to the pan, cover and simmer for a further 15 minutes. Stir in the cornflour and cook for 5 minutes or until the soup thickens slightly. Transfer the soup to a liquidiser or food processor and blend until smooth.

3. Return to the saucepan. Season to taste, with salt and pepper. Reheat gently for 3–4 minutes.
4. Serve in warm soup bowls.

Variation

For a spicy soup, add a teaspoon of mild curry powder, or a teaspoon of cumin or coriander seeds at step 1.

Cook's note

This is delicious served chilled, too. Swirl a tablespoon of low-fat plain Bio-yogurt into each portion before serving, which doesn't add any Points.

Weight Watchers note

Non-stick saucepans can help reduce the amount of fat you need to use; some fat is needed to prevent food from sticking. So, always read through the method carefully and decide whether there are Points to be saved by reducing the fat content. Spray oils are another great way to reduce Points.

Accompaniments for Soups

Here's a selection of breads and garnishes to enjoy with soup.

Breads	Points	Calories
2 extra-thin crispbreads	1/2	50
slice of low-calorie bread	1/2	30
medium-size slice of bread, toasted and cut into croûtons	1	40
6 small, thin Melba toasts	1	90
mini pitta	1	80
3 rice cakes	1	90
1/2 medium-size naan bread	4	185
medium-size roll, soft or crusty	2	110
15 cm (6-inch) slice of French stick	4 1/2	480
5 cm (2-inch) slice of garlic bread	3 1/2	145
1 heaped tablespoon croûtons	1/2	85
Creams – per tablespoon		
low-fat plain fromage frais	1	7
single cream	1	25
double cream or crème fraîche	2	55
half-fat cream or half-fat crème fraîche	1/2	25
Yogurt – per 2 tablespoons		
low-fat Bio	1/2	7
Greek-style	1	25
low-fat plain	1/2	55
Quark (rounded tablespoon)	1/2	25
Miscellaneous		
rasher of grilled streaky bacon, crumbled	2	115
1 teaspoon of parmesan cheese	1/2	10
5 cashew nuts or hazelnuts, chopped and toasted	1/2	50
1 tablespoon of pumpkin, sunflower or sesame seeds	1	80
1 teaspoon of desiccated coconut	1	10
1 anchovy-stuffed olive, sliced	1/2	5

'Point-Free' garnishes include

grated carrot

shredded celery, spring onion or cucumber

herbs, chopped fresh or fresh sprigs

julienne strips of lemon zest

chopped red, yellow or green pepper

a sprinkling of spices e.g. paprika or curry powder

mustard and cress

sliced gherkins

Garlic Croûtes

4 × 1 cm (½-inch) slices of
    French bread
1 small garlic clove, crushed
2 teaspoons half-fat butter or
    low-fat spread

1. Toast the bread lightly on
both sides. Meanwhile, mix
together the garlic and the
butter or spread.
2. Divide the garlic 'butter'
evenly between the four toasted
slices. Serve immediately,
floating two slices on each
serving of soup.

Cook's note
Look out for ready-prepared
garlic in tubes or small jars.
*Garlic croûtes are ideal to
accompany the following soups:
Provençal Tuna Soup (page 10),
Iced Tomato and Basil Soup
(page 21), Mediterranean
Roasted Vegetable Soup (page
17), Cream of Celeriac, Potato
and Chive Soup (page 18),
Creamy Cheese, Watercress and
Mushroom Soup (page 23),
Smoked Cod Bisque (page 12),
Mushroom Soup with Dijon
Mustard (page 21)*

Ⓥ

Creamy Cheese & Herb Croûtons

1 thick slice of wholemeal or
    brown bread
50 g (1¾ oz) low-fat soft cheese
1 teaspoon chopped fresh chives
    or parsley

1. Toast the bread lightly on
both sides.
2. Cream together the soft
cheese and chives or parsley.
Evenly spread over the toast.
3. Cut the toast into about 1 cm
(½-inch) cubes. Divide between
bowls of soup.

Cook's note
Look out for the flavoured soft
cheeses, e.g. garlic or chives,
for added variety.
*These croûtons are ideal to
accompany: Cream of
Cauliflower and Broccoli Soup
(page 20), Tomato and Lentil
Soup (page 13), Iced Tomato
and Basil Soup (page 21),
Mediterranean Roasted Vegetable
Soup (page 17), Golden
Vegetable Soup (page 24),
French Onion Soup (page 19),
Carrot and Apple Soup (page
25), Curried Apple and Leek
Soup (page 23)*
Ⓥ if using vegetarian soft
cheese

Potato Cake Croûtons

1 small, ready-made potato cake
1 teaspoon whole-grain mustard
    or tomato purée
a pinch of dried parsley or chive
    flakes (or 1 teaspoon chopped
    fresh parsley or chives)

1. Lightly toast the potato cake
on both sides. Spread evenly
with a thin coating of mustard
or tomato purée. Sprinkle on
the herbs and press them on
to the surface, with a knife.
2. Cut into small squares or very
fine strips and serve with soup.

Cook's note
Potato cakes are usually bought
in packs of 6; they freeze well.
*These are ideal to accompany:
Scotch Broth (page 8), Tomato
and Lentil Soup (page 13),
Farmhouse Vegetable Soup
(page 24), Smoked Cod Bisque
(page 12), Spicy Tomato Soup
(page 19), Curried Apple and
Leek Soup (page 23), Carrot
and Apple Soup (page 25),
French Onion Soup (page 19),
Creamy Cheese, Watercress and
Mushroom Soup (page 23)*

Ⓥ

Curried Pitta Pieces

1 mini pitta bread
2 teaspoons mango chutney
1 teaspoon low-fat plain yogurt
¼ teaspoon curry powder

1. Toast the pitta bread on
both sides.
2. Mix together the chutney,
yogurt and curry powder. Spread
over one side of the pitta bread.
3. Cut the pitta bread into small
wedges. Serve with the soup.

Variation
Use a spicy chutney or lime
pickle, instead of the sweet
mango chutney and curry
powder.
*Suitable to accompany:
Tomato and Lentil Soup
(page 13), Spicy Fish Soup
with Potato (page 16), Cream
of Leek and Potato Soup with
Shredded Chicken (page 16),
Spiced Lamb and Chick-pea
Soup (page 11), Mushroom
Soup with Dijon Mustard (page
21), Spicy Tomato Soup (page
19), Curried Apple and Leek
Soup (page 23), Cream of
Celeriac, Potato and Chive Soup
(page 18), Carrot and Apple
Soup (page 25)*

Ⓥ

Crispy Turkey Rashers

Turkey rashers are virtually fat free, so get grilling and crumble into airtight containers. Either refrigerate for a few days or freeze (without the onion) for up to a month.

4 turkey rashers
1 spring onion, chopped finely
(optional)

1. Preheat the grill and line with a piece of foil. Grill the rashers, turning once, until golden brown and crisp.
2. Allow to cool slightly before crumbling and mixing with the onion if using.
3. Divide between bowls of soup.
Suitable to accompany:
Tomato and Lentil Soup (page 13), Farmhouse Vegetable Soup (page 24), Three-Bean and Parsley Potage (page 9), Smoked Cod Bisque (page 12), Mushroom Soup with Dijon Mustard (page 21), Cream of Cauliflower and Broccoli Soup (page 20), Golden Vegetable Soup (page 24), French Onion Soup (page 19)

Parmesan Wafers

4 sheets of frozen filo pastry
(25 × 23 cm/10 × 9 inches)
4 teaspoons olive oil
4 teaspoons finely grated
parmesan cheese

1. Preheat the oven to Gas Mark 5/190°C/375°F. Have ready a large, lined baking sheet.
2. Layer the four sheets of pastry on a board, brushing each layer lightly with the olive oil and sprinkle it with 1/2 teaspoon of parmesan cheese. Press the layers together, to ensure they connect.
3. Sprinkle the remaining parmesan cheese evenly over the surface. Using a sharp knife, cut the pastry into 16 equal squares (kitchen scissors are handy for this).
4. Using a palette knife, transfer the squares to the baking sheet. Bake for 5 minutes or until golden brown and crisp.
5. Cool on the baking tray before transferring to an airtight container. Serve separately as an accompaniment to soup.

Weight Watchers note
Filo pastry can be used to make pastry and tartlet cases, savoury roulades and a variety of party-style food. Being fat-free, it's a real bonus – but do count the Points you use when brushing the pastry with low-fat spreads or oil.

Cook's note
Place any unused filo sheets in a sealed plastic bag and store in the refrigerator for up to 2 days, or freeze.
Ⓥ if using vegetarian cheese

Mini Herb Dumplings

Points per serving: 1
Total Points per recipe: 10

Makes: 20 dumplings
Preparation time: 10 minutes
Cooking time: 10–15 minutes
Freezing: recommended (see below)
Calories per dumpling: 55

Serve 2 of these mini dumplings as a tasty addition and experiment with the variations below.

100 g (3¹/₂ oz) self-raising flour
a pinch of baking powder
¹/₂ teaspoon dried mixed herbs
2 tablespoons hard margarine
salt

1. Sift the flour and a pinch each of baking powder and salt into a bowl. Mix in the dried herbs and then rub in the margarine, until the mixture resembles breadcrumbs. Add just enough water to make a soft, but not sticky, dough.
2. Shape 20 mini dumplings.
3. To cook, either drop into a pan of simmering water, cover and cook for 10 minutes or until light and fluffy. Alternatively, add to the soup, cover and simmer, as above.

Variations

For bacon dumplings: add 1 crisp grilled rasher of streaky bacon, crumbled at step 1. For horseradish dumplings: add a teaspoon of horseradish sauce. For mushroom dumplings: add 50 g (1³/₄ oz) mushrooms, very finely chopped. For mint dumplings: add ¹/₂ teaspoon dried mint.
Suitable to accompany:
Farmhouse Vegetable Soup (page 24), Mushroom Soup with Dijon Mustard (page 21), Cream of Cauliflower and Broccoli Soup (page 20).

Cook's Note
For best results, open-freeze the uncooked dumplings and then store in plastic bags in the freezer.

Ⓥ if using vegetarian margarine

Starters and Light Meals

Many of us enjoy 'grazing' or eating snacks at fairly frequent intervals, perhaps purely out of habit or because it suits our lifestyle. You may be too busy to spend time preparing food, or perhaps the family all eat at different times, so it proves virtually impossible to enjoy a main meal together.

Luckily, *1,2,3 Success Plus* allows you to snack throughout the day. Just stick to the number of Points you have available and plan your day so that you have sufficient Points to enjoy other delicious foods, apart from an abundance of 'free' foods to curb the hungriest of appetites!

But, whilst Weight Watchers can offer all the help needed to achieve success, it's up to you to plan how to 'spend' your Points. So, take some time each week, to look at your diary and decide if you need to save and carry over Points for a special occasion, plan for tricky days and for that 'rainy' day when you will need to depend upon store cupboard ingredients.

Both this chapter and Packed Lunches (see pages 53–70) offer you delicious, quick and simple-to-prepare light meals. It has starters, too, with minimal Points, so you can look forward to easy entertaining for all occasions. So, you see, there is no need to miss out on your favourite foods when following *1,2,3 Success Plus*.

Many of the meals serve two as a light lunch or four as a starter. The light meals or snacks cover meals suitable for brunch, right through to late-night suppers. They are quick to prepare too!

As you become familiar with this book, you will discover delicious recipes in Vegetables and Salads (see pages 71–94) that are also ideal for starters, snacks and light meals, such as Cherry Tomato, Green Bean and Hazelnut Salad (see page 94). Grilled Asparagus with Onion and Herb Dressing (see page 82), is a perfect accompaniment to grilled or cold meats or for entertaining with friends but, equally, it makes a delicious starter or light meal.

You have the flexibility and choice to add a little grated parmesan cheese, or some cooked prawns for your own finishing touch, without adding too many Points.

chapter 2

Avocado and Orange Salad with a Tomato and Tarragon Dressing

Points per serving: 3½	
Total Points per recipe: 7	
Serves: 2	
Preparation time: 10 minutes	
Freezing: not recommended	
Calories per serving: 140	

A colourful salad with a creamy tarragon dressing – tarragon is a classic French herb.

6 tablespoons very-low-fat plain
    fromage frais
1 tomato, de-seeded and diced
2 teaspoons chopped fresh
    tarragon or ½ teaspoon
    dried tarragon
1 medium-size orange
1 small avocado
1 teaspoon lemon juice
salt and freshly ground black
    pepper
green salad leaves, to serve

1. In a bowl, mix together the fromage frais, tomato and tarragon. Season with salt and pepper and chill whilst preparing the salad.

2. Peel the orange, carefully removing all the pith. Segment the orange, over a small bowl to catch the juice.

3. Peel, quarter and slice the avocado. Add the lemon juice to the reserved orange juice and gently fold in the avocado slices.

4. Arrange a few green leaves on each plate and scatter the orange and drained avocado slices over the top.

5. Whisk any remaining fruit juices into the tomato and tarragon dressing and drizzle the dressing over the salad. Serve at once.

Variations

Replace the tarragon with mint or coriander leaf.

    Smoked ham, turkey, chicken or prawns would all taste delicious with this salad – remember to calculate those Points.

Guacamole with Crudités

Points per serving: 2	
Total Points per recipe: 8	
Serves: 4	
Preparation time: 10 minutes+chilling	
Freezing: not recommended	
Calories per serving: 100	

This is a great dish to enjoy in the summer, as a starter or snack, particularly when you are entertaining outdoors and the barbecue season is in full swing!

1 small onion, halved
1 garlic clove
1 cm (½-inch) piece of fresh
    root ginger (optional)
1 large, ripe avocado, stoned
2 tablespoons low-fat plain
    fromage frais
finely grated zest and juice of
    1 lime
2 tablespoons chopped fresh
    coriander
1 teaspoon ground coriander
1 teaspoon ground cumin
½ teaspoon chilli powder
1 ripe tomato, de-seeded and
    chopped
chilli sauce (optional)
350 g (12 oz) fresh vegetables
    (see opposite)
salt and freshly ground black
    pepper

1. Place the onion, garlic and ginger in a food processor and blend until finely chopped. Add the next seven ingredients. Process until smooth.

2. Stir the tomato into the mixture. Season to taste, with salt and pepper. For the less faint-hearted, add a dash of chilli sauce.

3. Transfer to a serving bowl, cover tightly with clingfilm and chill for at least 30 minutes. Serve, on a large plate, surrounded by fresh, crisp crudités.

Cook's note

Select crisp, raw vegetables from the 'free' list, including: carrots, celery, radishes, cucumber, chicory, cauliflower florets, mushrooms, red or yellow peppers and cherry tomatoes. Wash and drain thoroughly. Prepare the vegetables as necessary and cut into finger-dipping or bite-size pieces.

    Guacamole is best eaten on the day of making. Reserve the avocado stone and leave it in the mixture, as this is thought to help maintain a brilliant colour.

    Use a teaspoon to scrape the bright green 'lining' on the avocado skin. Add this to the mixture for extra colour and flavour.

Weight Watchers note

For a more substantial light meal, serve a portion of guacamole and the crudités with a pitta bread or on its own as a topping for a jacket potato, accompanied with a crisp mixed salad.

30

Pear and Blue Cheese Salad (*page 34*)
Avocado and Orange Salad with a Tomato and Tarragon Dressing (*opposite*)

Mushroom Medley with a Herb Dressing

Points per serving: 1/2
Total Points per recipe: 2

Serves: 4
Preparation time: 10 minutes +
15 minutes chilling
Freezing: not recommended
Calories per serving: 25

A simple salad of mushrooms in a herb dressing, this is delicious as a starter with garlic bread, or as an accompaniment to cold cooked meats. Serve with crusty bread and add the extra Points.

225 g (8 oz) mushrooms,
quartered
1 small garlic clove, chopped
(optional)
2 tablespoons lemon juice
3 tablespoons low-fat
vinaigrette dressing
1 spring onion, chopped finely
1 tablespoon chopped fresh
parsley
1 tablespoon torn fresh basil
leaves
2 teaspoons chopped fresh
oregano or marjoram or
1/2 teaspoon dried oregano
or marjoram
salt and freshly ground black
pepper
assorted lettuce leaves, to serve

1. Toss the mushrooms with the garlic and lemon juice in a bowl, until all the mushrooms are moistened.
2. Mix the vinaigrette dressing, spring onion and herbs. Toss into the mushrooms, coating them well. Season with salt and pepper. Cover and chill for 15 minutes.
3. Divide the salad leaves between small plates and arrange the mushrooms on top.

Variations

Crumble a crisp cooked medium-size turkey rasher over each serving of mushrooms and add 1/2 Point.

For a creamy dressing, replace 2 tablespoons of the vinaigrette dressing with 4 tablespoons of low-fat plain Bio-yogurt or very-low-fat fromage frais (add 1/2 Point per serving).

Cook's note

If you have fresh tarragon available, use this in place of the basil.

Fresh Grapefruit and Crab Salad with Honey and Poppyseed Dressing

Points per serving: 2 1/2
Total Points per recipe: 10

Serves: 4
Preparation time: 10 minutes
Freezing: not recommended
Calories per serving: 130

The memory of delicious fresh crab sandwiches in Cornish fishing villages still lingers. Nowadays, crab is much more widely available, ready prepared. Here is an unusual combination for a tasty starter or light lunch.

1 small lettuce, e.g. Little Gem
or lollo rosso, torn
1 pink or white grapefruit
4 tablespoons low-fat plain
yogurt
2 tablespoons low-fat
mayonnaise
2 teaspoons clear honey
1/2 teaspoon poppy seeds
225 g (8 oz) fresh crab meat
2 celery sticks, sliced finely
salt and freshly ground black
pepper

1. Divide the torn salad leaves between two plates.
2. Using a serrated knife, remove all the peel and pith from the grapefruit. (Do this over a small bowl, to catch any juice.) Segment the grapefruit, removing any membrane. Arrange the segments over the salad leaves.
3. Add the yogurt, mayonnaise, honey and poppy seeds to the collected juice. Mix well.
4. Fold in the flaked crab meat and celery. Season with salt and pepper and spoon on to the bed of salad leaves. Serve immediately.

Variations

When crab meat is unavailable, replace with peeled cooked prawns or a seafood cocktail.

Replace the poppy seeds with 1/2 teaspoon grated fresh root ginger – a superb partner for crab.

This serves 2 as a light meal. Points per serving will be 5. Calories per serving will be 260.

Cook's note

Canned crab works well. Chill the crab in the can before use, then drain thoroughly and proceed as in step 4.

ⓥ

Minty Melon Cocktail

50 g (1¾ oz) caster sugar
4 tablespoons lemon juice
1 large cantaloupe melon
2 tablespoons chopped fresh mint

1. First, prepare a light syrup. Put the sugar, lemon juice and 125 ml (4 fl oz) of water in a small saucepan. Heat gently, until the sugar has dissolved. Transfer to a large bowl to cool.

2. Quarter the melon, remove the seeds and peel. Cut into bite-size pieces and combine with the mint in the cooled syrup. Cover and chill for an hour.

3. Serve in individual glass dishes.

Variation

Juicy watermelons make a refreshing change. You will need 450 g (1 lb) of flesh. The Points will be the same.

Cook's note

Do not worry if there appears to be insufficient syrup. The chilling time will draw out the melon's natural juice, too.

Weight Watchers note

If you use a honeydew melon instead of a canteloupe, add another ½ Point per serving.

Chicory and Orange Salad with Creamy Cheese Dressing

A colourful, refreshing starter: alternatively, divide it between two (don't forget to double the Points), for a refreshing light lunch.

2 chicory heads, separated into leaves and washed
½ bag of watercress
75 g (2¾ oz) medium-fat soft cheese, e.g. Philadelphia Light
2 rounded tablespoons low-fat plain fromage frais
1 teaspoon chopped fresh tarragon or chives
2 oranges
salt and freshly ground black pepper

1. Arrange the chicory leaves and watercress on small plates.

2. In a small bowl, cream together the soft cheese and fromage frais until smooth. Stir in the tarragon or chives and season with salt and pepper.

3. Remove the peel and pith from the oranges. Cut the orange into segments, removing all the membrane. Do this over a bowl to catch any juice. Add the juice to the dressing.

4. Spoon the dressing over the salad leaves and arrange the orange segments on top. Serve at once.

Variations

This serves 2 as a light lunch. Points per serving will be 1. Calories per serving will be 175.

For a more substantial lunch, add 25 g (1 oz) of wafer-thin sliced ham or chicken to the salad and be sure to add the Points.

Cook's note

To cut away peel and pith from citrus fruit, first cut both ends off the fruit and stand upright on a board. Use a small, sharp knife to slice the peel and pith away in strips.

33

Melon and Grape Salad with Ginger, Honey and Lime Dressing

Points per serving: 1½
Total Points per recipe: 6

Serves: 4
Preparation time: 15 minutes
Freezing: not recommended
Calories per serving: 55

Cool, refreshing melon has a long-standing partnership with the 'warming' spice ginger. Enjoy the combination in this salad.

1 medium-size cantaloupe melon
125 g (4½ oz) green grapes, halved and de-seeded
4 teaspoons clear honey
juice of 2 limes and finely grated zest of 1 lime
1 teaspoon finely grated fresh root ginger or ½ teaspoon ground ginger
fresh mint sprigs, to garnish

1. Halve and de-seed the melon. Remove the rind and cut the flesh into bite-size pieces.
2. Divide the melon and grapes between 4 small dishes.
3. In a small bowl, whisk together the honey, lime juice and zest and ginger. Drizzle over the fruit. Garnish with a sprig of mint and serve at once.

Cook's notes

Melons are ready to eat when they have a perfumed aroma and each end of the fruit is slightly soft when pressed lightly.

1 teaspoon of ground ginger is equivalent to about 2.5 cm (1 inch) of fresh root ginger.

Weight Watchers note

If you use a honeydew melon instead of a canteloupe, add another ½ Point per serving.

Pear and Blue Cheese Salad

Points per serving: 4½
Total Points per recipe: 9

Serves: 2
Preparation time: 15 minutes
Freezing: not recommended
Calories per serving: 170

The combination of tangy blue cheese and sweet juicy pears is a delicious starter.

55 g (2 oz) blue Stilton cheese, crumbled
5–6 tablespoons skimmed milk
1 large pear
2 teaspoons lemon juice
salt and freshly ground black pepper
assorted salad leaves or young spinach leaves, to serve

1. Blend the cheese and milk together in a liquidiser, to form a creamy, pouring consistency. Season with salt and pepper and chill until required.
2. Peel, core and slice the pear into wedges. Toss lightly in the lemon juice.
3. Divide the salad leaves between two plates. Arrange the pears alongside and drizzle over the blue cheese dressing. Serve immediately.

Variations

When in season, fresh apricots are delicious instead of pears. Allow 3 apricots per serving.

For a special occasion, 3 walnut halves, chopped, will add some crunch to the salad, and also ½ Point per serving! Scatter over the dressing at step 3.

Weight Watchers note

Serve with a slice of crusty brown bread but remember that Granary bread is 1½ Points per medium slice but brown or wholemeal bread is 1 Point.

(v) if using vegetarian cheese

(v)

Minted Citrus Salad

This refreshing fruit salad is good at any time of the day – perfect for breakfast, ideal to whet the appetite as a starter or to cleanse the taste buds at the end of a meal.

1 white grapefruit
1 ruby red or pink grapefruit
2 large oranges
1 tablespoon chopped fresh mint
fresh mint sprigs, to garnish

1. Use a serrated knife to remove all the peel and pith from the grapefruits and oranges. Hold the fruit over a bowl, to catch any juice, and cut into segments, removing all membrane.
2. Mix all the fruit with the chopped mint. Cover and chill.
3. Divide the fruit between small plates and garnish each with a mint sprig.

Cook's note
This fruit salad will keep well for 2–3 days. Cover with clingfilm and refrigerate.

Weight Watchers note
Juicy, sweet fruit will eliminate the need for added honey or sugar. Choose brightly coloured fruit that feel heavy for their size.

Smoked Trout Pâté

Always popular, this is a light, soft pâté to suit all occasions, from the lunch box to the dinner table. Serve with melba toast (page 204).

200 g (7 oz) smoked trout fillets
    (about 2 fillets)
4 tablespoons half-fat crème
    fraîche or half-fat cream
55 g (2 oz) cottage cheese
1 tablespoon lemon juice
1 teaspoon horseradish sauce
salt and freshly ground black
    pepper
lemon wedges, to serve

1. Remove any skin and fine bones and flake the fish into a liquidiser or food processor. Add the cream, cottage cheese, lemon juice and horseradish sauce. Blend until smooth.
2. Season to taste with salt and pepper. Divide between small dishes, cover with clingfilm and chill for an hour.
3. Allow the pâté to stand at room temperature for 10 minutes before serving, with small wedges of lemon.

Variation
This serves 2 as a light lunch. Points per serving will be 3, Calories per serving will be 260. Accompany with a crisp mixed salad or crudités of celery, cucumber, green pepper and cherry tomatoes.

Weight Watchers note
Ideal for a packed lunch, packed straight from the freezer in the morning! You could include crispbreads, a medium-size pitta bread or a small, crusty brown roll. Remember to add the Points.

Cook's note
Ready-prepared smoked trout fillets are available from supermarkets. Look out for them in the chilled fish cabinet.

Melon and Parma Ham with Honey and Mustard

Points per serving: 9
Total Points per recipe: 18
Serves: 2
Preparation time: 5 minutes
Freezing: not recommended
Calories per serving: 110

A classic combination with a delicious dressing. Serve with crusty bread.

For the dressing:
1 teaspoon olive oil
1 teaspoon whole-grain mustard
2 teaspoons runny honey
2 teaspoons white-wine vinegar or lemon juice
salt and freshly ground black pepper

For the salad:
1/2 ripe melon, e.g. honeydew, de-seeded
4 medium slices of Parma ham
salad leaves, to serve

1. In a small bowl, mix together the olive oil, mustard, honey and vinegar. Season with a little salt and pepper.
2. Cut the half melon into two quarters and then cut each quarter into five slices.
3. Fan the slices out on two serving plates. Arrange the Parma ham alongside, together with a few salad leaves. Sprinkle on the dressing.

Variation
Replace the mustard with grated fresh root ginger.

Marinated Mushroom and Prawn Salad

Points per serving: 1½
Total Points per recipe: 3
Serves: 2
Preparation time: 5 minutes + 30 minutes chilling
Freezing: not recommended
Calories per serving: 160

An excellent special-occasion starter.

50 g (1¾ oz) button mushrooms, sliced thinly
4 baby plum or cherry tomatoes, halved
55 g (2 oz) cooked peeled prawns
1 teaspoon capers
6 fresh basil leaves, torn
½ teaspoon balsamic vinegar
1 tablespoon vinaigrette dressing, e.g. Italian
salt and freshly ground black pepper

To serve:
assorted salad leaves
2 heaped tablespoons croûtons

1. In a bowl, gently mix the mushrooms, tomatoes, prawns, capers and basil leaves.
2. Mix together the vinegar and Italian dressing. Season with salt and pepper and sprinkle over the salad. Cover and chill for 30 minutes.
3. Arrange the salad leaves on a plate and spoon on the salad. Garnish with crisp croûtons.

Spicy Roasted Aubergine Dip

Points per serving: 1
Total Points per recipe: 4
Serves: 4
Preparation time: 5 minutes + chilling
Cooking time: 45 minutes
Freezing: not recommended
Calories per serving: 60

A delicious spicy dip which is perfect to serve with crisp vegetable crudités (see page 30) or pieces of toasted pitta bread as a starter.

1 large aubergine, cut into chunks
1 onion, sliced
1–2 garlic cloves, sliced thinly
100 ml (3½ fl oz) tomato juice
½ teaspoon hot chilli powder
½ teaspoon ground coriander
½ teaspoon ground cumin
1 tablespoon olive oil
juice of ½ lemon or 1 lime
salt and freshly ground black pepper

1. Preheat the oven to Gas Mark 6/200°C/400°F. Place all the ingredients in a shallow, non-stick roasting tray and toss to mix well. Cover with foil.
2. Bake for 30–45 minutes, stirring twice. Leave to cool, with the foil cover on.
3. When cool, purée in a liquidiser or food processor. Adjust the seasoning, to taste. Spoon into a bowl, cover and chill before serving.

Variations
At step 2, serve the aubergine in its chunky form as a spicy vegetable accompaniment.

Spoon the dip on to a split jacket potato and top with a tablespoon of low-fat plain yogurt and chopped spring onion or coriander. Remember to add the Points.

36

Spicy Roasted Aubergine Dip *(opposite)*
Smoked Trout Pâté *(page 35)* with **Melba Toast** *(page 204)*

Butter Bean, Lime and Chive Dip

Points per serving: 4
Total Points per recipe: 8

Serves: 2
Preparation time: 5 minutes
Freezing: not recommended
Calories per serving: 180

400 g (14 oz) canned butter
    beans, drained
1 garlic clove, crushed
freshly squeezed juice of 1 lime
    (about 2 tablespoons)
1 tablespoon olive oil
2 tablespoons low-fat plain
    Bio-yogurt
1 tablespoon snipped fresh
    chives
salt and freshly ground black
    pepper

1. Using a food processor or liquidiser, blend the butter beans, garlic, lime juice, olive oil and yogurt together, to a smooth purée.
2. Season to taste with salt and pepper. Stir in the chives, cover and chill until required.

Variations

This serves 4 as a starter. Points per serving will be 2, Calories per serving will be 90. If you prefer to use dried butter beans, soak 125 g (4½ oz) overnight and cook as per the pack instructions.

Greek Pepper Salad with Feta Cheese and Mint Dressing

Points per serving: 4
Total Points per recipe: 16

Serves: 4
Preparation time: 15 minutes
Freezing: not recommended
Calories per serving: 215

For the dressing:
2 tablespoons chopped fresh
    mint
1 garlic clove, chopped
2 tablespoons lemon juice
2 tablespoons vinaigrette
    dressing

For the salad:
1 cucumber
1 red pepper, de-seeded and
    sliced
1 green pepper, de-seeded and
    sliced
1 yellow pepper, de-seeded and
    sliced
450 g (1 lb) tomatoes, de-seeded
    and quartered
4 spring onions, chopped
175 g (6 oz) feta cheese,
    crumbled
10 black olives in brine, drained
    and sliced
salt and freshly ground black
    pepper

1. First, make the dressing. Whisk together the mint, garlic, lemon juice and vinaigrette dressing. Season with salt and plenty of pepper.
2. Halve the cucumber lengthways, scoop out and discard the seeds and then cut the cucumber into 1 cm (½-inch) slices.
3. Layer in a large bowl, with the peppers, tomatoes and spring onions. Top with the feta cheese and olives.
4. Pour the dressing over the salad. Serve with crusty bread.

Variation

For a delicious tuna salad, replace the mint with basil and the feta cheese with 400 g (14 oz) of canned tuna in brine, drained. You will save 2½ Points per serving.

Cook's note

This salad will keep, covered, in the refrigerator for a couple of days.

Weight Watchers note

Leftovers make a delicious packed lunch, stuffed into a medium-size pitta bread just before serving. Add 2½ Points for the medium pitta bread.

Ⓥ

Ⓥ if using vegetarian cheese

Cheese and Courgette Puff

Points per serving: 4
Total Points per recipe: 8

Serves: 2
Preparation time: 20 minutes
standing + 10 minutes
Cooking time: 25 minutes
Freezing: not recommended
Calories per serving: 220

Here's one way to take advantage of the summer glut of courgettes. Serve with crusty brown bread or fresh vegetables.

225 g (8 oz) small courgettes, grated coarsely
115 g (4 oz) ricotta cheese
2 eggs, separated
2 teaspoons chopped fresh parsley or ¹/₂ teaspoon dried parsley
2 teaspoons snipped fresh chives or ¹/₂ teaspoon dried chives
25 g (1 oz) half-fat Cheddar cheese, grated finely
salt and freshly ground black pepper

1. Spread the courgettes on a double layer of kitchen paper, sprinkle with a teaspoon of salt and set aside for 20 minutes.
2. Preheat the oven to Gas Mark 5/190°C/375°F. Lightly spray a 1.2-litre (2-pint) shallow gratin dish.
3. Squeeze out as much liquid as possible from the courgettes.
4. Blend the ricotta cheese, egg yolks, herbs and half the Cheddar cheese in a liquidiser or food processor for 10 seconds, or until smooth. Add the courgettes and give the liquidiser a short burst, to mix. Season with pepper (you may not need any extra salt).
5. Using a balloon or rotary whisk, whisk the egg whites in a clean, grease-free bowl until they form soft peaks. Lightly fold into the courgette mixture.
6. Spoon into the gratin dish and sprinkle on the remaining cheese. Bake for 20–25 minutes or until puffed and golden. Serve immediately.

Variations

Replace the Cheddar cheese with 25 g (1 oz) of chopped, cooked ham or 55 g (2 oz) of chopped cooked prawns.

This serves 4 as a starter. Points per serving will be 2. Calories per serving will be 110.

Cook's note

Divided between four ramekin dishes, this light meal is perfect as a first course or as an accompaniment to cold sliced ham or chicken.

Weight Watchers note

Serve with a large plateful of freshly cooked 0 Point carrots and cauliflower, for a substantial lunch or supper.

Ⓥ if using vegetarian cheese and free-range eggs

Scrambled Egg and Bacon Pitta Pocket

Points per serving: 6¹/₂
Total Points per recipe: 6¹/₂

Serves: 1
Preparation and cooking time:
10 minutes
Freezing: not recommended
Calories per serving: 490

This needs to be eaten warm it makes an ideal late-evening snack.

1 medium-size pitta bread
1 rindless rasher of streaky bacon, cut into small pieces
1 teaspoon sunflower margarine
1 egg, beaten
1 tomato, de-seeded and chopped
1 teaspoon snipped fresh chives
salt and freshly ground black pepper

1. Lightly toast the pitta bread; then wrap it in foil to keep warm.
2. Heat a small non-stick saucepan. Dry-fry the bacon pieces, stirring frequently, until crisp and golden brown. Remove with a slotted spoon.
3. Melt the margarine in the saucepan and lightly scramble the egg, until just beginning to set. Return the bacon to the saucepan, with the tomato and chives and gently fold the mixture together. Season well.
4. Spoon the egg mixture into the warm pitta bread and serve immediately.

Weight Watchers note

For an extra-tasty pitta, spread 2 tablespoons of tomato ketchup or brown sauce inside the pitta bread, before spooning in the filling. Add ¹/₂ Point per serving.

Mediterranean Cheese and Tomato Filo Tartlets

Points per serving: 4½
Total Points per recipe: 18
Serves: 4
Preparation time: 15 minutes
Cooking time: 20 minutes
Freezing: not recommended
Calories per serving: 225

Delicious to serve as a first course or light lunch, with a green salad.

6 sheets of filo pastry
1 tablespoon olive oil or
*   vegetable oil*
8 cherry tomatoes halved, or
*   4 small tomatoes, quartered*
175 g (6 oz) ricotta cheese
½ yellow or green pepper,
*   de-seeded and cut into*
*   thin strips*
4 teaspoons chilli sauce
5 black olives, stoned and
*   quartered*
salt and freshly ground black
*   pepper*
1 tablespoon chopped fresh basil
*   or tarragon, to garnish*

1. Preheat the oven to Gas Mark 5/190°C/375°F. Lightly spray four individual Yorkshire pudding tins (about 10 cm/4 inches in diameter).
2. Cut each filo sheet into four squares each about 12 cm (4½ inches) across. Brush each square very lightly with oil, layer four into each tin, off-setting the corners of each square so that they do not overlap. Gently press the pastry into the tins to form a case.
3. Bake for 10–15 minutes or until golden. Remove from the oven.
4. Divide the tomatoes, ricotta cheese, pepper and chilli sauce between each pastry case. Scatter on the olives. Season with salt and pepper.
5. Cook for a further 10–15 minutes, or until the pastry is crisp and golden brown, and the vegetables have softened.
6. Serve warm, garnished with the chopped basil or tarragon.

Cook's note
If you haven't any suitable tins, leave the filo sheets whole and make one 18 cm (7-inch) tart, 'scrunching' any overlapping pastry to form a rim.

Weight Watchers note
These tartlets are delicious served with a crisp green salad or freshly cooked green beans.

Ⓥ if using vegetarian ricotta cheese

Baked Egg and Mushroom Filo Tarts

Points per serving: 5
Total Points per recipe: 20
Serves: 4
Preparation time: 15 minutes
Cooking time: 30 minutes
Freezing: not recommended
Calories per serving: 280

This is a stunning way to serve eggs and a dish to suit all occasions. Accompany with a crisp green salad or brown bread.

6 sheets of filo pastry
4 teaspoons vegetable oil
1 small onion or 2 shallots,
*   chopped finely*
1 garlic clove, crushed
175 g (6 oz) open-cap or brown
*   (chestnut) mushrooms,*
*   chopped finely*
3 sun-dried tomatoes in oil,
*   drained and chopped finely*
2 teaspoons lemon juice
2 teaspoons chopped fresh
*   parsley or chives*
4 eggs
2 teaspoons freshly grated
*   parmesan cheese*
salt and freshly ground black
*   pepper*

1. Preheat the oven to Gas Mark 5/190°C/375°F. Lightly spray four 9 cm (3½-inch) wide, 2.5 cm (1-inch) deep flan tins.
2. Cut each filo sheet into four squares, each about 11 cm (4½ inches) across. Use 2 teaspoons of oil to brush each square very lightly as you layer four into each tin, off-setting the corners of each square so that they do not overlap. Gently press the pastry into each tin to form a case. Bake for 10–15 minutes, until golden.
3. Heat the remaining 2 teaspoons of oil and gently cook the onion or shallots and garlic for 4–5 minutes or until softened and transparent. Add the mushrooms and continue cooking until their juices begin to run.
4. Stir in the sun-dried tomatoes, lemon juice and fresh herbs. Season, to taste, with salt and pepper.
5. Divide the filling between the four pastry cases, pushing the filling to the sides to form a well in the centre. Break an egg into a cup and then gently slide it into the well. Repeat with the other eggs. Sprinkle evenly with the parmesan cheese.
6. Return to the oven and cook for a further 12–15 minutes or until the eggs are softly set. Serve straight away.

Variation
Replace the sun-dried tomatoes with ¼ red pepper, de-seeded and chopped finely. Deduct 1 Point per serving.

Ⓥ if using vegetarian parmesan cheese and free-range eggs

Toasted Muffin with Scrambled Egg, Bacon and Tomato

41

Points per serving: 7
Total Points per recipe: 7

Serves: 1

Preparation and cooking time:
10 minutes

Freezing: not recommended

Calories per serving: 490

The speediest of snacks for any time of the day. For a touch of luxury, replace the bacon with smoked salmon (see below).

1 rindless rasher of streaky
  bacon
1 muffin, halved
1 teaspoon half-fat butter or
  low-fat spread
1 egg, beaten
1 tablespoon skimmed milk
1 small tomato, de-seeded and
  chopped
1 teaspoon low-fat mayonnaise
1 teaspoon snipped fresh chives
salt and freshly ground black
  pepper

1. Set the grill to the highest setting. Grill the bacon until crisp. Lightly toast the muffin halves alongside the bacon. Switch the grill off, keeping the food on a warm serving plate under the residual heat.

2. Meanwhile, melt the butter or spread in a small non-stick saucepan. Beat together the egg and milk. Season to taste with salt and pepper and then cook gently in the saucepan until lightly scrambled. Stir in the tomato and mayonnaise.

3. Spoon the scrambled egg on to one muffin half. Top with the bacon rasher and garnish with the chives. Put the other half-muffin on top. Serve immediately.

Variations

Replace 1 bacon rasher with 2 turkey rashers and save 1 Point!

Replace the bacon with 55 g (2 oz) of smoked salmon, and save 1/2 Point.

Cook's note

If using smoked salmon, look for the more economical smoked salmon trimmings, sold pre-packed or loose at delicatessen counters.

Grilled Goat's Cheese Toasties

Points per serving: 7½
Total Points per recipe: 15

Serves: 2

Preparation and cooking time:
10 minutes

Freezing: not recommended

Calories per serving: 370

Goat's cheese has become very popular over recent years, with milder varieties now available. It is particularly delicious eaten warm.

6 × 2 cm (3/4-inch) diagonal
  slices of French bread
2 tomatoes, sliced thinly
115 g (4 oz) soft goat's cheese
2 teaspoons pesto (optional)
85 g (3 oz) assorted salad
  leaves
1 tablespoon fat-free vinaigrette
  dressing
freshly ground black pepper

1. Preheat the grill to its hottest setting and toast the bread slices on both sides.

2. Place one or two tomato slices on each toast, spread with the goat's cheese and drizzle a little pesto over the top. Season with ground black pepper.

3. Return to the grill for 2–3 minutes, or until the cheese is warm and starting to soften.

4. Meanwhile, toss the salad leaves in the dressing and divide between two plates. Arrange three toasties on each one and serve immediately.

Variation

Replace the pesto with 1/4 red pepper, de-seeded and diced. Deduct 1/2 Point per serving.

Ⓥ if using vegetarian cheese

Mustard-Grilled Tomatoes with Mozzarella Toasts

Points per serving: 5
Total Points per recipe: 10

Serves: 2
Preparation and cooking time:
20 minutes
Freezing: not recommended
Calories per serving: 325

Enjoy these grilled tomatoes over a leisurely brunch. See the end of the recipe for a delicious variation, too.

For the tomatoes:
4 large, ripe tomatoes, halved
2 teaspoons low-fat spread or half-fat butter
2 teaspoons whole-grain mustard
1 tablespoon chopped fresh parsley, chives or basil
salt and freshly ground black pepper

For the toasts:
2 crusty white or brown rolls, halved
55 g (2 oz) medium-fat soft cheese, e.g. Philadelphia Light
55 g (2 oz) half-fat mozzarella cheese, chopped or grated

1. Preheat the grill to a medium setting. Place the tomatoes, cut-side down, in a shallow gratin dish and grill for 5 minutes.
2. Meanwhile, lightly toast the bread rolls. (This can be done alongside the tomatoes.) Remove the grill pan. Increase the grill setting to high. Turn the tomatoes over. Season with salt and pepper.
3. Mix together the butter, mustard and chopped herbs. Place a knob of the mixture on each tomato half. Replace under the grill, to cook for a further 5 minutes. Transfer to two warm plates.
4. Meanwhile, thinly spread the cheese over the toasted rolls. Scatter on the mozzarella cheese. Place under the hot grill for 3–4, minutes or until the cheese is bubbling and tinged golden.
5. Serve the crusty cheese toasts with the warm tomatoes.

Variation
Spread a thin layer of Marmite on the toasts before topping them with the cheese. Replace 2 tomatoes with 1 small courgette, halved and then sliced in half lengthways, and 1 small yellow pepper, de-seeded and cut into quarters. Par-boil in boiling water for 3 minutes, drain thoroughly, and then proceed from step 3. The Points will be the same.

Cook's note
Mozzarella cheese is available ready-grated and in a re-sealable bag – ideal for storing in the freezer and weighing out small quantities when required.

V if using vegetarian cheese

Ciabatta with Spinach and Brie Melt

Points per serving: 10½
Total Points per recipe: 10½

Serves: 1
Preparation and cooking time:
10 minutes
Freezing: not recommended
Calories per serving: 490

The variations on this tasty snack are endless. You could try replacing the spinach with curly kale, the Brie with mozzarella or the cranberry sauce with mango chutney or a teaspoon of raisins. Who said losing weight can't be fun and easy? See the Weight Watchers note for low-Point variations.

2 thin slices of ciabatta bread
55 g (2 oz) fresh baby spinach leaves
1 teaspoon olive oil
1 tablespoon cranberry sauce
55 g (2 oz) firm Brie, sliced very thinly
salt and freshly ground black pepper

1. Set the grill to its highest setting and toast the bread. Leave the grill on but remove the tray.
2. Meanwhile, briskly cook the spinach in a saucepan with the olive oil for 1–2 minutes, or until the leaves just wilt. Season with salt and freshly ground black pepper. Drain thoroughly.
3. Spread the cranberry sauce over the slices of toast, spoon the spinach on top and finally arrange the slices of Brie over the spinach.
4. Flash under the hot grill for 1–2 minutes or until the cheese just starts to melt. Serve immediately.

Weight Watchers note
If you need to save some Points, replace the Brie with 40 g (1½ oz) medium-fat soft cheese. Melt this into the hot, drained spinach before piling on the toasted ciabatta and save 3 Points.

Or replace the ciabatta with 1 thick slice of wholemeal bread and save 2½ Points!

V if using vegetarian cheese

Baked Tomatoes with Sweetcorn and Mozzarella

Points per serving: 5
Total Points per recipe: 20
Serves: 4
Preparation and cooking time: 25 minutes
Freezing: not recommended
Calories per serving: 150

Based on the popular summer salad, here is a hot version for winter suppers in front of the fire.

4 large plum tomatoes
198 g (7 oz) canned sweetcorn
    kernels, drained
4–5 fresh basil leaves, torn
125 g (4¹/₂ oz) half-fat
    mozzarella cheese, drained
    and sliced into 8
salt and freshly ground black
    pepper
4 crusty rolls, to serve

1. Preheat the oven to Gas Mark 6/200°C/400°F. Halve the tomatoes lengthways. Scoop out and discard the core and seeds. Place the tomatoes in a shallow roasting tin and lightly season their cavities with salt and pepper.
2. Spoon the sweetcorn into the tomato shells, top with the basil and a slice of mozzarella cheese.
3. Bake for 15 minutes, until the tomatoes have softened. Flash under a hot grill, just to brown the cheese. Serve at once, accompanied by the crusty rolls.

Ⓥ if using vegetarian cheese

Smoked Haddock, Bacon and Potato Frittata

Points per serving: 5¹/₂
Total Points per recipe: 11
Serves: 2
Preparation and cooking time: 20 minutes
Freezing: not recommended
Calories per serving: 345

Serve this savoury omelette with green peas or a salad. Delicious cold, too. Frittata is the Italian name for a firmly set omelette, known as *tortilla* in Spain.

175 g (6 oz) potato, cut into
    1 cm (¹/₂-inch) cubes
2 celery sticks, sliced
2 rindless rashers of streaky
    bacon, cut into 4 pieces
200 g (7 oz) smoked haddock,
    skinned and cut into 2.5 cm
    (1-inch) cubes
2 spring onions, chopped
2 eggs, beaten
salt and freshly ground black
    pepper
Worcestershire sauce, to serve
    (optional)

1. Cook the potato in lightly salted boiling water for about 6 minutes, or until just tender. Add the celery and cook for a further 3 minutes. Drain well.
2. Meanwhile, dry-fry the bacon in a hot 20 cm (8-inch), non-stick frying-pan, until just cooked. Add the fish and gently stir-fry for 1 minute. Then add the potato, celery and spring onions.
3. Season the eggs well with salt and pepper and mix with 2 tablespoons of cold water. Add to the frying-pan, shaking the pan to distribute the egg mixture evenly. Reduce the heat and cook for 5 minutes or until lightly set. Pop under a hot grill if the surface of the frittata is still a little wet.
4. Divide between two warm plates and serve with a dash of Worcestershire sauce, if you like.

Variation

Replace the bacon with 55 g (2 oz) of low-fat Cheddar cheese, adding this with the eggs at step 3. You will need to melt 2 teaspoons of low-fat spread at step 2 to stir-fry the haddock in. Add 2 Points per serving.

Cook's note

You can leave the frittata to set like an omelette or, if you prefer, you can lightly scramble the mixture.

Garlicky Mushroom Bruschettas

Points per serving: 4
Total Points per recipe: 8

Serves: 2
Preparation and cooking time:
15 minutes
Freezing: not recommended
Calories per serving: 350

Mushrooms are so versatile and very tasty, too. Experiment with some of the more unusual varieties, e.g. shiitake, oyster and the flavoursome brown (chestnut) mushrooms.

15 cm (6-inch) slice of French bread, halved lengthways
2 teaspoons half-fat butter or low-fat spread
2 spring onions, chopped
1–2 garlic cloves, crushed
225 g (8 oz) open-cap mushrooms, sliced
1/2 teaspoon dried thyme or tarragon
1 tablespoon skimmed milk
4 tablespoons half-fat crème fraîche
salt and freshly ground black pepper
1 tablespoon chopped fresh parsley, to garnish

1. Preheat the grill to its hottest setting and toast the French bread.
2. Melt the butter or spread in a saucepan and gently sauté the spring onions and garlic for 3–4 minutes. Brush a little of the cooking juice over the cut sides of the bread.
3. Set the grill to a low heat and place the toasts on the lowest shelf, to keep warm and dry out a little.
4. Add the mushrooms, dried herbs and milk to the saucepan and cook gently for about 5 minutes, or until the mushrooms have softened and the liquid has evaporated. If the mushrooms have released a lot of juice, increase the heat to evaporate it.
5. Stir in the crème fraîche. Season with salt and plenty of pepper. Cook gently for a further minute.
6. Arrange the toasted breads on two serving plates and spoon the mushroom mixture on top. Garnish with chopped parsley and serve immediately.

Cook's note
These bruschettas are delicious served with a crisp mixed salad.

Weight Watchers note
Italian breads are traditionally used for bruschetta, but do check the Points per slice – these doughs usually include olive oil.

Soft-Boiled Egg with Prawns and Watercress Sauce

Points per serving: 5
Total Points per recipe: 5

Serves: 1
Preparation time: 5 minutes
Cooking time: 10 minutes
Freezing: not recommended
Calories per serving: 190

If you prefer, you can lightly poach the egg: either way, it is a delicious combination and very colourful.

25 g (1 oz) fresh watercress, chopped finely
3 tablespoons low-fat plain fromage frais
teaspoon lemon juice
1 egg
25 g (1 oz) cooked, peeled prawns, chopped
salt and freshly ground black pepper

1. Mix together the watercress, fromage frais and lemon juice in a large heatproof mixing bowl. Season to taste with salt and pepper.
2. Gently lower the egg into a pan of boiling water and boil for 4–5 minutes. Meanwhile, place the mixing bowl over the saucepan, to warm the sauce through.
3. Lift out the cooked egg and remove the shell when cool enough to handle. Halve the egg and place, yolk-down, on a warm plate. Mix the prawns into the watercress sauce, then spoon this over and around the eggs. Serve immediately.

Variation
Replace the watercress with a tablespoon of chopped fresh tarragon or chives.

Weight Watchers note
This is delicious served with fresh Granary bread (1 medium slice = 1 1/2 Points).

Parma Ham and Tomato Pinchos

Points per serving: 3¹/₂
Total Points per recipe: 3¹/₂

Serves: 1
Preparation and cooking time:
10 minutes
Freezing: not recommended
Calories per serving: 240

Pinchos are the Spanish equivalent of an open toasted sandwich. Parma ham really does taste good or choose your own favourite cured ham.

1 teaspoon olive oil
¹/₂ small garlic clove, chopped
*   finely*
a large pinch of cumin seeds
115 g (4 oz) plum tomatoes,
*   peeled, de-seeded and*
*   chopped*
1 medium-size slice of brown
*   or white bread*
40 g (1¹/₂ oz) Parma ham,
*   cut into pieces*
salt and freshly ground black
*   pepper*

1. Heat the oil in a non-stick frying-pan and sauté the garlic and cumin seeds for 1 minute. Add the tomatoes and cook for 1–2 minutes, to heat through. Season to taste.
2. Toast the bread on both sides and then spoon the tomato mixture on top.
3. Arrange the Parma ham on the tomato. Sprinkle with a little extra pepper and serve immediately.

Variations

Replace the cumin seeds with a pinch of dried, crushed chilli flakes. Serve with a crisp green salad.

Weight Watchers note

For a larger portion, replace the slice of toast with 2 slices of toasted low-calorie bread. Increase the quantity of tomatoes and seasoning and divide between the 2 slices.

Parmesan-Glazed Eggs in a Nest

Points per serving: 4¹/₂
Total Points per recipe: 4¹/₂

Serves: 1
Preparation and cooking time:
15 minutes
Freezing: not recommended
Calories per serving: 335

A lightly poached egg in a nest of spaghetti – so simple and delicious. The runny yolk forms the pasta sauce.

55 g (2 oz) spaghetti
1 egg
85 g (3 oz) baby spinach leaves,
*   washed and drained*
1 teaspoon low-fat spread
1 teaspoon grated parmesan
*   cheese*
salt and freshly ground black
*   pepper*

1. Cook the spaghetti in plenty of salted, boiling water for 8–10 minutes or until *al dente* (tender but still with a slight bite).
2. Meanwhile, poach the egg in a small saucepan of barely simmering water, for about 4 minutes or until the white is lightly set. (Do not be tempted to over-cook at this stage.)
3. Preheat the grill to its highest setting. Drain the spaghetti and spoon into small gratin dish, forming a slightly hollowed 'nest'.
4. Add the spinach to the hot spaghetti saucepan, without any water, and briskly cook for 2–3 minutes or until it wilts. Drain thoroughly, pressing out as much moisture as possible. Mix in the low-fat spread and season well with salt and pepper. Spoon into the 'nest'.
5. Drain the poached egg and lay on top of the spinach. Sprinkle the parmesan cheese over the egg and spaghetti. Place under the hot grill for 1–2 minutes, to melt the cheese. Serve immediately.

Variation

Replace the spinach with a tomato, halved and lightly grilled. Omit the low-fat spread and save ¹/₂ Point.

Cook's note

Eggs need to be fresh to poach successfully. Older eggs will sometimes poach better if they are first boiled for 20 seconds. This usually makes the whites just firm enough to cling to the yolk, rather than spreading into the water.

Ⓥ if using a free-range egg and vegetarian cheese

47

Spanish Tortilla

Points per serving: 4½
Total Points per recipe: 9
Serves: 2
Preparation and cooking time: 30 minutes
Freezing: not recommended
Calories per serving: 270

A Spanish 'vegetable omelette' that is delicious hot or cold, served with a tomato salad, a low-calorie coleslaw, or just some pickle. Ideal for packed lunches, picnics or a quick supper dish.

100 g (3½ oz) potato
1 small onion, sliced thinly
1 small red pepper, cored and sliced finely
2 garlic cloves, crushed
2 teaspoons olive oil
100 g (3½ oz) frozen peas, thawed
3 eggs
a good pinch of dried thyme or tarragon
salt and freshly ground black pepper

1. Boil the potato in lightly salted water until just tender. Drain, cool and slice thinly.
2. Heat a medium-size, non-stick frying-pan, until quite hot. Meanwhile, mix the onion, pepper and garlic with the oil.
3. Add the vegetables to the pan and cook, stirring occasionally, for about 5 minutes or until lightly browned. Then add the sliced potato and cook for a further 3 minutes.
4. Sprinkle in the peas. Beat the eggs with the dried herbs. Season well with salt and pepper. Pour into the pan, tipping the pan so the mixture covers all the vegetables.
5. Cook gently, without stirring, until the egg sets. If the surface looks a little wet, flash the pan briefly under a hot grill.
6. Cut the tortilla into four wedges and serve hot or cold.

Cook's note
This is a good recipe for using up odd vegetables, e.g. courgettes, mushrooms or cooked carrot or celeriac. The combinations are endless.

Sunday Brunch Special

Points per serving: 4
Total Points per recipe: 8
Serves: 2
Preparation time: 5 minutes
Cooking time: 15 minutes
Freezing: not recommended
Calories per serving: 225

For a special, leisurely brunch, serve this after Minted Citrus Salad (see page 35) and don't forget the morning newspapers and a fresh brew!

2 rindless rashers of streaky bacon
150 g (5½ oz) brown (chestnut) mushrooms, sliced
2 eggs
2 tablespoons half-fat crème fraîche
1 teaspoon whole-grain mustard
salt and freshly ground black pepper

1. Dry-fry the bacon in a non-stick frying-pan, until crisp and brown. Transfer to serving plates and keep warm.
2. Add the mushrooms to the frying-pan. Stir-fry for a minute. Pour on 150 ml (¼ pint) of water and leave the mushrooms to cook in the boiling water until all but a tablespoon of water has evaporated.
3. Meanwhile, poach the eggs in a small saucepan of gently simmering water for 4–5 minutes, or until lightly set.
4. Stir the crème fraîche and mustard into the mushrooms. Season to taste with salt and pepper.
5. Divide the poached eggs and the creamy mushrooms between the plates of bacon. Serve immediately.

Cook's note
Brown (chestnut) mushrooms have a firm texture and bags of flavour. Open-cap or 'button' mushrooms can be used, if preferred.

ⓥ if using free-range eggs

Toasted Granary Bread with Watercress, Pear and Cheese Melt

Points per serving: 5½
Total Points per recipe: 11

Serves: 2
Preparation time: 5 minutes
Cooking time: 2 minutes
Freezing: not recommended
Calories per serving: 230

Using flavours that really complement each other, this hot snack is simple and satisfying.

2 medium-size slices of Granary bread
25 g (1 oz) fresh watercress
1 large ripe pear, peeled, halved and cored
55 g (2 oz) mature blue Stilton cheese, crumbled

1. Preheat the grill to its hottest setting. Toast the bread on one side only.
2. Arrange the watercress on the untoasted side of the bread.
3. Slice the pear halves lengthways. Lay over the watercress and then crumble the Stilton over the top.
4. Pop under the grill for 1–2 minutes, until the cheese just begins to melt. Serve immediately.

Variation

Spread each slice of toast with a tablespoon of redcurrant jelly or cranberry sauce – a sweet contrast to the peppery watercress. Add ½ Point per slice.

Cook's note

The peppery notes from the watercress and the saltiness from the cheese should eliminate the need to add extra seasoning.

Ham, Tomato and Parsley Pancake Pockets

Points per serving: 5
Total Points per recipe: 10

Serves: 2
Preparation time: 10 minutes
Freezing: not recommended
Calories per serving: 255

4 pancakes (see page 204)
55 g (2 oz) wafer-thin ham
2 tomatoes, de-seeded and diced
1 spring onion, chopped
1 tablespoon chopped fresh flat-leaf parsley
2 teaspoons mild mustard, e.g. honey mustard
150 ml (¼ pint) low-fat plain Bio-yogurt
salt and freshly ground black pepper
salad leaves and celery sticks, to serve

1. Wrap the pancakes in foil and place in a preheated warm oven, or on a plate set over a saucepan of simmering water to warm through. (Alternatively, reheat in a microwave oven.)
2. Gently combine the ham, tomatoes, spring onion and chopped parsley in a bowl. Mix together the mustard and yogurt. Season with salt and pepper. Fold this into the tomatoes and ham.
3. Fold each pancake into four, like a cornet and spoon the filling into the pocket. Arrange two pancakes on each serving plate, with assorted salad leaves and some crisp celery. Serve.

Cook's note

If you wish to serve these pancakes with a warm filling, cover with foil and heat in a moderate oven (Gas Mark 4/180°C/350°F) for 15 minutes. They should not be piping hot.

49

Ⓥ if using vegetarian cheese

◆ **Light Meals**

Mushroom, Leek and Sweetcorn Pancakes

Points per serving: 5½
Total Points per recipe: 22

Serves: 4
Preparation time: 15 minutes
Cooking time: 20 minutes
Freezing: recommended
Calories per serving: 360

8 pancakes (see page 204)
2 teaspoons sunflower oil
2 leeks, shredded
1 red pepper, de-seeded and
  chopped
198 g canned sweetcorn kernels,
  drained
450 g jar of low-in-fat creamy
  mushroom cook-in sauce
1 tablespoon chopped fresh
  parsley
50 g (1¾ oz) half-fat Cheddar
  cheese, grated
salt and freshly ground black
  pepper

1. Preheat the oven to Gas Mark 5/190°C/375°F.
2. Heat the oil in a saucepan, add the leeks and sauté for 5 minutes or until just beginning to soften and colour. Add the red pepper and cook for a further 2–3 minutes.
3. Remove the saucepan from the heat. Stir in the sweetcorn and the mushroom sauce. Adjust the seasoning, to taste. Stir in all but a teaspoon of the parsley.
4. Spoon the filling along the centre of each pancake. Fold in the sides, to encase the filling. Place the pancakes, seam-side down, in a shallow, oblong ovenproof dish. Sprinkle with the cheese.
5. Cook for 20 minutes, until golden brown and bubbling. Sprinkle with the remaining chopped parsley, to serve.

Spinach and Edam Pancake Parcels with Tomato Sauce

Points per serving: 7½
Total Points per recipe: 15

Serves: 2
Preparation and cooking time:
20 minutes
Freezing: not recommended
Calories per serving: 435

Here's a short cut to the dinner table – without compromising on a tasty meal!

4 pancakes (see page 204)
For the filling:
1 teaspoon vegetable oil
1 small onion, chopped finely
225 g (8 oz) frozen leaf spinach
110 g tub of cottage cheese
55 g (2 oz) Edam cheese, grated
a pinch of grated nutmeg
To serve:
150 g (5½ oz) fresh tomato
  pasta sauce
1 tablespoon dried breadcrumbs
salt and freshly ground black
  pepper

1. Heat a small frying-pan. Mix together the oil and onion and add to the hot frying-pan. Sauté for a few minutes, until beginning to soften. Add the frozen spinach leaf. Increase the heat and stir fry for 5–7 minutes, to cook and dry out the spinach.
2. Remove from the heat. Stir in the cottage cheese and half the grated Edam cheese. Season well with a little nutmeg, salt and pepper. Divide between the pancakes. Fold in the sides and ends and place, seam-down, in a shallow gratin dish. Place in the grill pan (remove the grid).
3. Preheat the grill to a medium setting. Set the grill pan on its lowest position and just warm the pancakes through.
4. Meanwhile, gently heat the tomato sauce. Pour the hot sauce over the pancakes.
5. Sprinkle on the remaining cheese and breadcrumbs and pop back under the hot grill for 3–4 minutes or until the cheese has melted and the surface is golden and bubbling.

Variation
Replace the tomato sauce with a low-in-fat Creamy Mushroom Cook-in Sauce. Add 1 Point.

Ⓥ if using vegetarian cheese

Ⓥ if using vegetarian cheese

Ham, Tomato and Parsley Pancake Pockets *(page 49)*

Celeriac, Mushroom and Cheese Bake

Serves: 4
Preparation time: 20 minutes
Cooking time: 20 minutes
Freezing: recommended
Calories per serving: 210

A warming winter bake: accompany it with carrots or green peas for a satisfying supper.

1 celeriac, cut into 2.5 cm
   (1-inch) chunks
4 teaspoons hard margarine
1 onion, chopped
225 g (8 oz) button mushrooms,
   sliced
50 g (1³/₄ oz) plain white flour
425 ml (³/₄ pint) skimmed milk
75 g (2³/₄ oz) half-fat Cheddar
   cheese, grated
1 teaspoon whole-grain mustard
2 tablespoons fresh breadcrumbs
1 tablespoon grated parmesan
   cheese
salt and freshly ground black
   pepper

1. Preheat the oven to Gas Mark 5/190°C/375°F.
2. Cook the celeriac in lightly salted, boiling water for 10 minutes or until just tender. Drain.
3. Meanwhile, melt the margarine in a saucepan and gently sauté the onion for 5 minutes, or until softened. Add the mushrooms and cook for a further 5 minutes, allowing any juice to evaporate.
4. Blend in the flour, using a wooden spoon. Then gradually add the milk. Heat, stirring constantly, until the sauce thickens. Remove from the heat. Stir in the Cheddar cheese and mustard and season to taste, with salt and pepper. Fold in the celeriac.
5. Spoon the mixture into an ovenproof baking dish. Sprinkle on the breadcrumbs and parmesan cheese.
6. Bake for 20 minutes, until golden and bubbling.

Cook's note

Celeriac looks like a large knobbly turnip and, as the name implies, it has the flavour of celery.

Ⓥ if using vegetarian cheese

Packed Lunches

Eating 'on the hoof' is too common in today's frantic world. We no longer seem to take time to enjoy a lunchbreak and, worse still, what we eat often goes unnoticed.

Preparing packed lunches is another job to fit into a busy evening, so planning quick and easy lunches is important. Have a check list to hand each week; writing a weekly menu is one of the easiest ways to plan your Points, feed the family well and look forward to delicious food – all with **1,2,3 Success Plus**.

Here are plenty of ideas for packed lunches and snacks. Whether you require a well balanced, satisfying lunch box or a low-Points snack, something to tide you over the children's tea time or to fit around unexpected arrangements, you will find a delicious recipe to fit the bill. Here are a few helpful tips to see you through the week.

chapter 3

♦ Keep your favourite selection of store-cupboard ingredients topped up – cans of salmon or tuna, tomatoes and baked beans, low-calorie soups and sauces, rice and pasta and dried herbs and spices.

♦ Buy fresh ingredients for maximum taste – particularly bread and salads. If they taste good to start with, you are less likely to need spreads and dressings – which saves Points. Breads freeze successfully, so keep a selection of rolls and pitta breads handy.

♦ On the days you rely on popping in to the local supermarket or delicatessen for lunch, look out for the clearly labelled low-calorie sandwiches or salads. You can then calculate the Points – and enjoy it, knowing that **1,2,3 Success Plus** does not deprive you of choice.

♦ Invest in a small, insulated cool bag or sandwich box and some freezer blocks, to keep food well chilled throughout the year. Save small disposable food containers with lids for packing salads in and invest in a good-quality Thermos flask for keeping soups warm through the cold months.

♦ Batch-bake some of the tasty tea breads and biscuits (see Cakes and Bakes, pages 187–203). Individually wrap and freeze them. It's a good idea to label them with their Points, to help you plan ahead and save time later.

Creamy Egg and Watercress Bap

Points per serving: 7
Total Points per recipe: 7

Serves: 1

Preparation time: 15 minutes

Freezing: not recommended

Calories per serving: 230

1 egg

2 tablespoons Quark or low-fat
*   soft cheese*

3–4 tablespoons chopped fresh
*   watercress*

1 brown bap, split

salt and freshly ground black
*   pepper*

1. Hard-boil the egg. Leave to
cool and then shell it.

2. Chop the egg finely and mix
in the Quark or low-fat soft
cheese. Season well with salt
and pepper.

3. Fold the watercress into the
egg mixture and spoon into the
split bap. Wrap in clingfilm and
refrigerate until required.

Ⓥ if using vegetarian soft
cheese and a free-range egg

Pastrami, Pickled Dill and Tomato Sandwich

Points per serving: 6½
Total Points per recipe: 6½

Serves: 1

Preparation time: 10 minutes

Freezing: not recommended

Calories per serving: 310

Pastrami is a delicious, spicy,
cured, smoked beef that is
available in supermarkets and
delicatessens.

2 medium-size slices of Granary
*   bread*

2 teaspoons low-fat mayonnaise

25 g (1 oz) low-fat soft cheese

2 iceberg lettuce leaves, shredded

50 g (1¾ oz) wafer-thin
*   pastrami*

1 dill cucumber, sliced, or 2
*   gherkins, halved lengthways*

1 tomato, sliced thinly

salt and freshly ground black
*   pepper*

1. Lightly toast the bread slices.
Leave to cool.

2. Mix together the mayonnaise
and soft cheese. Season well
and spread on each slice of toast.

3. Layer the iceberg lettuce,
pastrami, dill pickle or gherkins
and tomato slices, seasoning
well with salt and pepper.

4. Top with the second slice
of toast and cut into quarters.
Secure each quarter with a
cocktail stick.

Crunchy Chicken, Coleslaw and Peanut Butter Roll

Points per serving: 4½
Total Points per recipe: 4½

Serves: 1

Preparation: 5 minutes

Freezing: not recommended

Calories per serving: 290

This is a tasty way of making
a little peanut butter stretch
further.

2 tablespoons reduced-calorie
*   coleslaw*

2 teaspoons peanut butter

a pinch of chilli powder

2 lettuce leaves, shredded

1 soft, white roll, split

35 g (1¼ oz) wafer-thin
*   chicken (½ pack)*

salt and freshly ground black
*   pepper*

1. In a bowl, mix together the
coleslaw, peanut butter and a
little chilli powder, to taste.
Season with salt and pepper.

2. Arrange the salad leaves in
the roll, top with the chicken
and finally the coleslaw mixture.
Top with the roll 'lid'.

3. Wrap in clingfilm and
refrigerate until required.

Marmite and Cream Cheese Sandwich

Points per serving: 4
Total Points per recipe: 4

Serves: 1

Preparation time: 5 minutes

Freezing: not recommended

Calories per serving: 260

2 medium-size slices of white or
*   brown bread*

Marmite, to taste

75 g (2¾ oz) low-fat soft cheese

2 iceberg lettuce leaves, shredded

1. Spread each slice of bread
with Marmite, to taste. Then
spread the soft cheese evenly
over each slice.

2. Sandwich the lettuce
between the two prepared
slices. Keep chilled until
required.

Variation

Mix 1 chopped spring onion or
some chopped celery with the
cream cheese.

Cook's note

Don't be tempted to season
the sandwich, as the Marmite
should suffice.

Ⓥ if using vegetarian soft
cheese

Smoked Salmon and Cucumber with a Creamy Dill Spread

Points per serving: 3½
Total Points per recipe: 7

Serves: 2
Preparation time: 5 minutes
Freezing: not recommended
Calories per serving: 315

A classic combination – great for a picnic. Smoked trout is equally as delicious.

2 tablespoons low-fat plain Bio-yogurt
1 teaspoon chopped fresh dill or ½ teaspoon dried dill
¼ – ½ teaspoon mild mustard, e.g. honey mustard or Dijon, to taste
4 thin slices of brown bread
115 g (4 oz) smoked salmon slices or trimmings
2.5 cm (1-inch) piece of cucumber, cubed
salt and freshly ground black pepper

1. In a small bowl, mix together the yogurt, dill and mustard to taste. Season to taste with salt and pepper.
2. Spread the dressing evenly over the four slices of bread. Arrange half the smoked salmon on two slices of bread, sprinkle on the cucumber and then top with the remaining salmon (this helps prevent the bread from becoming too soggy). Season with extra pepper.
3. Sandwich the bread together and cut into four triangles. Serve.

Cook's note
Look out for smoked salmon trimmings, which are ideal for adding to sandwiches, kedgeree and scrambled egg, at a much more economical price.

Weight Watchers note
Bio-yogurt has a delicious sharp note to contrast with the richness of smoked salmon.

Cottage Cheese, Mint and Apricot Bap

Points per serving: 4
Total Points per recipe: 4

Serves: 1
Preparation time: 5 minutes
Freezing: not recommended
Calories per serving: 245

1 wholemeal bap
2 crisp lettuce leaves
85 g (3 oz) cottage cheese
2 ready-to-eat dried apricots, sliced thinly
1 teaspoon chopped fresh mint
1 teaspoon low-fat mayonnaise
1 spring onion, chopped (optional)
salt and freshly ground black pepper

1. Split the bap and arrange a salad leaf on each cut half.
2. Fold together the cottage cheese, apricots, mint, mayonnaise and spring onion and season with salt and pepper.
3. Pile the filling on to the bap and top with the lid. Serve.

Variation
Omit the mint and low-calorie mayonnaise and replace with a teaspoon of spicy chutney or sweetcorn relish. Add 1 Point per serving.

ⓥ

Beef, Beetroot and Horseradish Sandwich

Points per serving: 4
Total Points per recipe: 4

Serves: 1
Preparation time: 10 minutes
Freezing: not recommended
Calories per serving: 260

A perfect start to the week, if there are any leftovers from the Sunday joint.

2 teaspoons low-fat spread
1 teaspoon horseradish sauce
2 medium-size slices of brown or white bread
25g (1 oz) slice of roast beef
55 g (2 oz) pickled or cooked beetroot, drained and sliced thinly
1 large lettuce leaf
salt and freshly ground black pepper

1. Mix together the low-fat spread and horseradish sauce and spread on the slices of bread.
2. Arrange the beef and beetroot on one slice of bread and then add the lettuce, seasoning the layers to taste.
3. Top with the second slice of bread.

Variation
Replace the beetroot with 2 tablespoons of reduced-calorie coleslaw. Add 1 Point per serving.

Cottage Cheese, Carrot and Raisin Baguette

> **Points per serving: 8**
> **Total Points per recipe: 8**
>
> Serves: 1
> Preparation time: 5 minutes
> Freezing: not recommended
> Calories per serving: 445

Make the most of the few Points that cottage cheese has, to enjoy this delicious, fruity filling in half a fresh, crusty baguette.

1 small carrot, grated coarsely
110 g tub of cottage cheese
2 teaspoons raisins or sultanas
1/2 baguette (French bread)
iceberg lettuce leaves, shredded
salt and freshly ground black
pepper

1. Combine the carrot, cottage cheese and raisins or sultanas. Season with salt and pepper.
2. Split the baguette in half and lay the shredded lettuce over the bottom half. Spread the cheese mixture evenly over the lettuce and top with the baguette lid.

Weight Watchers note
Half a baguette is 5 Points. If you wish to save 3 Points, whilst still having a hearty sandwich, replace with 4 slices of low-calorie bread.

Smoked Mackerel and Apple Open Sandwich

> **Points per serving: 7**
> **Total Points per recipe: 14**
>
> Serves: 2
> Preparation time: 5 minutes
> Freezing: not recommended
> Calories per serving: 350

Not so convenient for a packed lunch, but a delicious alternative to the sandwich – and, with a generous two rounds per serving, it will take longer to eat. This is delicious with cherry tomatoes and red pepper crudités.

2 tablespoons low-fat mayonnaise
4 teaspoons horseradish sauce
4 thin slices of brown bread
1 crisp, tart apple, e.g. Cox's,
cored and sliced thinly
1 teaspoon lemon juice
100 g (3 1/2 oz) peppered smoked
mackerel, skinned and flaked
salt

1. Mix together the mayonnaise and horseradish and spread over each slice of bread.
2. Toss the apple slices in the lemon juice. Arrange the flaked mackerel and apple slices on the bread, seasoning with a little salt.

Weight Watchers note
Weight Watchers from Heinz 90% fat-free, mayonnaise-style dressing only contains 1/2 Point per 2 tablespoons, compared with 2 Points for the same amount of low-fat mayonnaise.

Smoked Turkey Roll with Cranberry

> **Points per serving: 5**
> **Total Points per recipe: 10**
>
> Serves: 2
> Preparation time: 5 minutes
> Freezing: not recommended
> Calories per serving: 245

2 crusty medium-size white
rolls, split
4 tablespoons low-fat plain
fromage frais
4 teaspoons cranberry sauce
iceberg lettuce, shredded
55 g (2 oz) (about 8 slices)
wafer-thin smoked turkey
salt and freshly ground black
pepper

1. Spread each half-roll with a tablespoon of fromage frais and then with a teaspoon of cranberry sauce.
2. Put some shredded iceberg lettuce on the roll bases and then arrange the turkey on top. Season with salt and pepper.
3. Sandwich the half-rolls together.

Variation
Replace the turkey with 60 g (2 oz) of wafer-thin ham. The Points remain the same.

Weight Watchers notes
1 rounded tablespoon of low-fat fromage frais = 1 Point.
2 rounded tablespoons of very-low-fat fromage frais = 1/2 Point.

Banana, Cheese and Honey Sandwich

> **Points per serving: 6 1/2**
> **Total Points per recipe: 6 1/2**
>
> Serves: 1
> Preparation time: 5 minutes
> Freezing: not recommended
> Calories per serving: 365

A sweeter sandwich than the usual savoury fillings – which makes it a great boon when you crave something sweet.

1 ripe medium-size banana
1 teaspoon lemon juice
2 medium-size slices of brown
bread
40 g (1 1/2 oz) ricotta cheese
1 teaspoon runny honey
1 teaspoon sultanas or raisins

1. Mash the banana with the lemon juice until smooth. Spread over the slices of bread.
2. Mix together the ricotta cheese, honey and sultanas or raisins. Spread over one slice of bread and sandwich the slices together.
3. Cut into quarters and wrap in clingfilm, until required.

Variation
Divide the filling between four small slices of currant bread. Add 2 Points.

Cook's note
The riper the banana, the sweeter and creamier it will taste.

Ⓥ if using vegetarian cheese

56

Chinese Prawn and Sweetcorn Pitta

Points per serving: 4½
Total Points per recipe: 9

Serves: 2

Preparation and cooking time: 10 minutes

Freezing: not recommended

Calories per serving: 295

Delicious eaten warm or cold, this filling for a pitta bread makes a few tiger prawns go a long way.

1 small carrot, grated
2 tablespoons canned sweetcorn kernels, drained
2 teaspoons sesame oil
2 teaspoons light soy sauce
2 medium-size pitta breads
100 g (3½ oz) cooked tiger prawns
freshly ground black pepper
1 teaspoon chilli sauce (optional), to serve

1. Mix together the carrot, sweetcorn and 1 teaspoon each of sesame oil and soy sauce.
2. Lightly toast and split two pitta breads. Meanwhile, heat the remaining oil in a small frying-pan. Add the tiger prawns and stir-fry for 2 minutes, to heat through; then add the remaining teaspoon of soy sauce. Season with a little pepper.
3. Split and fill the toasted pitta breads with the carrot salad. Top with the tiger prawns.
4. Serve drizzled with a little chilli sauce, if you like.

Tuna Niçoise Pitta

Points per serving: 3½
Total Points per recipe: 7

Serves: 2

Preparation time: 10 minutes

Freezing: not recommended

Calories per serving: 265

100 g (3½ oz) canned tuna in brine, drained
2 tomatoes, de-seeded and chopped
1 small onion, sliced thinly into rings
1 celery stick, chopped
4 black olives in brine, drained, pitted and sliced
2 teaspoons chopped fresh parsley
5 fresh basil leaves, torn
radicchio or lollo rosso lettuce leaves or iceberg or round lettuce, torn
2 tablespoons low-fat vinaigrette dressing
2 medium-size pitta breads
salt and freshly ground black pepper

1. In a large bowl, gently combine the tuna, tomatoes, onion, celery, olives, parsley and basil. Season well with salt and pepper.
2. Toss the salad leaves in half the dressing. Mix the remainder into the tuna mixture.
3. Split the pitta breads and divide the salad leaves and tuna between the pockets. Wrap in clingfilm until required.

Curried Chicken, Celery and Nut Stuffed Pitta

Points per serving: 7½
Total Points per recipe: 7½

Serves: 1

Preparation time: 5 minutes

Freezing: not recommended

Calories per serving: 415

Make use of ready-prepared salads and coleslaw – low-fat alternatives are usually available, too.

4 tablespoons reduced-calorie celery, nut and sultana salad
1 teaspoon mild curry paste
1 apple, cored and chopped
75 g (2½ oz) cooked, boneless, skinless chicken, chopped
1 medium-size pitta bread
salt and freshly ground black pepper

1. Mix the celery, nut and sultana salad with the curry paste and apple. Season lightly.
2. Fold in the chicken pieces. Pile into the split pitta bread. Wrap in clingfilm and refrigerate until required.

Tandoori Chicken Pitta with Raita

Points per serving: 6
Total Points per recipe: 6

Serves: 1

Preparation time: 5 minutes

Freezing: not recommended

Calories per serving: 365

Raitas are Indian-style yogurt salads; this mint salad is like the Greek tzatziki or Turkish caçik.

75 g (2¾ oz) cooked tandoori chicken pieces
2 teaspoons lemon juice
4 tablespoons low-fat or lite tzatziki dip
1 spring onion, chopped
2.5 cm (1-inch) piece of cucumber, cubed
4 iceberg lettuce leaves, shredded
1 medium-size pitta bread
salt and freshly ground black pepper

1. Chop the chicken into small pieces. Sprinkle with lemon juice and season lightly with salt.
2. Mix together the dip, spring onion and cucumber. Season with salt and pepper.
3. Stuff the lettuce, chicken and raita into the pitta, ending with lettuce. Wrap in clingfilm until required.

Cheese, Orange and Date Pitta Pocket

Points per serving: 6½
Total Points per recipe: 6½

Serves: 1

Preparation time: 10 minutes

Freezing: not recommended

Calories per serving: 300

1 small orange, peeled,
    segmented and chopped
2 dates, stoned and chopped
1 spring onion, chopped
25 g (1 oz) half-fat Cheddar
    cheese, grated finely
2 tablespoons very-low-fat plain
    fromage frais
1 medium-size pitta bread
crisp salad leaves, e.g. frisée, torn
salt and freshly ground black
    pepper

1. Mix together the orange, dates, spring onion and cheese. Add any collected juice, together with the fromage frais. Season lightly, to taste.
2. Split the pitta bread and alternately fill it with the salad leaves and orange and date filling. Wrap in clingfilm and refrigerate until required.

Variation

Replace the half-fat Cheddar cheese with a small tub (110 g) of cottage cheese and add ½ Point.

Sardine, Fennel and Red Onion Salad

Points per serving: 3
Total Points per recipe: 6

Serves: 2

Preparation time: 10 minutes

Freezing: not recommended

Calories per serving: 145

1 small fennel bulb, outer
    leaves and root discarded
125 g (4¼ oz) canned sardines
    in brine, drained and flaked
½ red onion, sliced thinly
1 tablespoon chopped fresh
    parsley
2 tablespoons low-fat thousand-
    island dressing
4 lollo rosso lettuce leaves, torn
salt and freshly ground black
    pepper

1. Thinly slice the fennel across the bulb. Put the slices in a bowl, with the sardines, onion, parsley and thousand-island dressing. Fold the ingredients together.
2. Season with salt and pepper, to taste. Stuff each pitta pocket with a bed of salad leaves and top with the sardine mixture.

Dips and Pâtés

Dips and pâtés are ideal for social events, picnics, outdoor entertaining or eating whilst sitting around the kitchen table with friends or family.

They are easily transportable, and can be portioned into small containers.

They make a tasty change in the lunch box. Serve them with crispbreads and plenty of fresh, Point-free vegetable crudités.

See page 25 for a list of breads ideal for serving with these dips and pâtés.

Tuna, Tomato and Basil Dip

Points per serving: 3
Total Points per recipe: 6

Serves: 2

Preparation time: 10 minutes

Freezing: not recommended

Calories per serving: 190

Accompany this dip with crisp 'Points-free' crudités, such as celery, peppers, radish, carrots and a choice of bread and 'dippers' (see page 25). Great for packed lunches, picnics or as a snack.

200 g (7 oz) low-fat soft cheese,
    softened
100 g (3½ oz) canned tuna in
    brine, drained
2 small tomatoes, de-seeded
    and chopped
5 fresh basil leaves, shredded
1 teaspoon lemon juice
salt and freshly ground black
    pepper

1. Cream the softened cheese with a fork, until smooth.
2. Carefully fold in the tuna, tomatoes and basil. Season with the lemon juice and salt and pepper, to taste.
3. Divide between four small ramekins or two small containers, cover with clingfilm and chill until required.

Ⓥ if using vegetarian cheese

Sardine and Spring Onion Dip

Points per serving: 5
Total Points per recipe: 10

Serves: 2
Preparation time: 5 minutes
Freezing: not recommended
Calories per serving: 190

A little creativity with the endless varieties of low-fat 'goodies' now available makes losing weight more enjoyable.

125 g (4½ oz) canned sardines
    in brine, drained
170 g tub of low-fat tzatziki dip
2 spring onions, chopped finely
salt and freshly ground black
    pepper

1. Lightly mash the sardines. Mix in the tzatziki and spring onions. Season with salt and pepper.
2. Cover and chill until required.
3. Serve with crisp fresh crudités and other 'dippers' (see Cook's note page 30).

Variation

This serves 4 as a starter. Points per serving will be 2½ and Calories per serving will be 95.

Creamy Cheese and Mango Dip

Points per serving: 4
Total Points per recipe: 8

Serves: 2
Preparation time: 10 minutes +
30 minutes chilling
Freezing: not recommended
Calories per serving: 190

Fresh ripe mangoes are juicy, brightly coloured and absolutely delicious. Treat yourself to one for this creamy dip. Chop any remaining mango into a fruit salad or low-fat plain yogurt for a quick dessert.

125 g carton of medium-fat soft
    cheese, e.g. Philadelphia
2 tablespoons low-fat plain
    yogurt
¼ teaspoon chilli sauce, to taste
½ small ripe mango, peeled
    and chopped
2 teaspoons chopped fresh
    coriander
salt and freshly ground black
    pepper

1. In a bowl, beat together the soft cheese and yogurt, until smooth. Add the chilli sauce and mix well. Season, to taste.
2. Fold in the mango and chopped coriander. Cover and chill for 30 minutes

Ⓥ if using vegetarian soft cheese

Bombay Egg Spread

Points per serving: 2½
Total Points per recipe: 5

Serves: 2
Preparation and cooking time:
15 minutes
+ 2 hours chilling
Freezing: not recommended
Calories per serving: 135

1 tablespoon fresh breadcrumbs
1 teaspoon sunflower oil
1 small onion, chopped finely
1 teaspoon mild curry powder
2 eggs, beaten
25 g (1 oz) low-fat soft cheese
2 teaspoons chopped fresh
    parsley, coriander or chives
salt and freshly ground black
    pepper

1. Heat a non-stick frying-pan, add the breadcrumbs and stir-fry continuously for 1–2 minutes, or until golden.
2. Mix together the sunflower oil and onion and then add to the hot pan. Sauté for 4–5 minutes, until softened and slightly coloured. Add the curry powder and cook for a minute.
3. Stir in the eggs and stir-fry over a moderate heat, until lightly scrambled. Spoon the mixture into a small bowl.
4. Add the breadcrumbs, soft cheese and herbs. Beat well. Season to taste.
5. Divide the soft mixture between two small ramekin dishes, pressing down firmly. Cover and chill for 2 hours.

Ⓥ if using free-range eggs and vegetarian soft cheese

Carrot Pâté

This is a colourful, fresh-tasting, soft pâté, which will be popular with the children, too. As it freezes well, make a batch and freeze in individual portions. Serve with crispbreads or Melba toast.

1 teaspoon sunflower oil
1 small shallot or onion, chopped
150 g (5½ oz) carrots, sliced
    thinly
½ teaspoon grated orange zest
1 tablespoon medium-fat soft
    cheese, e.g. Philadelphia
    light
a pinch of ground coriander
1 teaspoon chopped fresh chives
    or parsley
salt and freshly ground black
    pepper

1. Heat the oil in a small saucepan and cook the shallot or onion for 5 minutes, until softened but not coloured. Add the carrots and just enough cold water to cover them.
2. Cover and cook gently for 15–20 minutes or until the carrots are soft. For the last 3–5 minutes, cook uncovered, to evaporate all the liquid. Leave to cool.
3. Place in a liquidiser or food processor and blend until very smooth. Add the orange zest, soft cheese, ground coriander and a little salt and pepper. Blend together thoroughly and then stir in the fresh herbs. Spoon the mixture between 2 small ramekins. Cover and chill for 2–3 hours.

Ⓥ if using vegetarian soft cheese

Quick Mushroom Pâté

4 teaspoons olive oil
225 g (8 oz) button mushrooms,
    chopped roughly
125 g (4½ oz) open-cup
    mushrooms, chopped
    roughly
2 garlic cloves, crushed
½ teaspoon paprika
½ teaspoon salt
¼ teaspoon ground bay leaf or
    ½ teaspoon dried thyme
1 egg, beaten

1. Heat 3 teaspoons of the olive oil in a large, non-stick frying-pan. Add the mushrooms and garlic and stir-fry over a medium heat for 5 minutes or until the mushrooms start to release their liquid. Increase the heat and continue to cook, shaking the pan from time to time, until most of the liquid has evaporated and the mushrooms look dry.
2. Transfer the mushrooms to a food processor. Add the paprika, salt and herbs.
3. Heat the remaining teaspoon of olive oil in the frying-pan, stir in the egg and scramble until set. (The egg will mop up any remaining mushroom residue.) Add this to the mushrooms.
4. Blend until the mixture has a fine, grainy consistency. Adjust the seasoning, to taste.
5. Divide the mushroom pâté into four individual ramekins. Cover with clingfilm and chill for at least 4 hours, before serving with crispbreads and crudités.

Cook's note
Look out for small jars of ready-prepared puréed garlic, chilli and ginger. This saves time and smelly chopping boards and fingers – and means you always have a teaspoonful to hand in the fridge.

Ⓥ if using a free-range egg

Layered Chicken and Watercress Salad with Orange and Mustard Dressing *(opposite)*
Cottage Cheese, Prawns and Asparagus Salad *(opposite)*

Cottage Cheese, Prawns and Asparagus Salad

Points per serving: 3
Total Points per recipe: 3

Serves: 1
Preparation and cooking time: 10 minutes
Freezing: not recommended
Calories per serving: 185

This salad also makes a delicious filling for a pitta bread or sandwich.

4 young asparagus tips (or 2 asparagus spears)
110 g tub of cottage cheese with prawn cocktail
5 cm (2-inch) piece of cucumber, cubed
1/2 Little Gem lettuce, shredded
3 cherry tomatoes, halved
1/2 teaspoon chopped fresh dill
salt and freshly ground black pepper

1. Plunge the asparagus into a pan of lightly salted, boiling water and cook for 2 minutes. Drain. Refresh under cold running water and then drain thoroughly again. Chop into 1 cm (1/2 inch) lengths, reserving the tips.
2. Mix together the cottage cheese, cucumber and asparagus. Season well with salt and pepper.
3. Arrange the lettuce in the base of a small bowl. Spoon on the cottage cheese mixture. Top with the cherry tomatoes and asparagus tips. Sprinkle with chopped dill and season with salt and pepper, to taste.
4. Cover and chill, until required.

Layered Chicken and Watercress Salad with Orange and Mustard Dressing

Points per serving: 5
Total Points per recipe: 5

Serves: 1
Preparation time: 10 minutes
Freezing: not recommended
Calories per serving: 295

If you have leftover roast chicken and new potatoes, here is a tasty way of using them up.

1 small orange, peeled
75 g (2³/₄ oz) cooked, boneless, skinless chicken breast, cut into bite-size pieces
100g (31/2 oz) small new potatoes, cooked and cubed
3 tablespoons low-fat plain Bio-yogurt
1/2 teaspoon whole-grain mustard
1 teaspoon chopped fresh chives or parsley
50 g (1³/₄ oz) fresh watercress, trimmed
2–3 radicchio leaves, torn
salt and freshly ground black pepper

1. Hold the orange over a bowl, to catch any juices, and, using a sharp knife, segment the orange. Chop each segment in half and place in a bowl, with the chicken and potatoes.
2. Stir the plain yogurt into the orange juice. Whisk in the mustard and chopped herbs. Season with salt and pepper.
3. Add the salad leaves to the dressing and toss lightly, to coat.
4. Place one-third of the dressed salad leaves in a bowl or container. Spoon on the chicken mixture and top with the remaining salad.
5. Cover and chill, until required.

63

Ham, Pineapple and Celery Salad

Points per serving: 2½
Total Points per recipe: 2½

Serves: 1
Preparation time: 5 minutes
Freezing: not recommended
Calories per serving: 310

Use a really tasty ham – just a small amount will give a delicious flavour to the salad.

2 canned pineapple rings in
natural juice
1 tablespoon low-fat
mayonnaise
40 g (1½ oz) slice of honey-
roast ham, chopped
1 celery stick, chopped
¼ red pepper, de-seeded and
chopped
1 spring onion, chopped
salt and freshly ground black
pepper

1. Cut the pineapple rings into bite-size pieces.
2. Mix 2 tablespoons of pineapple juice with the mayonnaise in a bowl.
3. Mix the pineapple, ham, celery, red pepper and spring onion. Toss the salad ingredients in the dressing. Season with salt and pepper. Cover and chill until required.

Paprika, Mushroom and Courgette Salad

Points per serving: 1½
Total Points per recipe: 1½

Serves: 1
Preparation time: 10 minutes
Freezing: not recommended
Calories per serving: 135

This salad is ideal made ahead of time. Serve with crispbreads.

1 tomato, sliced thinly
½ small courgette, sliced thinly
1 tablespoon vinaigrette dressing
2 tablespoons salad cress
4 tablespoons low-fat plain
yogurt
1 teaspoon tomato purée
1 teaspoon snipped fresh chives
¼ teaspoon mustard seeds
¼ teaspoon paprika
55 g (2 oz) button mushrooms,
quartered
salt and ground black pepper

1. Arrange the tomato and courgette slices in the base of a small pot or bowl. Sprinkle on the dressing and season with a little salt and pepper. Arrange the salad cress on top.
2. In a small bowl, mix together the yogurt, tomato purée, chives, mustard seeds and paprika. Season to taste. Fold in the mushrooms, coating them thoroughly with the dressing.
3. Pile the mushrooms on top of the salad. Cover and chill.

(v)

Ham and Potato Salad with a Curried Mango Dressing

Points per serving: 4½
Total Points per recipe: 4½

Serves: 1
Preparation time: 10 minutes
Freezing: not recommended
Calories per serving: 140

1 iceberg lettuce leaf, shredded
1 large tomato, de-seeded and
chopped
25 g (1 oz) wafer-thin ham
3 tablespoons potato salad
½ teaspoon mild curry paste
1 tablespoon mango chutney
1 teaspoon snipped fresh chives
2.5 cm (1-inch) piece of red or
yellow pepper, chopped
salt and freshly ground black
pepper

1. Arrange the shredded lettuce and tomato in the base of a small container or bowl. Place the ham on top.
2. Mix together the potato salad, curry paste, mango chutney and chives. Season with a little salt, if required. Spoon on top of the ham.
3. Scatter the chopped pepper on top. Cover and chill until required.

Weight Watchers note
Wafer-thin ham gives you a generous 25 g (1 oz) helping for just ½ Point. 1 medium-size slice of honey-roast or canned ham (35 g/1¼ oz) carries twice the amount of Points, so if you use this in preference, add ½ Point per serving.

Cottage Cheese Crunch with Spicy Grapes

Points per serving: 2½
Total Points per recipe: 2½

Serves: 1
Preparation time: 10 minutes
Freezing: not recommended
Calories per serving: 180

*110 g tub of diet cottage cheese
    with chives
1 celery stick, chopped
1 carrot, grated
25 g (1 oz) bean sprouts or
    shredded iceberg lettuce
2 teaspoons oil-free vinaigrette
    dressing, e.g. honey and
    mustard
6 seedless green grapes, quartered
1 tablespoon spicy fruit chutney,
    e.g. mango
salt and freshly ground black
    pepper*

1. Mix together the cottage cheese and celery. Season with salt and pepper and then spoon into the base of a small bowl or pot.
2. Mix together the carrot and bean sprouts or lettuce. Add the dressing and toss lightly, to coat. Layer on top of the cottage cheese.
3. Finally, mix together the grapes and the chutney and spoon on top of the salad. Cover and chill until required.

Ⓥ

Creamy Prawn and Tomato Salad with Coriander

Points per serving: 2
Total Points per recipe: 2

Serves: 1
Preparation time: 10 minutes
Freezing: not recommended
Calories per serving: 125

*1 iceberg lettuce leaf, shredded
3 slices of cucumber, cut into
    strips
½ small green pepper, de-seeded
    and chopped
4 tablespoons low-fat plain
    Bio-yogurt
1 tablespoon chopped fresh
    coriander
1 teaspoon lemon juice
1 large tomato, de-seeded and
    chopped
55 g (2 oz) cooked peeled
    prawns, thawed if frozen
cayenne pepper
chilli sauce
salt*

1. Mix together the shredded lettuce, cucumber and green pepper. Arrange in the base of a small container or bowl (about 425 ml/¾-pint capacity).
2. In a bowl, fold together the yogurt, coriander, lemon juice, tomato, prawns and a pinch of cayenne. Add a dash of chilli sauce, if liked, and season with salt.
3. Spoon the prawn mixture over the salad. Cover and chill until required.

Tuna, Red Pepper and Sweetcorn Salad

Points per serving: 2
Total Points per recipe: 4

Serves: 2
Preparation time: 10 minutes
Freezing: not recommended
Calories per serving: 105

Tuna is nutritious, versatile, economical and a handy storecupboard ingredient – but choose tuna canned in spring water or brine.

*100 g (3½ oz) canned tuna in
    brine, drained
2 tablespoons low-fat mayonnaise
½ celery stick, chopped
1 teaspoon chopped fresh chives
½ small red pepper, de-seeded
    and chopped
4 tablespoons canned sweetcorn
    kernels, drained
4 iceberg lettuce leaves, shredded
salt and freshly ground black
    pepper*

1. Mix together the tuna, mayonnaise, celery and chives. Season with salt and pepper. Divide between two small containers (each about 350 ml/12 fl oz).
2. Mix together the red pepper and sweetcorn. Season well and spread over the tuna. Top with the shredded lettuce. Cover and chill.

Edam Cheese and Coleslaw

Points per serving: 5½
Total Points per recipe: 5½

Serves: 1
Preparation time: 10 minutes
Freezing: not recommended
Calories per serving: 185

*40 g (1½ oz) Edam cheese,
    grated
1 tomato, de-seeded and
    chopped
1 teaspoon snipped fresh chives
2 iceberg lettuce leaves,
    shredded finely
4 tablespoons reduced-calorie
    coleslaw
salt and freshly ground black
    pepper*

1. Place the cheese, tomato and chives in the base of a 300 ml (½-pint) bowl or plastic container. Mix together well and season with salt and pepper.
2. Press the shredded lettuce on top and then spoon on the coleslaw. Cover with clingfilm and refrigerate until required.

Ⓥ if using vegetarian cheese

Pasta and Rice to Go

Depending on your Points allowance, choose one of the quantities of either cooked pasta or rice and simply mix it with one of the following recipe ideas. It's easy!

Pasta shapes, e.g. macaroni, shells, twists

A small portion of pasta (about 25 g/1 oz uncooked or 75 g/2³/4 oz cooked) will be 1 Point or 90 Calories.

A medium portion (about 55 g /2 oz uncooked or 150 g/5¹/2 oz cooked) will be 2 Points or 180 Calories.

A large portion (about 90 g/3¹/4 oz uncooked or 225 g/8 oz cooked) will be 3 Points or 270 Calories.

Rice, e.g. brown, white, basmati

A small portion of rice (about 25 g/1 oz uncooked rice or 75 g/2³/4 oz cooked) will be 1¹/2 Points or 90 Calories.

A medium portion (about 55 g/2 oz uncooked or 150 g/5¹/2 oz cooked will be 3 Points or 180 Calories.

A large portion (about 90 g/3¹/4 oz uncooked or 225 g/8 oz cooked) will be 4¹/2 Points or 270 Calories.

Smoked Salmon and Cucumber with a Lemon and Mustard Dressing

> **Points per serving: 5¹/2**
> **Total Points per recipe: 5¹/2**
>
> Serves: 1
> Preparation time: 5 minutes
> Calories per serving: 215
> Freezing: not recommended

Delicately flavoured, this is an excellent way of making a little smoked salmon go a long way. Accompany with a green-leaf salad or crudités and a crusty brown roll.

For the dressing:

2 tablespoons low-fat plain yogurt
1 tablespoon lemon juice
1 teaspoon mild mustard, e.g. Dijon
1 teaspoon clear honey
¹/4 teaspoon mustard seeds
¹/4 teaspoon finely grated lemon zest (optional)
1 teaspoon chopped fresh dill or chives

For the salad:

55 g (2 oz) smoked salmon trimmings, chopped
5 cm (2-inch) piece of cucumber, cubed
150 g (5¹/2 oz) cooked rice
salt and freshly ground black pepper

1. Mix together the ingredients for the dressing in either a small jar with a screw top (simply shake everything well) or a small bowl. Season with salt and pepper.
2. Toss the dressing into the rice, with the salmon and cucumber. Cover and chill until required.

Variation

If you replace the cooked rice with a medium portion of cooked pasta, Points per serving will be 4.

Cook's note

Salmon trimmings are available pre-packed or at the delicatessen counter and are more reasonably priced than salmon slices.

Weight Watchers note

Bulk this salad up with chopped red pepper or tomato.

Bacon Bits and Tomato in a Herb Vinaigrette

> **Points per serving: 4¹/2**
> **Total Points per recipe: 4¹/2**
>
> Serves: 1
> Preparation time: 10 minutes
> Calories per serving: 260
> Freezing: not recommended

1 rindless rasher of streaky smoked bacon, chopped
2 button mushrooms, chopped
2 teaspoons lemon juice
150 g (5¹/2 oz) cooked pasta
1 spring onion, chopped
1 large tomato, de-seeded and chopped
2 tablespoons low-fat vinaigrette dressing, e.g. Italian
1 teaspoon chopped fresh parsley or basil
salt and freshly ground black pepper

1. Grill the bacon until crisp. Cool and drain on a piece of kitchen paper. Crumble into small pieces.
2. Mix together the mushrooms and lemon juice. Season well with salt and pepper.
3. Fold all the ingredients together with the pasta. Season well. Cover and chill until required.

Variation

If you replace the cooked pasta with a medium portion of cooked rice Points per serving will be 5¹/2.

Pilchard and Spring Onion in Spicy Tomato Sauce

1 small can of pilchards in tomato sauce

½ teaspoon chilli paste or a few drops of chilli sauce

300 g (10½ oz) cooked pasta

3 spring onions, chopped

¼ green or yellow pepper, de-seeded and chopped

2 tablespoons canned sweetcorn kernels, drained

1 teaspoon chopped fresh parsley

salt and freshly ground black pepper

1. Pour the pilchards and sauce into a small bowl. Gently transfer the fish to a plate. Halve the fish and remove any bones, then flake the fish into bite-size pieces.

2. Mix a tablespoon of water into the tomato sauce and then stir in the chilli paste or sauce, to taste. Season with salt and pepper. Mix well with the pasta.

3. Stir in the spring onions, yellow pepper and sweetcorn and fold in the pilchards. Divide between two small bowls or containers and sprinkle with the chopped parsley. Cover and chill, until required.

Mediterranean Vegetable Salad

½ yellow pepper, de-seeded and cut into large chunks

1 small courgette, sliced thickly

1 small onion or shallot, sliced

2 teaspoons olive oil

2 tomatoes, quartered and de-seeded

2 olives in brine, pitted and sliced

3 tablespoons vinaigrette dressing

¼ – ½ teaspoon chilli sauce

½ teaspoon dried mixed herbs

300 g (10½ oz) cooked pasta

6 fresh basil leaves, torn

salt and freshly ground black pepper

1. Toss the pepper, courgette and onion in the olive oil. Heat a non-stick frying-pan and, when it is very hot, stir-fry the vegetables for 3–4 minutes, until they begin to soften and brown. Remove the pan from the heat.

2. Add the tomatoes and olives to the vegetable mixture.

3. Mix the vinaigrette dressing with the chilli sauce and the herbs. Season with salt and pepper and drizzle over the vegetables.

4. Fold the pasta and basil leaves into the vegetable mix. Divide between two bowls or containers. Cover and chill until required.

Variation

If you replace the cooked pasta with 2 medium portions of cooked rice, Points per serving will be 5.

Curried Prawn and Apple Salad

Points per serving: 5
Total Points per recipe: 5

Serves: 1
Preparation time: 5 minutes
Freezing: not recommended
Calories per serving: 215

2 teaspoons lemon juice
55 g (2 oz) cooked, peeled prawns,
   thawed if frozen
1 small eating apple, cored
   and chopped
1/2 small celery stick, chopped
1 tomato, de-seeded and chopped
150 g (5 1/2 oz) cooked rice
For the dressing:
1 small spring onion, chopped
1 teaspoon mild curry powder
2 tablespoons low-fat plain
   yogurt
salt and freshly ground black
   pepper

1. Sprinkle the lemon juice over the prawns and apple and toss them to coat. Add the celery and tomato. Season with a little salt and pepper.
2. Mix together all the ingredients for the dressing. Fold into the prawn mixture. Mix with the rice. Cover and chill until required.

Variation

If you replace the rice with a medium portion of cooked pasta, Points per serving will be 4. Replace the prawns with wafer-thin slices of chicken or ham.

For another fishy alternative, replace the prawns with flakes of smoked mackerel; replace the curry powder with horseradish sauce. Add 2 1/2 Points.

Roast Chicken Salad with Cucumber and Sweetcorn Relish

Points per serving: 6 1/2
Total Points per recipe: 13

Serves: 2
Preparation time: 10 minutes
Freezing: not recommended
Calories per serving: 235

Small amounts of leftovers can go a long way, with a little imagination.

100 g (3 1/2 oz) cooked, boneless,
   skinless chicken, chopped
100 g (3 1/2 oz) cucumber, cubed
50 g (1 1/2 oz) canned sweetcorn
   kernels, drained
2 spring onions, chopped
4 teaspoons chopped fresh
   coriander
300 g (10 1/2 oz) cooked basmati
   rice
2 tablespoons low-fat
   mayonnaise
1/2 teaspoon chilli paste or a few
   drops of chilli sauce
1–2 teaspoons skimmed milk
salt and freshly ground black
   pepper
finely shredded lettuce, to serve

1. Fold together the chicken, cucumber, sweetcorn, spring onions and chopped coriander. Season with salt and pepper. Mix with the rice.
2. Mix the mayonnaise with the chilli paste or sauce. Dilute with a drop of milk. Fold into the salad.
3. Divide between two containers or bowls, spooning the salad on to a bed of shredded lettuce.

70

Vegetables and Salads

Over the last ten years, the range of fresh fruits and vegetables available to us has grown and grown. The seasons have become longer as vegetables and fruit are imported from all over the world. The quality has, in many cases, improved and our own supermarkets and retailers are ready with advice on how to use these vegetables in delicious recipes.

At one time, vegetable dishes and salads were often described as 'rabbit food'. But now, with more and more people, and particularly the teenage population, eating less or no meat at all, a plateful of fresh vegetables or salad is not only for rabbits to dream about! This chapter is packed with nutritious and simply delicious dishes – hot gratins or vegetable accompaniments, which can double up as satisfying meals, and some well-dressed salads too. Enjoy them on their own, or serve with grilled meats, fish or poultry.

If you enjoy a particular salad dressing, make up a quantity and keep it handy in the fridge. Commercially produced, oil-free dressings can be spiced up, too, by adding extra herbs or lemon juice. Make a dressing go further, by adding an extra tablespoon of low-fat plain yogurt or natural fruit juice. Just keep a record of any extra Points added in the process.

Use recipes as a basis and experiment with different vegetables. Swap the root vegetables around, replacing carrots with celeriac, or try out different salads and greens, most of which have their own unique flavour.

Steaming and microwaving vegetables helps preserve vitamins and minerals, which are otherwise washed out in the cooking water. So, try to shop on a regular basis for fresh produce and choose quick cooking methods, to keep in as much goodness as possible.

Finally, a hint on storing vegetables and salads. A cool, dark place – a utility room or garage – is a good home for vegetables; or wrap small quantities in food bags and store in the salad/crisper drawers at the bottom of the refrigerator. The longer vegetables are stored, the less nutritious they become. Vitamins start to deteriorate from the moment of harvesting.

Cauliflower Cheese

A traditional family favourite! It is a great accompaniment to fresh grilled plaice or cod and equally as satisfying served on its own or with crusty bread.

1 cauliflower, broken into florets
1 tablespoon half-fat butter or
*   margarine*
3 tablespoons plain flour
425 ml (³/4 pint) skimmed milk
125 g (4¹/2 oz) half-fat
*   Cheddar cheese, grated*
a pinch of mustard powder
2 teaspoons natural-colour
*   dried breadcrumbs*
salt and freshly ground black
*   pepper*

1. Cook the cauliflower, in lightly salted, boiling water for 8–10 minutes, or until just tender. Drain thoroughly.
2. Meanwhile, make the cheese sauce. Put the butter or margarine, flour and milk all together in a saucepan and slowly bring to the boil, stirring briskly all the time, until the sauce thickens and becomes smooth.
3. Remove from the heat, stir in half the cheese and the mustard. Season, to taste.
4. Preheat the grill to its highest setting. Transfer the cauliflower to a shallow 1.2-litre (2-pint) ovenproof dish. Pour the cheese sauce on top. Sprinkle on the cheese and breadcrumbs.
5. Place under the hot grill for 4–5 minutes or until the cheese sauce is golden brown and bubbling. Serve immediately.

Variation

This serves 4 as an accompaniment. Points per serving will be 4 and Calories per serving will be 195.

Golden Vegetable Stir-Fry with Warm Mustard Dressing

Stir-fries are a quick, no-fuss method of preparing vegetables. Serve this delicious combination on its own or with grilled salmon or chicken.

2 teaspoons olive oil
1 onion, cut into 8, layers
*   separated*
1 garlic clove, chopped
1 yellow pepper, de-seeded and
*   cut into wedges*
400 g (14 oz) canned new
*   potatoes, drained and*
*   halved*
1 large carrot
2 teaspoons snipped fresh chives
2 teaspoons whole-grain
*   mustard*
2 tablespoons half-fat crème
*   fraîche*
salt and freshly ground black
*   pepper*

1. Heat the oil in a large, non-stick frying-pan. Add the onion and stir-fry for 4–5 minutes, or until softened and slightly coloured.
2. Add the garlic, yellow pepper and potatoes and stir-fry for a further 4–5 minutes.
3. Meanwhile, using a potato peeler, shave long parings from the carrot and add to the pan. Season to taste, with salt and pepper.
4. Mix together the chives, mustard and crème fraîche and stir into the vegetables. Cook for a further minute. Serve.

Ⓥ if using vegetarian cheese

Aubergine Cannelloni with Tomato Sauce

The aubergine is a versatile vegetable. It absorbs flavours well (and – beware – soaks up oil!) and offers a variety of textures, depending on the cooking method. These cannelloni are delicious. Serve with fresh green beans or a green salad.

1 large aubergine
4 teaspoons olive oil
1 onion, chopped
1 courgette, chopped
2 garlic cloves, chopped
3 tomatoes, skinned, de-seeded and chopped
6 fresh basil leaves, torn
2 teaspoons sun-dried tomato paste
1 tablespoon capers, drained and chopped
150 g (5½ oz) half-fat mozzarella cheese, drained and chopped
2 tablespoons fresh breadcrumbs
4 teaspoons grated parmesan cheese
300 ml tub of fresh tomato pasta sauce
salt and freshly ground black pepper

1. Preheat the oven to Gas Mark 4/180°C/350°F.
2. Trim off the stalk end of the aubergine, remove and reserve the outer bulbous slices and then cut the aubergine lengthways into 8 thin slices (each about 5 mm/¼ inch thick). Chop the outer slices.
3. Arrange the slices on a non-stick baking tray. Brush with a little oil and season with salt and pepper. Cook for 15 minutes, until softened.
4. Place the onion, courgette and chopped aubergine in a saucepan, season with salt and pepper, add 4 tablespoons of water and cook, allowing the water to evaporate, whilst softening the vegetables.
5. Add the garlic, tomatoes, basil and tomato paste. Cook gently for a further 3–4 minutes. Add the capers. Remove from the heat to cool; season to taste.
6. Sprinkle the centre of each sliced aubergine with the mozzarella. Spoon the vegetable stuffing along the centre of each slice, then roll up and place each 'cannelloni', seam-down, in a shallow ovenproof dish.
7. Brush with the remaining oil and sprinkle over the breadcrumbs and parmesan cheese. Bake for 10 minutes.
8. Remove from the oven. Dilute the pasta sauce with 3 tablespoons of water and pour around the aubergine rolls. Cook for a further 10 minutes.

Ⓥ if using vegetarian cheeses

Moroccan Vegetable Stew

This is a spicy version of ratatouille – it can be made several days ahead of eating and tastes all the better for it! Delicious hot, or well chilled with barbecued meats or crusty bread.

1 small aubergine, sliced thinly
1 red pepper
1 green pepper
2 teaspoons olive oil
1 onion, sliced
1 garlic clove, crushed
1 fresh red chilli, de-seeded and chopped
1 teaspoon ground cumin
225 g (8 oz) plum tomatoes, skinned, de-seeded and chopped
150 ml (¼ pint) vegetable stock or tomato juice
salt and freshly ground black pepper
2 tablespoons chopped fresh coriander

1. Place the aubergine in a colander, sprinkling each layer with salt. Cover with a weighted plate and leave to stand for 15–20 minutes. Then, rinse and drain thoroughly.
2. Place the peppers under a hot grill, turning frequently, until the skin is charred and blistered. Pop in a plastic bag and leave to cool.
3. Heat the oil in a saucepan, add the onion, garlic and chilli and cook gently for 5 minutes, until softened but not coloured. Add the cumin and cook for 1 minute.
4. Halve the aubergine slices and add to the pan, with the tomatoes and stock. Season with salt and pepper. Part-cover and leave to simmer for 20 minutes, stirring occasionally.
5. Meanwhile, peel the peppers, discarding the cores and seeds. Cut into thin strips.
6. Five minutes before the end of cooking, stir in the pepper strips. Season to taste. Serve, garnished with chopped coriander.

Variations
Replace the tomatoes and stock with 400 g (14 oz) canned chopped tomatoes with herbs.

This serves 4 as an accompaniment. Points per serving will be ½. Calories per serving will be 65.

Ⓥ

Parsnip and Carrot Mash with a Crunchy Hazelnut Topping

Points per serving: 2½
Total Points per recipe: 10

Serves: 4
Preparation time: 20 minutes
Cooking time: 20 minutes
Freezing: recommended
Calories per serving: 140

Serve this colourful mash on its own with green vegetables or as an accompaniment with grilled chops or sausages.

450 g (1 lb) parsnips, sliced
450 g (1 lb) carrots, sliced
4 tablespoons low-fat plain
*   fromage frais*
freshly grated nutmeg
1 teaspoon chopped fresh parsley
2 tablespoons fresh white
*   breadcrumbs*
10 hazelnuts, chopped
salt and freshly ground black
*   pepper*

1. Cook the parsnips and carrots in separate saucepans of lightly salted, boiling water, for 15–20 minutes, or until tender. Drain thoroughly.
2. Preheat the oven to Gas Mark 5/190°C/375°F.
3. Mash the parsnip with 3 tablespoons of fromage frais and a little grated nutmeg. Season, to taste.
4. Mash the carrot with 1 tablespoon of fromage frais. Mix in the parsley. Season to taste.
5. Randomly spoon the parsnip and carrot into a shallow ovenproof dish, to create a marbled effect. (Use a small, round-edged knife to join together.)
6. Mix together the breadcrumbs and nuts and scatter over the vegetable mash. Bake for 15–20 minutes, or until heated through and the crunchy topping is golden.

Variation

Replace the hazelnut topping with 55 g (2 oz) of grated Gruyère cheese. Add 2½ Points per serving.

Cook's notes

If you use a food processor to purée the vegetables, do not over-purée them, particularly the carrots, which will become watery.

For speed, cook and mash the carrot and parsnip together.

Summer Vegetable Bake

Points per serving: 3
Total Points per recipe: 6

Serves: 2
Preparation time: 15 minutes
Cooking time: 45 minutes
Freezing: recommended
Calories per serving: 280

An assortment of fresh-tasting, oven-baked vegetables – good enough on its own or as a vegetable accompaniment to grilled salmon steaks.

juice of ½ lemon
1 tablespoon olive oil
1 garlic clove, crushed
1 red pepper, de-seeded and
*   chopped*
1 green pepper, de-seeded and
*   chopped*
1 courgette, cut into chunks
2 tomatoes, quartered
4 shallots, halved
225 g (8 oz) new potatoes, halved
For the topping
25 g (1 oz) fresh breadcrumbs
25 g (1 oz) half-fat Cheddar
*   cheese, grated finely*
2 tablespoons chopped fresh
*   mixed herbs, e.g. parsley,*
*   thyme, chives*
salt and finely ground black
*   pepper*

1. In a large bowl, mix together the lemon juice and olive oil. Add the garlic, peppers, courgette, tomatoes, shallots and potatoes. Season with salt and pepper. Toss thoroughly, to coat with the oil.
2. Preheat the oven to Gas Mark 6/200°C/400°F.
3. Spoon the vegetables into a gratin dish and cook for 30 minutes, turning half way through.
4. Mix together the breadcrumbs, cheese and herbs and sprinkle over the vegetables. Cook for a further 15 minutes, or until golden and crisp on the surface.

Variation

This serves 4 as an accompaniment. Points per serving will be 1½ and Calories per serving will be 140.

Ⓥ

Ⓥ if using vegetarian cheese

Roasted Vegetables with Toasted Greek Cheese

You can enjoy these roasted vegetables hot or cold, on their own or as an accompaniment, and with the option of transforming them into a supper dish, with toasted bread and grilled cheese.

1 small red pepper, de-seeded
    and quartered
1 small yellow pepper, de-seeded
    and quartered
2 red onions, quartered
1 fennel bulb, trimmed and
    sliced thickly
2 large courgettes, sliced thickly
4 large, flat mushrooms
4 large tomatoes
4 asparagus spears
2 tablespoons lemon juice
1 tablespoon olive oil
2 garlic cloves, chopped
salt and freshly ground black
    pepper

To serve:
4 medium-size slices of sun-dried
    tomato bread
125 g (4½ oz) feta cheese,
    sliced into 4
8 fresh basil leaves, torn

1. Preheat the oven to Gas Mark 6/200°C/400°F. Arrange the vegetables in one layer in a shallow roasting tin.
2. Mix together the lemon juice and olive oil. Season with salt and pepper and brush a little over the vegetables. Sprinkle on the chopped garlic.
3. Roast for 45 minutes or until well browned and tender. Turn the vegetables once during cooking, brushing with a little more of the lemon juice and oil. Remove from the oven.
4. Preheat the grill to a high setting. Toast the bread lightly and then arrange on individual plates.
5. Lightly brush a piece of foil with lemon and oil, place in the grill pan and arrange the cheese slices on top. Grill for 1–2 minutes on each side.
6. Meanwhile, arrange the warmed vegetables on the toast. Using a spatula, place a piece of grilled cheese on top of the warm vegetables and drizzle with any remaining cooking juices or lemon/oil. Scatter on the basil.

Variation
Serve the vegetables on their own, without the bread and cheese, accompanied with 2 tablespoons of tzatziki dip per person. The Points will be 1 per serving.

Cook's note
These vegetables are delicious eaten chilled, either on their own or with grilled fish or chicken.
Ⓥ if using vegetarian cheese

Grilled Vegetable Kebabs with a Hot Tomato Glaze

These kebabs can be served on their own with crusty bread or pittas and a salad, or with a potato or vegetable bake.

1 medium-size aubergine
1 red or yellow pepper, halved
    and de-seeded
2 medium-size courgettes
4 teaspoons olive oil
2 tomatoes, skinned, de-seeded
    and chopped finely
1 shallot, chopped finely
4 teaspoons horseradish sauce
salt and freshly ground black
    pepper

1. Slice the aubergine into 2.5 cm (1-inch) thick rounds; then quarter each slice. Cut the pepper into chunks and thickly slice the courgettes.
2. Preheat the grill to a medium-high setting. Remove the grid and line the tray with foil. Thread the vegetables on to four small skewers. Brush with the oil and season with salt and pepper. Grill for 15–20 minutes, turning and brushing frequently, until the vegetables have softened and coloured.
3. Meanwhile, mix together the tomatoes, shallot and horseradish. Stir in any remaining oil and then brush a little over the vegetables for the last 5 minutes of grilling.
4. Dab the kebabs with the remaining glaze and season, to taste.

Ⓥ

Crisp Baked Florets with a Piquant Dip

Points per serving: 4½
Total Points per recipe: 9

Serves: 2
Preparation and cooking time:
30 minutes
Freezing: not recommended
Calories per serving: 270

Roasting vegetables seems to bring out their own unique flavour. Here is a delicious way of enjoying everyday vegetables with a twist! Serve with a small baked potato, a little pasta or some crusty bread.

½ medium-size cauliflower,
   broken into florets
225 g (8 oz) broccoli florets
1 egg, beaten
2 teaspoons plain flour
2 tablespoons fresh white
   breadcrumbs
1 tablespoon grated parmesan
   cheese
½ teaspoon mild chilli powder
2 teaspoons vegetable oil
For the dip:
175 g (6 oz) low-fat plain
   fromage frais
1 tablespoon tomato purée
1 tablespoon chopped fresh
   coriander or chives
1 teaspoon chopped capers or
   gherkins
chilli sauce
salt

1. Preheat the oven to Gas Mark 7/210°C/425°F. Par-cook the cauliflower and broccoli florets in lightly salted, boiling water for 7–8 minutes. Drain and refresh in ice-cold water. Drain and dry thoroughly with kitchen paper.
2. Place the florets in a bowl and drizzle on the beaten egg. Lightly turn the florets in the egg, using two forks.
3. Mix together the flour, breadcrumbs, parmesan cheese and chilli powder. Season with salt to taste. Sprinkle over the florets, continually turning the vegetables until very lightly dusted.
4. Brush a baking tray with a little of the oil. Arrange the florets on the tray in one layer and drizzle any remaining oil over them. Roast for 10–15 minutes or until crisp and tinged golden brown.
5. Meanwhile, mix together the fromage frais, tomato purée, fresh herbs, capers or gherkins, and chilli sauce, to taste. Season with salt. Divide between two small ramekin dishes.
6. Arrange the florets on two serving dishes, accompanying each with a ramekin of piquant dip. Serve immediately.

Variation

Use low-fat soft cheese instead of fromage frais and add 1 Point per serving.

Weight Watchers note

Make the most of all the brassica family – cauliflower, broccoli, cabbage and sprouts, to name but a few. Delicious and free from Points!

Cook's note

Pop four halved tomatoes in the oven alongside the florets and serve as an accompaniment. Alternatively, accompany with a crusty brown roll per serving or a medium-size jacket potato. Remember to add the Points.

Hot Broad Bean, Tomato and Tuna Salad

Points per serving: 2
Total Points per recipe: 4

Serves: 2
Preparation and cooking time:
20 minutes
Freezing: not recommended
Calories per serving: 135

Served with crusty bread or a jacket potato, this is a delicious way to enjoy tuna.

100 g (3½ oz) frozen broad
   beans
2 shallots, sliced into rings
4 tablespoons dry white wine
   or dry cider
2 tomatoes, skinned, de-seeded
   and sliced
1 teaspoon chopped fresh
   tarragon
1 teaspoon extra-virgin olive oil
100 g (3½ oz) canned tuna
   in spring water or brine,
   drained
salt and freshly ground black
   pepper

1. Cook the broad beans in lightly salted, boiling water for 8–10 minutes, or until just tender. Drain.
2. Meanwhile, place the shallots and wine or cider in a small saucepan, cover and simmer for 5 minutes. Stir in the beans, tomatoes, tarragon and olive oil. Season with salt and pepper.
3. Spoon the warm vegetables on to serving plates. Arrange the tuna on top and serve.

🅥 if using vegetarian cheese

Vegetables and Salads ♦ **Vegetable Main Meals**

Ratatouille-Stuffed Tomatoes

Points per serving: 2
Total Points per recipe: 8

Serves: 4
Preparation time: 15 minutes
Cooking time: 40 minutes
Freezing: not recommended
Calories per serving: 200

A tasty mid-week supper dish for all the family to enjoy with green vegetables. Delicious eaten well chilled, too.

8 small beef tomatoes
100 g (3¹/₂ oz) long-grain rice
300 ml (¹/₂ pint) vegetable stock or water
1 small onion, chopped
1 red or green pepper, de-seeded and chopped
2 small courgettes, chopped
100 g (3¹/₂ oz) button mushrooms, chopped finely
1 teaspoon dried herbes de Provence or dried mixed herbs
55 g (2 oz) reduced-fat Cheddar cheese, grated
salt and freshly ground black pepper

1. Cut a small slice off the top of the tomatoes and discard. Using a sharp, small knife, scoop out the flesh. Chop the flesh into a bowl. Invert and drain the tomato shells on a piece of kitchen paper. Preheat the oven to Gas Mark 5/190°C/375°F.

2. Place the rice, stock or water and onion in a saucepan. Cover and bring to the boil; then reduce the heat and simmer for 5 minutes. Add the red or green pepper, courgettes, mushrooms and herbs, and simmer gently, uncovered, for a further 10 minutes or until the rice is cooked, absorbing most of the stock. Season to taste with salt and pepper.

3. Pile the mixture into the tomato shells. Place in a shallow baking dish and cover lightly with foil. Bake for 15 minutes.

4. Remove the foil, sprinkle with the cheese and cook for a further 10 minutes.

Weight Watchers note

Stock up on half-fat products and save some Points. Alternatively, choose mature, strongly flavoured Cheddar cheese, which means you can use less and still enjoy a great taste.

Cook's note

If you choose four large beef tomatoes instead of 8 small ones, extend the cooking time at step 3 by 5 minutes.

Ⓥ if using vegetarian cheese

Summer Vegetable Risotto

Points per serving: 4
Total Points per recipe: 16

Serves: 4
Preparation time: 10 minutes
Cooking time: 30 minutes
Freezing: not recommended
Calories per serving: 285

225 g (8 oz) long-grain rice
350 ml (12 fl oz) vegetable stock
1 fennel bulb, trimmed and quartered
450 g (1 lb) assorted green vegetables, e.g. asparagus, mangetout, green beans, broccoli florets
4 heaped tablespoons frozen broad beans
2 heaped tablespoons frozen peas
1 yellow or red pepper, de-seeded and sliced
2 teaspoons olive oil
2 garlic cloves, crushed
¹/₄ teaspoon crushed dried chillies
2 tablespoons lemon juice
2 tablespoons chopped fresh parsley
salt and freshly ground black pepper

1. Put the rice and stock in a saucepan. Bring to the boil, lower the heat, cover and simmer for 15–20 minutes, or until all the liquid has been absorbed and the rice is tender.

2. Meanwhile, bring a large pan of lightly salted water to a steady boil. Add the fennel and blanch for 1 minute. Add the remaining vegetables, bring the water back to the boil and blanch for a further 2 minutes, or until barely tender. Drain and refresh in ice-cold water. Drain thoroughly.

3. Heat the oil in a large pan. Add the garlic and dried chillies and cook gently for 2 minutes. Add the cooked rice and gently stir over a low heat for 2 minutes.

4. Add the blanched vegetables, increase the heat and cook, stirring, for 1 minute or until piping hot.

5. Toss in the lemon juice and parsley. Season, to taste with salt and pepper. Divide between warm plates and serve.

Variations

At step 4, add 8 pitted, sliced black olives.

At step 3, add 2 sun-dried tomatoes, drained from their oil, chopped. The flavoursome oil can also replace the olive oil. The Points will remain the same.

Cook's notes

There is a wonderful variety of rice widely available, including Thai or 'jasmine' and mixed-grain rices.

Wild rice is also available, packaged alone or mixed with long-grain rice. They all add their own unique flavour and variety to your favourite rice dishes.

Ⓥ

Grilled Asparagus with Onion and
Herb Dressing *(page 82)*

Pasta-Stuffed Aubergines

2 medium-size aubergines
1 onion, chopped
1 garlic clove, crushed
1 tablespoon sunflower or olive oil
1 teaspoon dried herbes de
    Provence or dried mixed
    herbs
2 tablespoons tomato purée
50 g (1³/₄ oz) small pasta shapes,
    e.g. fusilli or macaroni
1 egg, beaten
1 tablespoon grated parmesan
    cheese
1 tablespoon dried breadcrumbs
salt and freshly ground black
    pepper

1. Cut the aubergines in half lengthways. Then, using a small sharp knife and a spoon, scoop out as much of the flesh as possible, leaving the shells intact.
2. Chop the flesh finely. Blanch the shells in a saucepan of boiling water for 2 minutes just to soften them, then remove and drain upside-down.
3. Put the chopped aubergine flesh, onion, garlic and oil in a saucepan, with 2 tablespoons of water. Heat gently, until the mixture just starts to bubble; then cover and simmer for 5 minutes.

4. Remove from the heat. Season well with salt and pepper and stir in the dried herbs and tomato purée. Leave to cool. Preheat the oven to Gas Mark 4/180°C/350°F.
5. Cook the pasta according to the pack instructions. Drain well and stir into the aubergine mixture; then add the beaten egg and mix well.
6. Spoon the filling into the aubergine shells. Arrange in a shallow, ovenproof dish and sprinkle on the cheese and breadcrumbs. Bake for 30–40 minutes, until golden brown. Serve with a crisp green salad.

Variation

Add 125 g (4¹/₂ oz) extra-lean minced beef, lamb or pork at step 3 but don't add the water until the meat has browned. The extra Points will be 1 Point per serving for pork or beef and 2 Points per serving for lamb.

Weight Watchers note

This is an ideal recipe to batch bake; freeze each half individually. Delicious served with your favourite tomato sauce.

Ⓥ if using vegetarian cheese and a free-range egg

Cabbage Stir-fry with Cumin and Bacon

Here's one way to get your greens! Good as a light supper, accompanied with a tomato sauce and crusty bread, or as an accompaniment to grilled fish.

2 rindless rashers of smoked
    streaky bacon, chopped
1 teaspoon cumin seeds
175 g (6 oz) firm green
    cabbage, e.g. savoy, shredded
1 garlic clove, crushed
    (optional)
salt and freshly ground black
    pepper

1. Heat a non-stick frying-pan. Add the bacon and stir-fry for 3–4 minutes, or until golden brown. Add the cumin seeds and stir-fry for a further minute.
2. Add the cabbage, garlic (if using) and 4 tablespoons of water. Simmer for 5 minutes until the water has evaporated and the cabbage is just softening. Season to taste and serve hot.

Variations

This serves 1 as a light meal. Points per serving will be 4 and Calories per serving will be 190. For a creamy cabbage, stir in 150 ml (¹/₄ pint) of low-fat plain Bio-yogurt at the end of step 2 and gently heat the yogurt through for a further minute. Add 1 Point per serving if using as an accompaniment, and 2 Points per serving if serving as a light meal.

Cook's note

Cumin seeds have an earthy, aromatic flavour and are widely used in Middle-Eastern cookery. Lightly roasting or frying the seeds, at step 1, before use, really enhances their flavour and aroma. This applies to most whole spices.

Weight Watchers note

Although crisp smoked bacon partners cabbage particularly well, if you want to save some Points, replace the bacon with 4 turkey rashers, saving 1 Point per serving, or with 115 g (4 oz) of button mushrooms sautéed in a teaspoon of olive oil at step 1, saving 1¹/₂ Points per serving.

Grilled Asparagus with Onion and Herb Dressing

Tender young asparagus are delicious grilled. Enjoy this hot salad with crusty bread.

225 g (8 oz) fresh young
asparagus
1 garlic clove, chopped
2 teaspoons olive oil
1 small red onion or 1 shallot,
finely chopped
2 teaspoons chopped fresh
parsley or snipped fresh
chives
2 tablespoons low-fat vinaigrette
dressing
salt and freshly ground black
pepper

1. Preheat the grill to high. Line the grill with foil and lay the asparagus on top. Mix together the garlic and olive oil and brush over the asparagus. Grill for 6–8 minutes, turning half-way through cooking.
2. Meanwhile, mix together the onion or shallot, herbs and vinaigrette dressing. Season to taste with salt and pepper.
3. Divide the asparagus between warm plates and spoon the onion and herb vinaigrette over them. Serve immediately.

Variations

This serves 2 as a light meal. Points per serving will be 2, Calories per serving will be 65. Replace half the asparagus with baby sweetcorns.

This recipe makes an unusual salad accompaniment to poached salmon, prawns or chicken.

Cook's note

An oriental-style or mustard-based dressing would taste good with the asparagus. Remember to calculate the Points.

Cauliflower Florets with Roasted Red Pepper Sauce and Almond Crumbs

Brighten up cauliflower with this delicious red pepper sauce and a crunchy nut topping – perfect for special occasions.

For the sauce:
2 red peppers
2 tablespoons half-fat crème
fraîche
chilli sauce

For the cauliflower:
1 large cauliflower
2 teaspoons fresh breadcrumbs
2 teaspoons coarsely chopped
almonds (about 5)
salt and freshly ground black
pepper
chopped fresh parsley, to serve

1. To make the sauce, preheat the grill to its highest setting and grill the peppers, turning frequently, until the skins are charred and blistered. Remove and cover with kitchen towel or pop into a plastic bag until cool enough to handle. Peel off the skin and discard the core and seeds.
2. Place the peppers and crème fraîche in a food processor or liquidiser. Blend until smooth. Add a dash of chilli sauce and salt and pepper, to taste. Transfer to a bowl until required.
3. Cook the whole cauliflower in a saucepan, containing just enough salted, lightly boiling water to cook the stalk whilst steaming the florets.
4. Meanwhile, gently reheat the sauce in a small saucepan, or in the microwave oven.
5. Heat a non-stick frying-pan and, when very hot, sprinkle in the breadcrumbs and nuts. Cook, stirring frequently, until the crumb mixture turns golden brown.
6. Drain the cauliflower and transfer to a hot dish. Spoon over the sauce and garnish with the crumb mixture and chopped parsley. Serve immediately.

Weight Watchers note

If you need to save some Points, replace the crème fraîche with just enough good-quality vegetable stock or a little of the cauliflower water to produce a coating sauce.

82

Mixed Mushrooms with Thyme and White Wine

Points per serving: 1
Total Points per recipe: 4

Serves: 4
Preparation and cooking time:
30 minutes
Freezing: not recommended
Calories per serving: 100

Choose any combination of mushrooms for this. Serve hot or chilled.

1 tablespoon olive oil
2 onions, sliced
2 garlic cloves, crushed
600 g (1 lb 5 oz) assorted
    mushrooms, sliced thickly
150 ml (¼ pint) dry white
    wine
2 teaspoons mustard seeds
2 teaspoons chopped fresh
    thyme
1 tablespoon chopped fresh
    parsley
salt and freshly ground black
    pepper

1. Heat the oil in a large saucepan, add the onions and garlic and gently cook, without colouring, for 5 minutes or until just softening.
2. Stir in the mushrooms and gently cook for 10 minutes, or until the mushrooms begin to release their juices. Increase the heat to evaporate any excess moisture.
3. Pour on the white wine. Stir in the mustard seeds and thyme and season with salt and plenty of pepper.
4. Cover and simmer for 10 minutes, shaking the pan occasionally. Stir in the fresh parsley just before serving.

Variation

Serves 2 as a light meal. Points per serving will be 2 and Calories per serving will be 195.

Cook's note

This makes a delicious starter, served with garlic bread.

Parsnips and Apples in a Curry Dressing

Points per serving: 1½
Total Points per recipe: 4½

Serves: 3
Preparation and cooking time:
20 minutes
Freezing: not recommended
Calories per serving: 80

A delicious combination to ring the changes with the good old parsnip. Serve to accompany cooked ham, grilled plaice fillets or grilled chicken.

300 g (10 ½ oz) parsnips,
    peeled
2 teaspoons curry or tikka paste
ground cumin (optional)
1 large Cox's eating apple,
    peeled, cored and quartered
2 teaspoons lemon juice
1 teaspoon coriander seeds,
    crushed coarsely
1 tablespoon chopped fresh
    coriander
salt

1. Cut the parsnips into 1 cm (½-inch) slices and then again into sticks. Put in a medium saucepan, with 150 ml (¼ pint) of boiling water, curry or tikka paste and a good pinch of ground cumin. Season with a little salt. Bring to the boil, cover and simmer for about 8 minutes, or until the parsnips are just softening.
2. Thickly slice the apple quarters and toss in the lemon juice. Add to the parsnips and simmer, uncovered, for 5 minutes or until the liquid has reduced to about 4 tablespoons.
3. Stir in the coriander seeds and chopped coriander. Serve immediately.

Variation

Stir in 4 tablespoons of greek-style natural yogurt (2 Points), to make a creamy sauce. Serve as a light lunch, with pitta or naan bread.

83

Tomato-Baked Celery

Points per serving: 0
Total Points per recipe: 0
Serves: 4
Preparation time: 5 minutes
Cooking time: 1 hour
Freezing: recommended
Calories per serving: 80

1 small head of celery
1 small onion, chopped
300 ml (1/2 pint) passata
1 tablespoon chopped fresh
*   thyme or 1 teaspoon*
*   dried thyme*
1 tablespoon chopped fresh
*   oregano or 1 teaspoon dried*
*   oregano*
salt and freshly ground black
*   pepper*

1. Preheat the oven to Gas Mark 4/180°C/350°F.
2. Cut the celery into 7 cm (3-inch) lengths. Place in a small, lidded ovenproof dish.
3. Mix together the onion, passata and herbs. Season with salt and pepper and pour over the celery.
4. Cover and cook until very tender, about an hour.

Variation
For a light supper for two, at the end of step 4, arrange 100 g (3¹/₂ oz) of thinly sliced mozzarella cheese over the celery and cook for a further 10–15 minutes, or until the cheese has melted. Add 4 Points per serving.

Ⓥ

Orange-Braised Potato, Carrot and Shallots

Points per serving: 2½
Total Points per recipe: 5
Serves: 2
Preparation time: 10 minutes
Cooking time: 20 minutes
Freezing: not recommended
Calories per serving: 220

This is a good all-in-one vegetable accompaniment, to serve with pork or chicken dishes.

4 shallots, halved
1 large carrot, sliced
350 g (12 oz) potatoes, cubed
200 ml (7 fl oz) orange juice
1 bay leaf
a pinch of ground allspice
salt and freshly ground black
*   pepper*
snipped fresh chives, to garnish

1. Place all the ingredients in a saucepan and season with a little salt and pepper. Bring to the boil, cover tightly and simmer for 20 minutes or until the vegetables are tender. (Add an extra spoonful of orange juice, if necessary.)
2. Remove the bay leaf and adjust the seasoning, to taste, before serving, sprinkled with chives.

Ⓥ

New Potatoes in a Creamy Herb Dressing

Points per serving: 2½
Total Points per recipe: 5
Serves: 2
Preparation and cooking time:
20 minutes
Freezing: not recommended
Calories per serving: 165

Use your favourite fresh herbs for this potato dish.

250 g (9 oz) baby new potatoes,
*   scrubbed*
4 tablespoons low-fat plain
*   yogurt*
40 g (1¹/₂ oz) medium-fat soft
*   cheese, e.g. Philadelphia*
*   'Light'*
1 teaspoon chopped fresh mint
1 teaspoon chopped fresh
*   parsley*
1 teaspoon snipped fresh chives
salt and freshly ground black
*   pepper*

1. Cook the potatoes in salted, boiling water for 15 minutes, or until tender. Drain.
2. Blend the yogurt, soft cheese and herbs together in a food processor or liquidiser, until smooth and creamy. Season, to taste.
3. Toss the hot potatoes into the dressing.

Variation
This is delicious eaten cold.

Ⓥ if using vegetarian soft cheese

Oven-Baked Chips

Points per serving: 1½
Total Points per recipe: 6
Serves: 4
Preparation time: 10 minutes
Cooking time: 40 minutes
Freezing: not recommended
Calories per serving: 105

A great recipe for chips – with all the taste and 'crunch', but without the extra Calories.

1 teaspoon vegetable oil
2 × 100 g (3¹/₂ oz) baking
*   potatoes*
1 egg white, beaten lightly
salt

1. Preheat the oven to Gas Mark 6/200°C/400°F. Lightly brush a non-stick baking tray with the vegetable oil.
2. Cut the potatoes into thick slices and then into wedges. Parboil for 5 minutes. Drain thoroughly, patting dry with absorbent kitchen paper.
3. Dip the potato wedges into the egg white, drain and then lay them, cut-side down, on the baking tray.
4. Cook for 40 minutes, turning over half-way through. They will be puffed and golden brown when ready.
5. Serve hot, sprinkled with salt.

Ⓥ

Cauliflower Florets with Roasted Red Pepper Sauce and Almond Crumbs *(page 82)*

Orange-Braised Potato, Carrot and Shallots *(opposite)*

Irish Mashed Potatoes with Savoy Cabbage and Leeks

Known as 'colcannon' in Ireland and traditionally eaten on Hallowe'en, this is a tasty dish that can be prepared well in advance and will keep warm quite happily.

450 g (1 lb) potatoes, quartered
1 small savoy cabbage, cored
*   and shredded*
2 small leeks, sliced
150 ml (1/4 pint) skimmed milk
4 teaspoons half-fat butter
salt and freshly ground black
*   pepper*

1. Cook the potatoes, in salted, boiling water, for 15–20 minutes or until tender. Meanwhile, cook the cabbage in a saucepan with just a little boiling water for 5–8 minutes, until just tender. Drain both vegetables thoroughly.
2. Gently cook the leeks, in the milk, in a small, covered saucepan for 10–15 minutes, until softened. Pour into a large bowl, with the milk.
3. Add the potatoes to the leeks and milk and beat well, until mashed. Add the cabbage and butter and mix well. Season with plenty of salt and pepper. Serve immediately.

Variation

Replace the leeks with 4 spring onions, chopped and added uncooked to the mashed potato.
    Replace the savoy cabbage with 450 g (1 lb) curly kale.

Cook's note

You can transfer this vegetable mash to an ovenproof dish, cover it with foil and keep it warm in a moderate oven until required.

Bubble and Squeak Patties

Leftovers from the weekend meals often taste better than their predecessor! Here is just one example of simply delicious food.

450 g (1 lb) mashed potato
175 g (6 oz) cooked, shredded
*   cabbage or brussels sprouts*
2 lean rashers of rindless back
*   bacon, chopped*
4 spring onions, sliced
4 tablespoons hot skimmed milk
salt and freshly ground black
*   pepper*

1. Preheat the oven to Gas Mark 7/220°C/425°F.
2. Place the potatoes and greens in a bowl. Season with salt and pepper.
3. Heat a small, non-stick frying-pan and cook the bacon until browned and crisp. Add the spring onions and cook for a further 2–3 minutes. Add to the potato mixture. Add the hot milk and mix well.
4. Divide and shape into four equal patties, of about 10 cm (4-inch) diameter. Place on a lightly greased baking sheet.
5. Cook for 20 minutes, turning half-way through.

Variation

Replace the potato with parsnips or a combination of both.

Ⓥ if you omit the bacon

Potato and Rosemary Bake

Points per serving: 1½
Total Points per recipe: 6

Serves: 4
Preparation time: 10 minutes
Cooking time: 1¼ hours
Freezing: recommended
Calories per serving: 150

Did you know....? Rosemary is believed to grow well in the garden of a happy household!

600 g (1 lb 5 oz) potatoes, sliced thinly
2 onions, sliced thinly
4 teaspoons chopped fresh rosemary
300 ml (½ pint) hot vegetable stock
salt and freshly ground black pepper

1. Preheat the oven to Gas Mark 4/180°C/350°F.
2. Layer the potato and onion slices with the rosemary and seasoning in a large, shallow, ovenproof dish. Pour in the stock.
3. Place on the highest shelf in the oven and cook for 45–50 minutes. Baste with a little of the stock and cook for a further 15–20 minutes, until the potatoes are tender and the surface is golden.
4. Serve hot, with roast or grilled meat.

Variation
Replace the onion with 1 large leek, sliced.

Spanish-Style Potatoes

Points per serving: 2½
Total Points per recipe: 10

Serves: 4
Preparation and cooking time: 25 minutes
Freezing: not recommended
Calories per serving: 155

Garlicky and quite delicious, these 'patatas' are good hot or cold.

450 g (1 lb) new potatoes, scrubbed and halved
2 garlic cloves, crushed or chopped finely
4 teaspoons extra-virgin olive oil
4 spring onions, chopped finely
2 teaspoons sherry vinegar
2 tablespoons chopped fresh flat-leaf parsley
salt and freshly ground black pepper

1. Cook the potatoes, in lightly salted, boiling water, for 15–20 minutes, or until tender. Drain.
2. Meanwhile, mix together the garlic and olive oil and cook over a low heat for 10 minutes or until the garlic has softened but not coloured. Remove from the heat and toss in the spring onions.
3. Mix together the potatoes, garlic and onion, vinegar and parsley. Season, to taste.

Cook's note
Serve with cold cooked ham, pork or chicken.

Tropical Chicken Salad

Points per serving: 3
Total Points per recipe: 6

Serves: 2
Preparation time: 10 minutes
Freezing: not recommended
Calories per serving: 210

175 g (6 oz) cooked, skinless, boneless chicken breast
1 small kiwi fruit, peeled, halved and sliced
1 ripe mango, peeled
grated zest and juice of ½ lime
2 tablespoons low-fat plain yogurt
1 tablespoon chopped fresh coriander
½ teaspoon finely grated fresh root ginger
½ teaspoon red chilli paste
salt
1 small bag of salad leaves, to serve

1. Slice the chicken into strips. Place in a large bowl, with the kiwi slices. Using a small, sharp knife, cut the mango flesh away from the stone and then slice the flesh. Add to the bowl.
2. Mix together the lime zest and juice, yogurt, coriander, ginger, chilli paste and a little salt, to taste.
3. Carefully, fold the dressing into the chicken and fruit. Arrange the salad leaves on two plates and spoon the chicken salad on to the bed of leaves.

Variation
If you do not have a small jar of ready-prepared chilli paste, use ½ small fresh red chilli, de-seeded and chopped finely.

Cook's note
The flavour of mango has been likened to a combination of nectar and peaches. It is a delicious fruit, native to India – and a valuable source of Vitamin A. It also contains a very large stone, so don't be fooled by its size.

Mexican Avocado, Tomato and Pasta Salsa

Great for entertaining, the lunch box or picnics; served on its own or with grilled chicken or salmon, this salad is delicious. Salsas are fresh sauces, usually uncooked.

225 g (8 oz) pasta shapes,
*   e.g. penne, twists*

For the salsa:

1 red pepper, de-seeded and
*   chopped finely*
1 small, fresh green chilli,
*   de-seeded and chopped*
*   finely*
2 tomatoes, skinned, de-seeded
*   and chopped*
1 avocado, peeled, stoned and
*   chopped*
grated zest and juice of 1 lime
1 tablespoon olive oil
4 tablespoons chopped fresh
*   coriander*
salt and freshly ground black
*   pepper*

1. Cook the pasta in plenty of lightly salted, boiling water, for 8–10 minutes, or according to pack instructions. Drain and refresh under cold running water. Drain thoroughly.
2. In a large bowl, mix together all the remaining ingredients. Season well with salt and pepper.
3. Mix the pasta into the 'salsa'. Cover and chill until required.

Variations

This serves 4 as an accompaniment. Points per serving will be 3½. Calories per serving will be 350. If you want to serve this as a warm pasta salad, toss the 'salsa' into the freshly cooked hot pasta and, if you wish, add 300 ml (½ pint) of low-fat plain Bio-yogurt (add 2½ Points per serving).

Cook's note

Wash your hands thoroughly in soapy water after handling fresh chillies. Take care not to touch your eyes.

Egg and Beetroot Salad with Red Onion and Crème Fraîche

Here's a recipe to prove that you can't beat beetroot! Serve with plainly boiled new potatoes or crusty bread and a green salad.

175 g (6 oz) cooked beetroot,
*   sliced thinly*
1 dessertspoon balsamic or
*   sherry vinegar*
½ teaspoon chopped fresh mint
½ teaspoon chopped fresh
*   thyme*
½ teaspoon chopped fresh
*   parsley*
1 small red onion, sliced finely
2 eggs, hard-boiled and sliced
4 teaspoons half-fat crème
*   fraîche*
1 teaspoon snipped fresh chives
salt and freshly ground black
*   pepper*

1. Place the beetroot in a shallow dish. Sprinkle on the vinegar and the mint, thyme and parsley. Cover and leave to marinate for a minimum of 2 hours, but preferably overnight.
2. Arrange the beetroot in overlapping slices in the middle of two serving plates. Arrange the onion rings and sliced egg on top.
3. Spoon the crème fraîche in the centre of the eggs. Sprinkle on the chives and season well with salt and pepper. Serve at once.

Variation

Rollmop herrings or smoked salmon are delicious with this salad. Replace the eggs with 55 g (2 oz) of fish, and garnish with a hard-boiled egg, chopped and sprinkled over the top. Remember to add the Points.

Cook's note

Do try to use fresh cooked beetroot for this recipe. Pickled beetroot will be too acidic.

Ⓥ

Ⓥ if using free-range eggs

Country Salad Bowl

A big, hearty and serious salad is great to dig into! All you need is some crusty bread and an appetite.

*150 g (5¹/₂ oz) baby new
    potatoes*
*100 g (3¹/₂ oz) baby asparagus
    spears*
*2 Little Gem lettuces, chopped
    roughly*
*1 small head of raddichio,
    leaves separated*
¹/₂ bag lamb's lettuce
*2 plum tomatoes, cut into
    wedges*
*40 g (1¹/₂ oz) button
    mushrooms, sliced thinly*
*1 celery stick, cut into 5 cm
    (2-inch) lengths and thinly
    sliced lengthways*
*1 tablespoon chopped fresh
    chervil or parsley*
8 fresh basil leaves, torn
1 egg, hard-boiled and halved
*4 tablespoons very low-fat plain
    fromage frais*
4 tablespoons skimmed milk
1 teaspoon Dijon mustard
*salt and freshly ground black
    pepper*

1. Cook the potatoes, in salted, boiling water for 12–15 minutes, or until just tender. Drain, cool and thickly slice. In a separate saucepan, cook the asparagus for 2 minutes in boiling water; then drain and refresh under cold running water. Drain thoroughly.
2. Place the salad leaves in a large bowl. Add the cool potatoes and asparagus, tomatoes, mushrooms and celery. Mix in the chervil or parsley and the torn basil leaves.
3. Using a teaspoon, scoop the egg yolk out into a bowl with the fromage frais, skimmed milk and mustard. Beat with a spoon, until the egg has broken down and forms a smooth dressing. Season well with salt and pepper.
4. Roughly chop the egg white.
5. Drizzle the dressing over the salad and gently toss into the ingredients. Scatter the chopped egg white over the top. Serve at once.

Variation

Try out the different varieties of mustards and add that extra something to dressings and sauces. Look out for tarragon-, honey-, red-pepper-, horseradish- or tomato-flavoured mustards – to name but a few!

Weight Watchers note

Virtually fat-free (very-low-fat) fromage frais has only half the Points of the low-fat variety – and you can hardly tell the difference when used in dressings.

Ⓥ if using a free-range egg

Chicken and Apricot Pasta Salad

Sometimes it is impossible to think what to do with leftovers! Here is a quick salad for starters.

*115 g (4 oz) cooked, boneless,
    skinless chicken breast, cut
    into bite-size pieces*
*150 g (5¹/₂ oz) pasta shapes, e.g.
    shells or spirals, cooked*
*200 g (7 oz) canned apricot
    halves in apple juice*
*2 tablespoons low-fat plain
    yogurt*
*1 tablespoon chopped fresh
    flat-leaf parsley*
*2 teaspoons flaked almonds,
    toasted*
*salt and freshly ground black
    pepper*
assorted salad leaves, to serve

1. Put the chicken and pasta into a bowl. Drain the apricots, reserving 3 tablespoons of the juice, and add the fruit to the pasta.
2. Mix the fruit juice with the yogurt and toss into the pasta, with the chopped parsley. Season to taste.
3. Divide the salad between small plates. Sprinkle on the almonds. Serve with salad leaves.

Chinese Vegetable and Sesame Seed Salad with Soy Dressing

Points per serving: 2
Total Points per recipe: 4
Serves: 2
Preparation and cooking time: 15 minutes
Freezing: not recommended
Calories per serving: 200

Many supermarkets now sell bags of mixed stir-fry vegetables, which will work well in this salad. Look out for pak-choi too – similar to chard and delicious eaten raw in salads or stir-fried.

1 tablespoon sesame seeds
115 g (4 oz) mangetout or
    sugar-snap peas
½ head of chinese leaves,
    shredded finely
115 g (4 oz) bean sprouts
2 carrots
3 tablespoons light soy sauce
1 tablespoon light olive oil or
    sunflower oil
1 tablespoon sherry vinegar or
    lemon juice
1 teaspoon clear honey
½ teaspoon ground ginger
    (optional)
¼ teaspoon dried garlic
    granules

1. Place the sesame seeds in a dry saucepan and heat, stirring, until they are brown. Transfer to a small bowl.
2. Cook the peas in lightly salted, boiling water for 3 minutes. Drain and refresh in ice-cold water, then drain thoroughly.
3. In a large bowl, mix together the chinese leaves, bean sprouts and peas. Using a potato peeler, pare the carrots into ribbons and add to the salad bowl.
4. Whisk the remaining ingredients, with the sesame seeds, to form a dressing. Fold into the salad.
5. Divide between plates and serve immediately.

Variations

This serves 4 as a starter. Points per serving will be 1. Calories per serving will be 100. Use ¼ white cabbage or ½ iceberg lettuce, instead of the chinese leaves.

Weight Watchers note

For a more substantial meal, add 55 g (2 oz) of cooked peeled prawns per serving. This will add 1 Point per serving.

Coronation Potato Salad

Points per serving: 1½
Total Points per recipe: 3
Serves: 2
Preparation time: cooking potatoes + 10 minutes
Freezing: not recommended
Calories per serving: 140

For the dressing:
1 tablespoon low-fat plain
    Bio-yogurt
1 tablespoon low-fat
    mayonnaise
1 tablespoon chopped fresh
    parsley
2 teaspoons mango chutney
1 teaspoon apricot jam
½ teaspoon curry paste
salt and freshly ground black
    pepper
For the salad:
225 g (8 oz) new potatoes
spring onion, chopped, to garnish
green salad leaves, to serve
a pinch of paprika or chilli
    powder, to serve

1. Cook the potatoes in lightly salted, boiling water, until only just tender. Drain and allow to cool. Slice thickly.
2. Place all the dressing ingredients in a bowl and whisk thoroughly. Season with salt and pepper, to taste.
3. Fold in the potatoes. Cover and chill until required.
4. To serve, spoon the potato salad on to a bed of salad leaves. Sprinkle with the spring onion. Dust lightly with paprika or chilli powder.

Variation

For a complete meal or light lunch, fold some cooked prawns, flakes of smoked mackerel or chopped chicken breast into the salad. Remember to add the Points.

Cook's note

Replace the cooked fresh potatoes with canned new potatoes, drained and halved or sliced.

Crunchy Coleslaw

While commercially available coleslaw is a great convenience, you can't beat a home-made version.

1 small white cabbage
1 fennel bulb
2 carrots, grated
4 spring onions, chopped, or
   1 small onion, chopped
1/2 teaspoon fennel seeds
   (optional)
10 ready-to-eat apricots,
   chopped, or 1 heaped
   tablespoon raisins
For the dressing:
200 g (7 oz) very-low-fat plain
   fromage frais
1 teaspoon Dijon mustard
2 teaspoons lemon juice or
   white-wine vinegar
salt and freshly ground black
   pepper

1. Remove the core and coarse outer leaves of both the cabbage and fennel. Shred finely and place in a large bowl.
2. Add the carrots, spring onions, fennel seeds (if using) and apricots or raisins. Season with a little salt and pepper.
3. Mix together the fromage frais, mustard and lemon juice or vinegar. Season with salt and pepper. Fold into the vegetables, mixing thoroughly.
4. Cover and chill for at least 2 hours, to allow the flavours to develop.

Cook's note

A coleslaw can include, apple, celery or nuts or be made with red cabbage – so experiment! Rather than the creamy dressing, you can use a fat-free or reduced-calorie vinaigrette or thousand-island dressing.

Weight Watchers note

Coleslaw is delicious with plain or ham omelettes, or with jacket potatoes, in sandwiches or accompanying cold meats. You can make it a meal in itself, by adding cubes of cheese or prawns. It will keep, refrigerated, for several days, so plan your meals and packed lunches to include some crunchy coleslaw.

Roasted Tomato Salad with Red Onion and Spinach

The contrast in texture of the juicy, soft tomatoes and the crisp onion come as quite a surprise!

8 small tomatoes
1 garlic clove, chopped finely
4 teaspoons olive oil
175 g (6 oz) baby spinach leaves
1 red onion, sliced finely into
   rings
6–8 fresh basil leaves, torn
1 teaspoon sherry or balsamic
   vinegar
salt and freshly ground black
   pepper

1. Preheat the oven to Gas Mark 5/190°C/375°F. Score the top of each tomato with a cross, cutting one quarter of the way down. Place on a baking sheet.
2. Mix together the garlic and 1 teaspoon of olive oil. Brush a little of the garlic just into the cut of the tomato. Cook for 8–10 minutes, until the tomatoes have softened but still hold their shape.
3. Meanwhile, mix together the spinach, onion and basil leaves. Mix together the remaining oil and vinegar, and season with salt and pepper. Toss into the salad.
4. Remove the tomatoes, season with a little salt and pepper and carefully spoon in amongst the leaves. Serve at once.

Variation

This serves 2 as a light meal. Points per serving will be 2 and Calories per serving will be 140.

Weight Watchers note

This makes a tasty light meal for two, served with shavings of fresh parmesan cheese or sliced low-fat mozzarella. A little parmesan goes a long way but remember to add the Points.

Cook's note

Treat yourself to a bottle of Balsamic vinegar – a tiny amount can transform salad dressings, cooked meat and grilled vegetables.

Strawberry and Cucumber Salad with Black Pepper (*opposite*)

Tropical Chicken Salad (*page 87*)

Strawberry and Cucumber Salad with Black Pepper

Points per serving: 0
Total Points per recipe: 0

Serves: 4

Preparation time: 10 minutes

+ 15 minutes chilling

Freezing: not recommended

Calories per serving: 35

It may sound an unlikely combination, but it works! This refreshing salad is great with poached salmon or turkey – and it looks stunning.

1 cucumber, peeled
2 tablespoons white-wine vinegar
16 large strawberries, washed and hulled
salt and freshly ground black pepper
fresh chervil or mint sprigs, to garnish

1. Cut the cucumber in half lengthways and, using a teaspoon, scoop out and discard the seeds. Slice the cucumber thickly and transfer to a bowl. Sprinkle over the vinegar.
2. Cut the strawberries into quarters or thick slices and mix them gently with the cucumber. Season lightly with salt, but grind on plenty of pepper (try to grind it coarsely).
3. Cover and chill for 15 minutes before serving, garnished with a sprig of fresh chervil or mint.

Chinese Leaf Salad with Oriental Dressing

Points per serving: 1/2
Total Points per recipe: 1

Serves: 2

Preparation time: 10 minutes

Freezing: not recommended

Calories per serving: 85

A fragrant salad, which would make a good accompaniment to Pork Kebabs (see page 102) or Beef Teriyaki (see page 96).

1 large orange
6 chinese leaves, shredded
125 g (4 1/2 oz) fresh bean sprouts
1 tablespoon light soy sauce
1/2 teaspoon grated fresh root ginger or a pinch of ground ginger
caster sugar

1. Using a sharp knife, remove the peel and pith from the orange. Hold the orange over a bowl and remove all but 3 segments. Catch any juice in the bowl. Squeeze the remaining segments and the pith, to extract some more juice.
2. Transfer the orange segments to a bowl. Add the chinese leaves and bean sprouts.
3. Mix together the orange juice (you should have about 3 tablespoons), the soy sauce and ginger. Add a pinch of sugar and stir well.
4. Lightly toss the dressing into the salad leaves. Serve.

Carrot and Poppy Seed Salad with Orange Vinaigrette

Points per serving: 1/2
Total Points per recipe: 1

Serves: 2

Preparation time: 10 minutes

+ 15 minutes chilling

Freezing: not recommended

Calories per serving: 30

The simplest of salads – perfect for pittas, filling sandwiches (delicious with water-thin chicken or ham) or to enjoy on its own.

2 medium-size carrots, grated finely
For the dressing:
2 tablespoons orange juice
1/2 teaspoon finely grated orange zest
1 teaspoon sugar
1/2 teaspoon poppy seeds
salt and freshly ground black pepper

1. Place the grated carrots in a bowl.
2. Whisk together the ingredients for the dressing. Season, to taste. Toss into the carrots. Cover and chill for 15 minutes, to allow the carrot to absorb the dressing.

Variation

Stir 2 tablespoons of low-fat plain Bio-yogurt into the dressing and add a 1/2 Point.

Cook's note

1 large orange will yield about 4 tablespoons of juice.

Warm Carrot, Raisin and Rice Salad

Points per serving: 4
Total Points per recipe: 8

Serves: 2

Preparation and cooking time: 20 minutes

Freezing: not recommended

Calories per serving: 280

100 g (3 1/2 oz) long-grain rice
25 g (1 oz) raisins
2 carrots, grated finely
grated zest and juice of 1/2 orange
2 teaspoons olive oil
1/4 teaspoon ground coriander
salt and freshly ground black pepper

1. Cook the rice according to pack instructions. Drain thoroughly.
2. Mix the raisins and carrots into the rice. Season with salt and pepper.
3. Mix together the orange zest and juice, the olive oil and the ground coriander. Toss into the rice salad, turning the ingredients well.
4. Serve the salad warm or chilled, as a light meal or as an accompaniment to cold meats.

Variation

Add a tablespoon of chopped fresh coriander at step 3. Use brown instead of white rice. This recipe works well with pasta, too.

Three Bean Salad with Garlic Dressing

Points per serving: 2
Total Points per recipe: 8

Serves: 4
Preparation and cooking time:
10 minutes
+ 30 minutes chilling
Freezing: not recommended
Calories per serving: 120

Serve this salad on its own, with pasta or a little grated cheese, or with cold meats or tuna.

125 g (4½ oz) fresh or frozen
    broad beans
125 g (4½ oz) fine green beans
425 g (15 oz) canned red
    kidney beans, rinsed and
    drained

For the dressing:
2 tablespoons chopped fresh
    parsley
1 garlic clove, crushed
2 teaspoons olive oil
2 teaspoons white-wine vinegar
1 teaspoon whole-grain mustard
salt and freshly ground black
    pepper

1. Cook the broad beans in lightly salted, boiling water for 5 minutes. Add the green beans and cook for a further 3–4 minutes. Drain and refresh under cold running water. Drain thoroughly. (The beans will have a crunchy bite.)
2. Place the beans in a bowl with the red kidney beans.
3. Mix together the ingredients for the dressing. Season to taste and then toss into the beans. Cover and chill for at least 30 minutes before serving.

94

Cherry Tomato, Green Bean and Hazelnut Salad

Points per serving: 1
Total Points per recipe: 4

Serves: 4
Preparation time: 15 minutes
Freezing: recommended
Calories per serving: 150

Here's a recipe you will really enjoy with tasty, toasted hazelnuts.

225 g (8 oz) dwarf green beans
3 tablespoons vinaigrette
    dressing
2 tablespoons lemon juice
1 teaspoon Dijon mustard
1 teaspoon caster sugar
12 cherry tomatoes, halved
1 tablespoon chopped fresh
    basil leaves
20 hazelnuts, toasted and
    chopped coarsely
salt and freshly ground black
    pepper

1. Cook the beans in lightly salted, boiling water for 5 minutes. Drain and refresh in ice-cold water. Then drain thoroughly and transfer to a large bowl.
2. Meanwhile, mix together the vinaigrette dressing, lemon juice, mustard and sugar. Season to taste with salt and pepper.
3. Toss the green beans with the dressing, mixing together well. Fold in the tomatoes and the chopped basil.
4. Divide the mixture between small plates. Scatter the hazelnuts evenly over the top. Serve at once.

Cook's note
Look out for the brilliant red, baby plum tomatoes, now available in major supermarkets – or combine red cherry tomatoes with the yellow or orange baby tomatoes.

Weight Watchers Note
Once a bag of nuts has been opened, it is all too tempting to nibble at the odd one... or two. Seal the opened bag and store it in the freezer: the nuts will remain fresher for longer and are less likely to disappear!

Meat and Poultry

This chapter is full of main-course meals for all occasions. From the quick mid-week stir-fry or much loved shepherd's pie, to meals with a touch of something special for entertaining. You will find lots of different flavours and recipes to suit the occasion and they are all straightforward to prepare!

As a nation, we are being encouraged to eat a healthier, more balanced diet and meat producers have responded magnificently to this, with low-fat sausages, extra-trimmed cuts of meat, extra-lean minced meat – and more besides. Lean and tender cuts, already flattened for rolling or stuffing, trimmed and cut for stir frying, cubed for kebabs and casseroles, mean you can spend less time preparing food and more time enjoying the end result!

In these recipes, you will find alternative suggestions and variations to extend your choice instantly. Pork and Chinese Vegetable Stir-fry (see page 106), will taste delicious if you use turkey, beef or chicken. Austrian-Style Minced Beef (see page 100) will work well with the extra-lean minced pork that is readily available now.

Finally, here are a few tips to help you on your way to reach Goal.

◆ Trim away visible fat from traditional cuts of meat before cooking, and remove fats from cooked cold meats, such as ham and beef.

◆ Seal meat by dry-frying wherever possible, using a non-stick frying-pan.

◆ Choose the new leaner, tender cuts of meat. They may appear a little more expensive but remember that there will be less wastage and shrinkage.

◆ Choose cooking methods that don't require additional fat, such as grilling chops, or roasting without any additional fat.

◆ Bulk up smaller portions of meat with more fresh vegetables and carbohydrates such as rice, pasta or potatoes.

1

2

3

4

chapter 5

6

7

8

9

Beef and Rice Balls in Chilli Sauce

Points per serving: 3
Total Points per recipe: 12

Serves: 4
Preparation and cooking time:
55 minutes
Freezing: recommended
Calories per serving: 240

A recipe that can be made well in advance and reheated – perfect on a cold winter's night. Serve hot, with fresh green vegetables, rice or mashed potatoes or a medium-size pitta bread.

55 g (2 oz) long-grain basmati rice
300 g (10¹/₂ oz) extra-lean minced beef
1 teaspoon salt
2 garlic cloves, crushed
¹/₂ teaspoon ground cumin
1 teaspoon ground coriander
For the sauce:
1 onion, chopped
1 red pepper, de-seeded and chopped
2 teaspoons sunflower oil
400 g (14 oz) canned chopped tomatoes with chilli
¹/₂ teaspoon dried marjoram or oregano
1 tablespoon barbecue relish or spicy chutney
salt and freshly ground black pepper

1. Boil the rice according to the pack instructions but allowing it to over-cook slightly so it is soft. Leave to cool completely.
2. Mix the rice with the beef, salt, garlic, cumin and coriander. Divide and shape into 12 balls, rolling them between wet hands.
3. Heat a large, non-stick saucepan. Brown the meatballs in the saucepan, turning them carefully as they colour. When evenly browned, transfer to a plate.
4. Add the onion, red pepper and oil to the saucepan. Stir well and cook gently for 5 minutes, or until softened.
5. Stir in the chopped tomatoes, herbs, relish or chutney and 200 ml (7 fl oz) water. Season to taste with salt and pepper, bring to the boil and then return the meatballs.
6. Reduce the heat to a simmer and cook for 12 minutes, stirring occasionally.

Cook's note
You can buy canned chopped tomatoes with added seasonings, e.g. mixed herbs, onions, chilli and so on. Look out for the varieties.

Weight Watchers note
Minced beef rarely requires additional fat to cook in, as it will express a surprising amount of its own. Look out for extra-lean mince.

Beef Teriyaki Skewers with Stir-Fry Vegetables

Points per serving: 3
Total Points per recipe: 12

Serves: 4
Preparation and cooking time:
15 minutes
+30 minutes marinating
Freezing: not recommended
Calories per serving: 170

350 g (12 oz) lean fillet or rump steak, cut into thin strips
2 tablespoons teriyaki marinade
1 small onion, quartered and separated into layers
2 teaspoons sunflower oil
¹/₂ red pepper, de-seeded and cut into matchsticks
¹/₂ green pepper, de-seeded and cut into matchsticks
100 g (3¹/₂ oz) mangetout, trimmed
2 teaspoons light soy sauce
4 teaspoons dry sherry
salt and freshly ground black pepper

1. Coat the steak with the teriyaki marinade in a shallow dish. Stir in the onion and leave to marinate for 30 minutes.
2. Preheat the grill to a medium-hot setting. Thread the steak on to four bamboo or metal skewers (see Cook's note). Reserve the onions.
3. Grill for 7–8 minutes, turning half-way through the cooking time. Add a couple more minutes if you prefer your beef well done.
4. Meanwhile, heat the oil in a non-stick wok or frying-pan. Add the onion, peppers and mangetout and stir-fry for 2–3 minutes, or until just starting to wilt. Stir in the soy sauce and sherry. Check the seasoning.
5. Divide the vegetables between warmed plates and place the skewer on top. Serve at once.

Variation
Use boneless, skinless chicken breast, cut into bite-size pieces, in place of the beef. Save 1 Point per serving!

Cook's note
Soak bamboo or wooden skewers in water for 10 minutes before use, to prevent them from charring under the grill.

96

Beef and Mushroom Stroganoff

A variation on the classic French theme; serve with plainly boiled rice or pasta and green vegetables or a green salad.

350 g (12 oz) lean fillet or
*   rump steak, cut into 2.5 cm*
*   (1-inch) strips*
2 tablespoons plain flour,
*   seasoned*
3 teaspoons sunflower oil
1 onion, sliced thinly
125 g (4¹/₂ oz) button
*   mushrooms, sliced*
3 tablespoons tomato purée
1 tablespoon Worcestershire
*   sauce*
1 teaspoon lemon juice
300 ml (¹/₂ pint) low-fat plain
*   Bio-yogurt*
salt and freshly ground black
*   pepper*
2 tablespoons chopped fresh
*   parsley, to garnish*

1. Place the beef and seasoned flour in a large plastic bag and shake to coat the meat.
2. Heat 2 teaspoons of oil in a large, non-stick frying-pan. Sauté the onion for 5 minutes and then add the mushrooms and cook for a further 5 minutes. Transfer to a plate, using a draining spoon.
3. Heat the frying-pan, add the remaining teaspoon of oil and, when the oil is just starting to smoke, add the meat. Stir-fry, to brown the strips evenly. Stir in the tomato purée, Worcestershire sauce and lemon juice.
4. Return the onion and mushroom to the frying-pan and gently cook for 5 minutes. Stir in the yogurt and allow to heat through. Season to taste with salt and pepper, and sprinkle with parsley.

Variation
Stir in a tablespoon of brandy at step 4.

Replace the beef with pork escalopes. Add 1 Point per serving.

Beef Stir-Fry with Black Bean Sauce

Stir-fry dishes are very versatile, naturally low in fat and quick to prepare, often using up odd leftover vegetables. Just keep a good stock of storecupboard ingredients, and you will always have something tasty to prepare at a moment's notice.

300 g (10¹/₂ oz) lean grilling
*   steak, trimmed of fat*
1 tablespoon soy sauce
1 tablespoon dry sherry
1 teaspoon sugar
1 teaspoon cornflour
2 tablespoons vegetable oil
1 onion, cut into chunks
1 yellow or red pepper, de-seeded
*   and cut into chunks*
1 carrot, sliced thinly
115 g (4 oz) mangetout, halved
2 tablespoons black bean sauce
2 teaspoons sesame seeds

1. Slice the steak into thin strips and then mix well with the soy sauce, sherry, sugar and cornflour. Set aside for 10 minutes.
2. Heat a non-stick wok or large frying-pan until very hot, add the oil and then heat until just smoking. Quickly stir in the marinated beef, tossing and turning in the pan for approximately 1 minute.
3. Remove the beef with a slotted spoon and reheat the pan, adding 3 tablespoons of water.
4. Stir in the vegetables and cook over a high heat for 2 minutes (most of the water will evaporate).
5. Return the beef to the pan, mix in the black bean sauce, reheat and serve immediately, sprinkled with sesame seeds.

Weight Watchers notes
Serve this tasty stir-fry with cooked rice or noodles.

Remember, 55 g (2 oz) uncooked rice or egg noodles is equal to a medium portion (140 g or 4 tablespoons) cooked rice – worth 3 Points.

Minced Beef Casserole with Horseradish
    Scones *(page 100)*
Beef and Rice Balls in Chilli Sauce *(page 96)*
Beef Stir-fry with Black Bean Sauce *(page 97)*

Minced Beef Casserole with Horseradish Scones

*450 g (1 lb) extra-lean minced
    beef*
1 onion, sliced thinly
2 carrots, chopped
2 celery sticks, chopped
*125 g (4½ oz) button
    mushrooms, sliced*
1 beef stock cube, crumbled
*salt and freshly ground black
    pepper*

For the scones:
175 g (6 oz) self-raising flour
½ teaspoon salt
*50 g (1¾ oz) half-fat butter or
    low-fat spread*
2 tablespoons skimmed milk
2–3 teaspoons horseradish sauce
extra flour, for dusting

1. Dry-fry the minced beef in a non-stick saucepan for 5 minutes, stirring frequently, until the meat is brown. Add the onion and cook for a further 3–4 minutes.
2. Stir in the carrots, celery, mushrooms, stock cube and 300 ml (½ pint) boiling water. Season with salt and pepper. Bring to the boil and then cover and simmer for 15 minutes.
3. Preheat the oven to Gas Mark 6/200°C/400°F. Pour the minced beef into an ovenproof casserole dish.
4. Make the scones. Sift the flour and salt together in a bowl. Rub in the butter or low-fat spread, until the mixture is crumbly.
5. Stir in the milk and horseradish and mix to a soft dough, adding a drop more milk, if necessary.
6. Press the dough out on to a lightly floured board, to a thickness of 4 cm (1½ inches). Using a 5 cm (2 inch) cutter, press out eight scones. Lightly dust each scone with flour.
7. Place the scones on top of the minced beef. Bake for 15–20 minutes, until golden brown.

Variation
Replace the horseradish with 1 teaspoon of dried mixed herbs.

Weight Watchers note
Divide the casserole into four portions and freeze, for delicious single servings.

Austrian-Style Minced Beef

Serve this savoury minced beef with potato cakes and fresh carrot.

*350 g (12 oz) extra-lean
    minced beef*
225 g (8 oz) onions, sliced
1 tablespoon paprika
300 ml (½ pint) passata
1 tablespoon tomato ketchup
2 tablespoons red-wine vinegar
1 teaspoon dried marjoram
1 teaspoon caraway seeds
*salt and freshly ground black
    pepper*

1. Heat a non-stick saucepan, add the minced beef and stir-fry for 5 minutes, until the meat browns and becomes crumbly. Stir in the onions and paprika and cook for a further 5 minutes.
2. Add the remaining ingredients. Cover and cook very gently for 35 minutes, stirring occasionally. Adjust the seasoning, to taste, and serve.

Variation
Add 1 green or red pepper, de-seeded and diced, 15 minutes before the end of cooking.

Bolognese Sauce

A good bolognese sauce can be used for so many dishes – stuffed peppers, pasta recipes, or as a jacket potato or pancake filling.

450 g (1 lb) extra-lean minced beef
2 onions, chopped
1 large carrot, grated coarsely
1 garlic clove, crushed
1/2 teaspoon mild chilli powder
400 g (14 oz) canned chopped tomatoes
1 tablespoon tomato purée
50 ml (2 fl oz) red wine
300 ml (1/2 pint) beef stock
1 teaspoon dried herbes de Provence or dried mixed herbs
salt and freshly ground black pepper

1. Heat a non-stick frying-pan until hot, then add the beef. Stir-fry for 3 minutes, browning the meat and breaking up any lumps.
2. Add the onions, carrot, garlic and chilli powder. Cover and gently cook for 10 minutes, stirring frequently.
3. Stir in the chopped tomatoes, tomato purée, wine, stock and herbs.
4. Bring to the boil and then reduce the heat to a simmer. Season with salt and pepper. Cover and cook over a low heat for 25 minutes or until the meat is tender.

Variations

Try extra-lean minced lamb or pork and don't forget Quorn or minced turkey. Try this all-in-one recipe.

Weight Watchers note

If you do not have the choice of extra-lean minced beef, use kitchen paper to 'blot' up any free oil from the surface of the meat sauce.

Spiced Beef Casserole

A rich, dark casserole of tender beef with a hint of orange and spices. Serve with Irish Mashed Potatoes with Savoy Cabbage and Leeks (see page 86) or mashed or jacket potatoes.

1 tablespoon sunflower oil
500 g (1 lb 2 oz) lean beef stewing steak, cubed
175 g (6 oz) button mushrooms
2 tablespoons plain flour
300 ml (1/2 pint) unsweetened orange juice
300 ml (1/2 pint) beef stock
2 teaspoons white-wine vinegar
2 teaspoons soft dark brown sugar
1/2 teaspoon ground cinnamon
1 bay leaf
1/2 teaspoon dried thyme
grated zest of 1/2 orange
salt and freshly ground black pepper
chopped fresh parsley, to garnish

1. Preheat the oven to Gas Mark 4/180°C/350oF.
2. Heat the oil in a flameproof casserole and brown the meat on all sides. Add the mushrooms and cook for 2 minutes.
3. Sprinkle on the flour and cook for 1 minute, stirring continuously.
4. Gradually, blend in the orange juice and stock. Stir in the remaining ingredients. Season to taste and then cover and transfer to the oven. Cook for 2 hours, until the meat is tender.
5. Serve, garnished with chopped fresh parsley.

Variation

This recipe is delicious made with chicken, pork or turkey.

Cook's note

If you are caught without orange juice or zest, add 2 tablespoons of marmalade instead. Omit the sugar and increase the beef stock by 200 ml (7 fl oz).

Pork Kebabs with Five Spices

Points per serving: 3½
Total Points per recipe: 14

Serves: 4
Preparation and cooking time:
25 minutes + 30 minutes marinating
Freezing: recommended at step 2.
Thaw thoroughly before grilling.
Calories per serving: 185

Five-spice seasoning is a blend of Eastern spices. It's the basis for the marinade for these delicious basted kebabs. Serve hot or cold, with a salad and crusty bread or rice.

400 g (14 oz) pork escalopes,
*   cut into strips*
4 teaspoons sunflower oil
1 shallot, chopped
1 garlic clove, crushed
2 tablespoons dry sherry
2 tablespoons light soy sauce
1 teaspoon grated fresh root
*   ginger*
1 teaspoon five-spice seasoning

1. Arrange the pork in a shallow dish in one layer.

2. Mix together the remaining ingredients. Drizzle over the pork, turning and coating the meat thoroughly. Cover and leave in a cool place for 30 minutes, to marinate.

3. Thread the pork on to four metal or bamboo skewers and cook under a preheated grill for 5 minutes on each side, brushing the kebabs with any remaining marinade.

Cook's note

For a change, replace the pork with chicken or beef fillet.

Weight Watchers note

There are lots of ways of serving these tasty kebabs. Here are just a few ideas:

    In a pitta bread with Carrot and Poppy Seed Salad (see page 93)

    In a lunch box with Chinese Leaf Salad (see page 93)

Mango-Roasted Pork with Oriental Vegetables

Points per serving: 3½
Total Points per recipe: 14

Serves: 4
Preparation time: 10 minutes
Cooking time: 45 minutes
Freezing: recommended for meat only
Calories per serving: 300

This makes a change from a traditonal Sunday roast, served with roasted oriental vegetables on a bed of mango.

225 g (8 oz) carrot
225 g (8 oz) mooli (white
*   radish)*
225 g (8 oz) pak choi, quartered
175 g (6 oz) broccoli florets
125 g (4½ oz) baby sweetcorn,
*   halved lengthways*
1 large, ripe mango, peeled and
*   cut into 2.5 cm (1-inch)*
*   pieces*
2 red chillies, de-seeded and
*   chopped*
grated zest and juice of 2 limes
4 tablespoons rice vinegar or
*   sherry vinegar*
1 tablespoon caster sugar
150 ml (¼ pint) dry sherry
2 tablespoons chopped fresh
*   coriander*
1 tablespoon light soy sauce
450 g (1 lb) pork fillet,
*   trimmed*

1. Preheat the oven to Gas Mark 6/200°C/400°F.

2. Cut the carrot and mooli lengthways into 8 cm (3-inch), narrow strips. Bring a large saucepan of lightly salted water to the boil and add the carrot, mooli, pak choi, broccoli and sweetcorn. Cook for 4–5 minutes. Drain and refresh under cold water. Drain until required.

3. In a bowl, mix together the mango, chillies, lime zest and juice, rice vinegar, sugar, sherry, coriander and soy sauce.

4. Place the mango and the chilli mixture in a small roasting tin. Lay the pork fillet on top. Roast for 30 minutes, turning half-way through cooking. Remove from the oven, mix in the vegetables and coat them well with the juices. Cook for a further 10–15 minutes.

5. Slice the pork fillet and arrange on a bed of assorted vegetables. Serve immediately, with plain rice.

Variation

Replace the pork fillet with 4 boneless, skinless chicken breasts. Reduce the cooking time at step 4 to 20 minutes.

Cook's note

Pak choi is similar to spinach or chard and used extensively in Chinese cooking. If you wish, you can substitute shredded chinese leaves or young tender spinach.

102

Pork and Leek Roulades with a Mushroom Sauce

4 small leeks, halved
8 × 25 g (1 oz) pork escalopes
1 teaspoon chopped fresh sage
2 tablespoons fresh breadcrumbs
grated zest of ½ lemon

For the sauce:

15 g (½ oz) low-fat spread
75 g (2¾ oz) mushrooms, sliced
½ teaspoon Dijon mustard
125 g (4½ oz) low-fat plain
    fromage frais
salt and freshly ground black
    pepper

1. Blanch the leeks in lightly salted, boiling water for 1 minute. Drain and set aside. Preheat the oven to Gas Mark 6/200°C/400°F.
2. Place the escalopes between two sheets of greaseproof paper or clingfilm. Use a rolling pin to beat and flatten the escalopes until very thin. Sprinkle the escalopes with a little chopped sage and season with salt and pepper.
3. Wrap two escalopes around each leek. Place, seam-down, in an ovenproof dish. Cover with foil and cook for 20 minutes.
4. Mix together the breadcrumbs and lemon zest. Sprinkle over the leek rolls and then return to the oven, uncovered, for a further 10 minutes.
5. Prepare the sauce: melt the low-fat spread in a small saucepan, add the mushrooms and mustard and cook gently for 4–5 minutes, until softened. Stir in the fromage frais. Season to taste with salt and pepper. Gently heat through, without boiling.
6. Spoon two pork roulades on to a serving plate and accompany with the mushroom sauce.

Variation

Replace the mustard sauce with a jar of ready-to-serve, low-in-fat tomato sauce.

Weight Watchers note

Remember that creams and yogurts or fromage frais that are very low in fat will separate if over-heated or boiled. Always heat them gently.

Crunchy Pork Chops with Glazed Apple Rings

Still a family favourite, and adaptable, too, for lamb, chicken or turkey breasts. Serve with traditional gravy and vegetables.

4 medium-size loin of pork
    chops, trimmed
1 egg, beaten
75 g (2¾ oz) dried sage and
    onion stuffing mix

For the glazed apples:

1 eating apple
3 teaspoons lemon juice
2 teaspoons clear honey

1. Preheat the oven to Gas Mark 6/200°C/400°F. Dip the chops first in the beaten egg, shaking off any excess and then in the stuffing mix, so that each chop is evenly coated.
2. Place in a shallow dish and cook for 40 minutes, until the chops are tender and the coating crisp.
3. Meanwhile, cut the apple into 4 rings. Remove the core. Brush each side with the lemon juice. Arrange one ring on each chop, glaze with the honey and cook for the last 10 minutes, with the pork. Serve immediately.

Cook's note

Look out for the various flavours of dried stuffing mixes, such as lemon and parsley, mint or lemon and tarragon – and ring the changes on this recipe.

Sausage, Red Onion and Apple Casserole

Points per serving: 7½
Total Points per recipe: 30

Serves: 4

Preparation time: 5 minutes

Cooking time: 30 minutes

Freezing: not recommended

Calories per serving: 400

Sausages are everybody's favourite – and the variety now available seems endless! Here is a delicious all-in-one meal for the family. Serve hot, with freshly cooked carrots.

450 g (1 lb) low-fat pork
    sausages
1 large red onion, sliced
1 teaspoon sunflower oil
400 g (14 oz) canned chopped
    tomatoes
2 Bramley cooking apples,
    peeled, cored and sliced
    thickly
1/4 teaspoon dried sage
150 ml (1/4 pint) unsweetened
    apple juice
500 g (1 lb 2 oz) canned new
    potatoes, drained
salt and freshly ground black
    pepper

1. Cook the sausages under a moderately hot grill for 6–8 minutes, turning half-way through cooking.
2. Meanwhile, heat a non-stick saucepan. Mix the onion with the oil. Add to the pan and fry for 2–3 minutes, stirring continuously.
3. Stir in the chopped tomatoes, apples, sage and apple juice. Gently bring to the boil and then add the sausages and potatoes. Season with salt and pepper.
4. Reduce the heat and simmer, covered for 10–15 minutes.

Pot-Roast Gammon with an Apple Gravy

Points per serving: 6
Total Points per recipe: 72

Serves: 12

Preparation time: 10 minutes

Cooking time: 2½ hours

Freezing: recommended

Calories per serving: 360

For a large number of hungry mouths to feed or special occasions, you can't beat a piece of gammon.

2.25 kg (5 lb) piece of gammon
1 bay leaf
6 juniper berries
2 onions, quartered
2 large cooking apples, peeled,
    cored and cut into wedges
425 ml (15 fl oz) unsweetened
    apple juice
1 teaspoon honey mustard or
    Dijon mustard
1 tablespoon sultanas
fresh watercress, to serve

1. Weigh the gammon. If larger or smaller than specified, calculate the cooking time at 20 minutes per 450 g (1 lb) plus 20 minutes extra.
2. Place the gammon in a large saucepan. Cover with cold water, add the bay leaf and juniper berries. Slowly bring to the boil. Drain and cover with fresh, cold water. Bring back to the boil and cook gently for an hour.
3. Preheat the oven to Gas Mark 4/180°C/350°F. Line a roasting tin with a large, thick sheet of foil. Place the joint in the centre and scatter the onions and apples around the joint. Pour on the apple juice. Wrap the foil up around the gammon, to form a sealed bag. Cook for an hour.
4. Carefully drain off the cooking juices, apple and onion. Continue to cook the gammon, uncovered for 30 minutes. Meanwhile, purée the apples, onion and cooking juices in a liquidiser or blender.
5. Stir the mustard and sultanas into the 'gravy'. Warm through gently.
6. Slice the ham thinly and serve, with a little of the sauce spooned alongside. Garnish with sprigs of watercress.

Weight Watchers note
1 medium-size slice (35 g/1¼ oz) of ham = 1 Point.

Cook's note
Any leftovers can be used in packed lunches, salads and risottos. Alternatively, freeze it in handy portions.

Pot-Roast Gammon with an Apple Gravy *(opposite)*
Sausage, Red Onion and Apple Casserole *(opposite)*

Pork and Chinese Vegetable Stir-fry

Prepare the pork, cover and leave it to marinate overnight in the refrigerator. This saves time the following day, particularly if you are out at work.

175 g (6 oz) pork tenderloin, sliced finely
1 tablespoon light soy sauce
1 tablespoon dry sherry
1 tablespoon five-spice seasoning

For the vegetable stir-fry:
2 teaspoons sunflower oil
1/2 red or green pepper, de-seeded and sliced thinly
1 celery stick, cut into matchsticks
2 carrots, cut into matchsticks or thin strips
55 g (2 oz) button mushrooms, sliced thinly
50 g (1 3/4 oz) sugar-snap peas or tiny broccoli florets
2 spring onions, chopped
125 g (4 1/2 oz) medium egg-noodles

1. Put the meat in a shallow dish. Mix together the soy sauce, sherry, five-spice seasoning and 2 tablespoons of water and brush over the pork, coating it well. Cover and leave to marinate for 1 hour.
2. Heat the oil in a large, non-stick frying-pan. Add the pepper, celery and carrots and stir-fry for 3 minutes. Add the mushrooms, sugar-snap peas or broccoli and spring onions and stir-fry for a further 2 minutes.
3. Remove the vegetables with a slotted spoon and put to one side. Add the pork to the hot saucepan and stir-fry for 3 minutes. Pour on any remaining marinade and cook for a further minute.
4. Meanwhile, cook the egg-noodles, according to the pack instructions. Drain and divide between hot serving plates.
5. Return the vegetables to the saucepan and lightly toss with the meat, to mix. Spoon the meat and vegetables on to the hot noodles. Serve immediately.

Tandoori Chicken with Mango Yogurt Relish

Here is a simple way of preparing your own tandoori style chicken. Alternatively, you can buy tasty ready-prepared and cooked tandoori chicken, but do remember to calculate the Points! Accompany with the relish and a mixed salad.

2 × 100 g (3 1/2 oz) skinless, boneless chicken breasts
2 tablespoons low-fat plain yogurt
2 teaspoons tandoori spice mix
1 garlic clove, crushed
1 small lemon or lime, cut into wedges
chopped fresh coriander or parsley

For the relish:
1 spring onion, chopped finely
3 tablespoons low-fat plain yogurt
1 teaspoon mild curry paste
2 teaspoons mango chutney
1 tablespoon chopped fresh mint
salt and freshly ground black pepper

1. Cut the chicken into neat, bite-size pieces. Mix the yogurt with the tandoori spice, garlic and a little seasoning. Leave to marinate for 30 minutes.
2. Preheat the grill until hot and thread the chicken on to two skewers. Cook the chicken for 5 minutes. Turn and cook the other side for 3–4 minutes. Allow to stand whilst you make the relish.
3. Mix all the relish ingredients together. Season well.
4. Serve the tandoori chicken with wedges of lemon or lime and a sprinkling of fresh herbs.

Chicken Supreme with a Tarragon Sauce

Points per serving: 3½
Total Points per recipe: 14

Serves: 4
Preparation and cooking time:
30 minutes
Freezing: not recommended
Calories per serving: 185

4 × 150 g (5½ oz) boneless,
skinless chicken breasts
300 ml (½ pint) chicken stock
grated zest of ½ lemon
8 fresh tarragon sprigs
2 teaspoons cornflour
150 ml (¼ pint) semi-skimmed
milk
salt and freshly ground black
pepper

1. Arrange the chicken in a shallow saucepan and pour over the stock. Bring to the boil. Add the lemon zest and 2 sprigs of tarragon. Reduce the heat and simmer gently for 10–15 minutes or until the chicken breasts are tender.
2. Using a slotted spoon, transfer the chicken to a sheet of foil and wrap up tightly, to keep warm.
3. Boil the stock further to reduce to about 150 ml (¼ pint). Strain the stock into a jug. Wipe the saucepan out with kitchen paper and return the stock to the pan.
4. Blend the cornflour with the milk. Add to the stock and bring to the boil, stirring, until the sauce thickens. Reduce the heat to a simmer.
5. Return the chicken breasts to the sauce, add the chopped leaves of 2 sprigs of tarragon (use scissors to snip them into the sauce) and season to taste.
6. Serve each chicken breast with a little sauce spooned over and a sprig of tarragon, to garnish. Accompany with green vegetables and rice or new potatoes, remembering to add the Points.

Variation
Stir 10 seedless and halved green grapes into the sauce at the end of step 4.

Chicken Bourguignonne Style

Points per serving: 4
Total Points per recipe: 16

Serves: 4
Preparation time: 20 minutes
Cooking time: 1 hour
Freezing: recommended
Calories per serving: 390

Ideal for special occasions, this casserole can be made a day or two ahead, and reheated. The flavours develop wonderfully. Serve with a parsnip or potato mash and green vegetables.

2 rindless rashers of streaky
bacon, cut into pieces
8 boneless, skinless chicken
thighs
8 shallots
1 tablespoon plain flour
200 ml (7 fl oz) red wine
100 ml (3½ fl oz) water
2 teaspoons chopped fresh
thyme
150 g (5½ oz) button
mushrooms
1 teaspoon sugar
salt and freshly ground black
pepper
4 fresh thyme sprigs, to garnish

1. Heat a non-stick frying-pan and sauté the bacon until browned and crisp. Transfer to a casserole dish. Add the chicken thighs to the pan and cook, turning frequently, until golden. Transfer to the casserole.
2. Preheat the oven to Gas Mark 4/180°C/350°F.
3. Add the shallots to the saucepan and stir-fry until coloured and slightly softened. Sprinkle on the flour and cook for 1 minute; then gradually blend in the red wine and water.
4. Bring to the boil, stirring, until the sauce thickens. Season to taste with salt and pepper. Add the thyme. Pour over the chicken.
5. Cook in the oven for an hour. After 30 minutes, add the mushrooms and sugar. Cook for the remaining time. Adjust the seasoning, to taste, before serving, garnished with fresh sprigs of thyme.

Variation
Replace the chicken with 500 g (1 lb 2 oz) beef, cut into cubes. Extend the cooking time by 40 minutes or until the meat is tender. Add 3½ Points per serving.

Rich Red Chicken with Rosemary and Cherry Tomatoes

Points per serving: 4½
Total Points per recipe: 18

Serves: 4

Preparation time: 30 minutes

Cooking time: 1 hour

Freezing: cool after step 4 and freeze

Calories per serving: 350

Once it's prepared, little attention is needed for this casserole, making it ideal for entertaining. The rich, sun-dried tomato flavour adds an element of surprise. Mop up the juices with mashed potato, Parsnip and Carrot Mash (see page 76) or jacket potatoes and serve some freshly cooked dwarf green beans as well.

4 onions, quartered

4 teaspoons olive oil

4 part-boned chicken breasts, skinned

2 garlic cloves, crushed

3 teaspoons chopped fresh rosemary

2 tablespoons sun-dried tomato paste

100 ml (3½ fl oz) red wine or sherry

2 teaspoons flour

450 ml (16 fl oz) chicken stock

350 g (12 oz) small, flat mushrooms

2 tablespoons whole-grain mustard

225 g (8 oz) cherry tomatoes

salt and freshly ground black pepper

flat-leaf parsley leaves, to garnish

1. Preheat the oven to Gas Mark 4/180°C/350°F. Heat a large, non-stick frying-pan until hot. Add the onions with 2 teaspoons of oil, reduce the heat and cook for 10 minutes, stirring, until just beginning to soften and turn golden. Remove with a slotted spoon, to a large, lidded, ovenproof casserole.

2. Add the remaining oil and chicken, breast-down and cook for 5 minutes, until the meat seals and lightly colours. Add the garlic and rosemary, turn the breasts over and cook for a further 5 minutes, to seal the underside. Transfer the chicken to the casserole.

3. Stir the tomato paste and wine or sherry into the garlic. Cook for 3–4 minutes, to reduce slightly, and then blend in the flour. Cook, stirring, for a further 2–3 minutes, until smooth. Blend in the stock. Bring to the boil and then pour over the chicken.

4. Cover tightly and cook in the oven for 50 minutes.

5. Meanwhile, wipe out the frying-pan and dry-fry the mushrooms over a gentle heat, until they begin to soften and release a little moisture. Continue to cook gently for 5 minutes.

6. Stir the mushrooms, mustard and tomatoes into the casserole. Season to taste with salt and pepper. Return to the oven, uncovered, for 10 minutes or until the tomatoes are just tender. Serve, garnished with parsley leaves.

Chicken and Fennel Braise with Bacon and Tomato

Points per serving: 3½
Total Points per recipe: 14

Serves: 4

Preparation time: 30 minutes

Cooking time: 40 minutes

Freezing: recommended

Calories per serving: 255

Serve this light, flavoursome casserole with Irish Mashed Potatoes, with Savoy Cabbage and Leeks (see page 86) or mashed potato and broccoli.

2 teaspoons olive oil

8 shallots

1 garlic clove

2 fennel bulbs, halved

2 rashers of rindless lean back bacon, cut into strips

4 small part-boned chicken breasts, skinned

2 teaspoons plain flour

300 ml (½ pint) chicken stock

150 ml (¼ pint) white wine

4 fresh thyme sprigs, plus extra sprigs to garnish

4 tomatoes, skinned, de-seeded and sliced

salt and freshly ground black pepper

1. Heat the oil in a large, non-stick saucepan or casserole dish and sauté the shallots, garlic and fennel for 10 minutes until golden. Shake the pan frequently and turn the fennel halfway through cooking. Remove to a plate with a slotted spoon.

2. Add the bacon and chicken (breast-side down), to the saucepan and sauté for 5 minutes or until the chicken is lightly coloured. Turn the breasts over and cook for a further 2–3 minutes.

3. Sprinkle in the flour and cook, stirring, for 1 minute. Return the shallots and fennel to the pan. Gradually, blend in the stock and wine. Add the thyme and season with salt and pepper. Cover tightly and simmer gently for 40 minutes.

4. Discard the thyme and garlic and adjust the seasoning, to taste. Stir in the tomatoes and simmer, uncovered, for a further 3–4 minutes, just to heat through.

5. Serve, garnished with sprigs of fresh thyme.

Cook's note

Take care not to trim off the root of the fennel bulb. You need to keep the halves intact.

Weight Watchers note

As much as we all love creamy, rich sauces, it is often the simple 'thin' sauces that are more flavoursome. Simplicity is a key to good, healthy cooking.

Lemon-Baked Chicken and Potatoes with Tzatziki

Points per serving: 5
Total Points per recipe: 20
Serves: 4
Preparation time: 10 minutes
Cooking time: 40 minutes
Freezing: not recommended
Calories per serving: 435

Enjoy a taste of Greece – this fragrant dish is ideal for informal eating on a summer's day. Accompany with tzatziki, crusty bread or pitta and a fresh green salad – and you are half-way there!

4 chicken leg portions, skinned
2 small red onions, quartered
4 garlic cloves, chopped
2 lemons, cut into chunks
450 g (1 lb) new potatoes,
*   halved*
1 tablespoon chopped fresh
*   thyme or 1/2 teaspoon*
*   dried thyme*
1 tablespoon chopped fresh
*   oregano or rosemary or*
*   1/2 teaspoon dried rosemary*
2 tablespoons olive oil
salt and freshly ground black
*   pepper*

For the tzatziki:
150 ml (1/4 pint) tub of Greek-
*   style natural yogurt*
1 teaspoon white-wine vinegar
5 cm (2-inch) piece of
*   cucumber, peeled, de-seeded*
*   and chopped*
1 tablespoon chopped fresh mint
*   leaves or 1 teaspoon dried*
*   mint*

1. Preheat the oven to Gas Mark 5/190°C/375°F.
2. Cut the chicken leg portions in two, and place in a large, shallow, ovenproof dish, with the onions, garlic, lemons, potatoes, thyme, oregano and olive oil. Season with salt and pepper. Toss the ingredients together well, to coat them evenly.
3. Cover with foil and cook for 20 minutes. Remove the foil and turn the potatoes and chicken over. Increase the oven temperature to Gas Mark 6/200°C/400° and cook, uncovered for a further 20 minutes, until the vegetables and chicken are well coloured.
4. Meanwhile, prepare the tzatziki. Mix together all the ingredients in a bowl and season with salt and pepper. Cover and chill until required.
5. Spoon the chicken, potato and onion on to warm plates, ensuring that all servings get a few wedges of lemon.

Variation

This is good eaten chilled, too, and makes an ideal packed lunch – but beware of the garlic!

Jerk Chicken with a Pineapple Salsa

Points per serving: 5
Total Points per recipe: 20
Serves: 4
Preparation and cooking time:
25 minutes
Freezing: recommended for chicken
breasts only
Calories per serving: 305

There is a marvellous selection of seasonings from every part of the globe, which certainly prevents boredom! Look for Jamaican 'jerk' or Cajun seasonings to spice up chicken breasts. Serve with this fresh pineapple salsa, a green salad and a jacket potato.

4 boneless, skinless chicken
*   breasts*
4 teaspoons sunflower oil
2 teaspoons lemon juice
1 tablespoon Jamaican jerk or
*   Cajun seasoning*

For the salsa:
175 g (6 oz) fresh pineapple,
*   finely chopped*
4 spring onions, chopped
50 g (11/4 oz) red pepper,
*   chopped*
5 mm (1/4-inch) piece of fresh
*   root ginger, chopped*
1 tablespoon cider vinegar
1 tablespoon soft brown sugar
4 tablespoons barbecue sauce

1. Make the salsa. Mix together all the ingredients and place in a small saucepan. Warm through over a gentle heat.
2. Preheat the grill to a medium-hot setting. Make 2–3 incisions into the chicken with a sharp knife. Rub in 2 teaspoons of oil. Mix the remaining oil with the lemon juice, for basting.
3. Sprinkle over the jerk or Cajun seasoning, rubbing it thoroughly into the breast. Grill, seasoning-side up, for 4–5 minutes, brushing occasionally with the oil and lemon juice. Turn the breasts over and grill for 3–4 minutes. Now turn the breasts back over, brush the seasoned side with the remaining baste, turn the grill up to its highest setting and grill for 5 minutes, until crisp and dark in colour. Serve the chicken with a little of the warm salsa.

Cook's notes

If you prefer, you can briskly stir-fry strips of the seasoned chicken for 8–10 minutes. Alternatively, cook the whole breasts at Gas Mark 5/190°C/375°F, for 15 minutes.

   Look out for ready-peeled and ready-to-eat, fresh pineapple, vacuum-packed, which is often displayed amongst the fresh exotic fruits in supermarkets. A large slice of pineapple is just 1/2 Point.

Thai-Style Chicken and Potato Curry

Points per serving: 7
Total Points per recipe: 28
Serves: 4
Preparation time: 20 minutes
Cooking time: 25 minutes
Freezing: recommended
Calories per serving: 395

Creamy and aromatic, this short-cut curry is delicious with sliced bananas or mango. Serve with fresh cooked spinach and carrots.

1 tablespoon cooking oil
2 onions, sliced
1 garlic clove, crushed
450 g (1 lb) boneless, skinless chicken thighs, cubed
2 tablespoons hot Thai curry paste
25 g (1 oz) creamed coconut
300 ml (¹/₂ pint) boiling water
1 tablespoon tomato purée
1 tablespoon soft light brown sugar
350 g (12 oz) potatoes, cut into chunks
150 ml (¹/₄ pint) low-fat plain yogurt
2 tablespoons chopped fresh coriander
salt

To serve:
2 medium-size bananas
grated zest and juice of 1 lime

1. Heat the oil in a large, non-stick saucepan. Gently sauté the onions and garlic, until softened and golden. Add the chicken and cook for 2–3 minutes, or until the chicken is sealed. Stir in the curry paste and cook for a further 2 minutes.
2. Dissolve the creamed coconut in the boiling water and add to the chicken, with the tomato purée, sugar and potato. Cover and gently simmer for 20–25 minutes, or until the potato is tender. (The starch released from the potato will help to thicken the sauce.)
3. Season, to taste, with salt. Stir in the yogurt and coriander and heat through, without boiling, for 5 minutes.
4. Spoon the curry on to warmed plates and serve. Accompany with the sliced banana, tossed in the grated lime zest and juice.

Variation
Replace the bananas with 1 large mango, peeled and chopped.

Cook's note
Chicken thigh is a much more succulent part of the chicken for casseroling. Breast meat tends to toughen and dry out if over-cooked. Thigh meat is also very economical to buy!

Orange-Glazed Sizzling Chicken

Points per serving: 4
Total Points per recipe: 16
Serves: 4
Preparation and cooking time:
30 minutes + marinating
Freezing: recommended
Calories per serving: 220

A harmony of flavours – orange, honey, ginger and the citrus note of coriander seeds – transforms chicken into a sizzling treat. Serve with rice salad and Crunchy Coleslaw (see page 91) or in a pitta bread with mixed leaves and a yogurt dressing.

8 boneless, skinless chicken thighs, halved
4 teaspoons sunflower oil
For the marinade:
grated zest and juice of 1 orange
1 tablespoon lemon juice
2 tablespoons white wine or sherry
1 tablespoon clear honey or stem-ginger syrup
¹/₂ teaspoon ground cinnamon
1 teaspoon ground ginger
1 teaspoon coriander seeds, crushed
1 teaspoon black peppercorns, crushed
To garnish:
1 orange, cut into 8
1 tablespoon chopped fresh coriander

1. Arrange the chicken, in one layer, in a shallow dish.
2. In a bowl, mix together all the ingredients for the marinade. Pour this over the chicken. Cover with clingfilm and leave to marinate for at least 4 hours and preferably overnight.
3. Heat a wok or large, non-stick frying-pan until it is radiating heat. Add 2 teaspoons of the oil and 4 pieces of chicken. Stir-fry briskly for 5 minutes, until golden brown. Remove to a plate.
4. Heat the remaining oil and add the remaining chicken pieces. Stir-fry for 5 minutes, until golden brown. Return the first batch of chicken to the frying-pan, with any remaining marinade, and cook briskly for a further 5–8 minutes, until the chicken has a glazed, dark colour.
5. Arrange the sizzling chicken and its juices on four individual plates. Serve with two orange wedges per serving and chopped fresh coriander.

Variation
Use turkey or pork instead of chicken. Gammon strips taste good, too.

Cook's notes
Prepare the chicken in its marinade the night before it is required and then simply sizzle it in a wok in no time at all.

Stem-ginger syrup is the syrup from a jar of preserved (not crystallised) stem ginger.

Chicken Chaat

Points per serving: 3
Total Points per recipe: 12

Serves: 4
Preparation and cooking time:
20–25 minutes
Freezing: recommended
Calories per serving: 160

Indian food can be either laboriously long to prepare and cook or, like this recipe, quick and simple, without compromising on flavour. Serve with a crisp green salad and Orange-Braised Potato, Carrot and Shallots (page 84), or with a yogurt dip or chutney and a jacket potato, as a change from the traditional boiled rice.

1 teaspoon salt
2 garlic cloves, chopped
1 tablespoon sunflower oil
450 g (1 lb) boneless, skinless
  chicken breast, cut into
  2.5 cm (1-inch) cubes
1 teaspoon ground coriander
1/4 teaspoon ground turmeric
1/2 teaspoon chilli powder
2 tablespoons lemon juice
2 tablespoons chopped fresh
  coriander

1. On a board, use a round-bladed knife to crush the salt and garlic together until they form a pulp. Heat the oil in a non-stick frying-pan. Add the garlic and fry for 3 minutes, or until lightly browned.
2. Add the chicken and stir-fry for 5–6 minutes, until sealed and lightly coloured.
3. Sprinkle on the ground coriander, turmeric and chilli powder and stir-fry for a further 3–4 minutes.
4. Remove from the heat and sprinkle on the lemon juice and chopped coriander.

Variation

For a saucier version, at step 3, stir in a light, tomato-based pour-over or cook-in sauce. Heat through, season to taste and serve on a bed of rice.

Or add 400 g (14 oz) of drained canned chick-peas, with the tomato sauce, and serve with pitta bread. Remember to add the extra Points.

Chinese-style Grilled Duck Breasts

Points per serving: 5
Total Points per recipe: 10

Serves: 2
Preparation time: 10 minutes
+ 2 hours marinating
Cooking time: 15 minutes
Freezing: not recommended
Calories per serving: 570

Duck à l'Orange with a difference!

For the marinade:
1 garlic clove, crushed
2 teaspoons grated fresh root
  ginger
1/4 teaspoon dried chilli flakes
  or 1 small fresh green chilli,
  de-seeded and chopped
grated zest and juice of 1 small
  orange
1 teaspoon sesame oil
1 teaspoon soy sauce
For the duck:
225 g (8 oz) duck breast
1 teaspoon clear honey
1 teaspoon sunflower oil
6 baby sweetcorn cobs, halved
  lengthways
1/2 red pepper, de-seeded and
  sliced
2 baby pak choi, leaves
  separated (see Cook's note)
light soy sauce, to serve

1. Mix together the marinade ingredients in a shallow dish. With a sharp knife, make 4 or 5 diagonal slashes in the duck breast. Coat in the marinade, then leave in a cool place for 1–2 hours.
2. Preheat the grill to medium hot. Shake any excess marinade off the duck, then grill the breast, skin-side up, for 5 minutes. Turn over and grill for a further 5 minutes.
3. Spread any remaining marinade and the honey over the duck breast (skin side), and grill for a final 5 minutes, until the skin is crisp and dark golden.
4. Meanwhile, heat a large, non-stick frying-pan. Add the oil and baby sweetcorn and stir-fry for 2 minutes. Add the pepper and pak choi and continue to cook briskly for a further 2 minutes.
5. Spoon the hot vegetables on to two plates. Slice the cooked duck and arrange the slices over the vegetables. Serve, offering soy sauce separately.

Cook's note

See the Cook's note for Mango-Roasted Pork with Oriental Vegetables (page 102) for substitutes for pak choi.

113

Lamb Jalfrezi with Carrot and Lemon Relish

Points per serving: 3¹/2
Total Points per recipe: 14
Serves: 4
Preparation time: 15 minutes
+ 30 minutes standing
Cooking time: 45 minutes
Freezing: recommended for jalfrezi only
Calories per serving: 305

Jalfrezi is traditionally a 'hot' curry, with red and green peppers; serve with the cooling carrot relish and plain-boiled basmati rice.

2 tablespoons desiccated coconut

300 g (10¹/2 oz) lean, boneless leg
    of lamb, cut into small cubes

1 tablespoon sunflower oil

2 garlic cloves, chopped

1 large onion, chopped

2 cm (³/4-inch) piece of fresh root
    ginger, peeled and chopped

1 large fresh green chilli,
    de-seeded and chopped
    (optional)

1 red pepper, de-seeded and sliced

1 green pepper, de-seeded and
    sliced

1 medium-size potato, peeled
    and cubed

1–2 tablespoons medium-
    strength curry powder

juice of 1 lemon

1 tablespoon tomato purée

salt and freshly ground black
    pepper

For the relish:

2 large carrots, grated coarsely

1 teaspoon black mustard seeds
    or poppy seeds

¹/2 teaspoon salt

1. Soak the coconut in 450 ml (16 fl oz) of boiling water for 30 minutes. Drain, reserving the liquid and discarding the coconut.
2. Heat a non-stick saucepan until hot and then dry-fry the lamb, stirring, until browned. Remove.
3. Heat the oil in the saucepan and sauté the garlic and onion, until browned. Stir in the ginger, chilli, peppers and potato.
4. Cover and cook for 10 minutes, until softened. Stir in the curry powder and cook for another minute.
5. Return the meat, stir in the reserved coconut water, juice of half the lemon, tomato purée and seasoning. Bring to the boil, cover and simmer very gently for 45 minutes or until the meat is very tender, stirring once or twice.
6. Meanwhile, mix the grated carrots with the remaining lemon juice, the mustard or poppy seeds and salt. Serve with the curry.

Cook's note

Curries benefit from being made 1 or 2 days ahead and then reheated. The flavours have time to mature, making quite a difference!

Weight Watchers note

Freeze individual portions of curry and weighed out bags of rice for an instant supper that simply requires reheating.

Shepherd's Pie with Parsnip and Potato Topping

Points per serving: 8
Total Points per recipe: 32
Serves: 4
Preparation time: 20 minutes
Cooking time: 1 hour
Freezing: recommended
Calories per serving: 310

A great favourite with the whole family. Use minced lamb, which is the traditional choice of meat for this, rather than beef.

350 g (12 oz) lean minced lamb

1 onion, chopped finely

2 carrots, sliced finely

300 ml (¹/2 pint) vegetable stock

Worcestershire sauce

1 teaspoon chopped fresh
    rosemary or ¹/2 teaspoon
    dried rosemary

450 g (1 lb) parsnips, peeled
    and cubed

350 g (12 oz) potatoes, peeled
    and cubed

4 tablespoons Greek-style
    natural yogurt

grated nutmeg

1 tablespoon cornflour, blended
    with 2 tablespoons water

salt and freshly ground black
    pepper

1. Dry-fry the minced meat in a large, non-stick saucepan until browned, stirring frequently. Add the onion and sauté for 5 minutes, then add the carrots, stock, about a teaspoon of Worcestershire sauce (or to taste) and

rosemary. Bring to the boil and then cover and simmer for about 20 minutes.
2. Meanwhile, place the parsnips and potatoes in a large saucepan. Cover with cold water, add a little salt and bring to the boil. Cover, reduce the heat and then simmer for about 15 minutes, or until the vegetables are tender.
3. Drain and mash the potatoes and parsnips. Beat vigorously, adding the yogurt, a pinch of grated nutmeg, salt and pepper, to taste (you will find a hand-held electric whisk will give a light and fluffy 'mash' without the effort!)
4. Preheat the oven to Gas Mark 5/190°C/375°F.
5. Add the blended cornflour to the lamb mixture, stirring until thickened. Remove from the heat.
6. Transfer the meat mixture to an ovenproof dish and top with the mash. Bake for about 20–25 minutes, until heated through and golden brown on top.

Vegetarian option

Substitute 300 g (10¹/2 oz) of minced Quorn or reconstituted soya mince for the lamb and save 2 Points per serving. Using extra-lean minced beef saves 3 Points per serving.

Weight Watchers note

This delicious recipe contains 8 Points per serving; but remember that shepherd's pie served in a restaurant may contain at least 9 Points for an average portion!

Roast Rack of Lamb with Flageolet Beans and Rosemary

A real treat – and ideal for the special occasion, as it requires little preparation and takes no time at all. Serve with mashed potato and carrots.

4 shallots, quartered
2 teaspoons olive oil
200 g (7½ oz) 'French-trimmed' rack of lamb (about 6 cutlets)
2 fresh rosemary sprigs
400 g (14 oz) canned flageolet beans
red-wine vinegar
salt and freshly ground black pepper

1. Preheat the oven to Gas Mark 6/200°C/400°F.
2. Toss the shallots and oil together in a small, shallow roasting tin. Roast for 10 minutes.
3. Add the rack of lamb, lightly seasoned with salt and pepper, and the rosemary sprigs. Roast for 10–15 minutes.
4. Pour the beans and their juice around the lamb. Season again and return to the oven for a further 5 minutes, just to heat the beans through. Sprinkle in ½–1 teaspoon of vinegar or to taste. Discard the rosemary sprigs.
5. Divide the beans and shallots between two hot plates. Slice the lamb into six small cutlets and arrange on top of the beans. Serve at once.

Cook's note
Replace the rack of lamb with 6 medium-size lamb cutlets. Reduce the roasting time at step 3 to 10 minutes.

Lamb and Spinach Filo Pie

This Mediterranean dish is ideal for buffet parties and entertaining. Alternatively, freeze any leftovers for a mid-week meal. Serve with a spicy tomato sauce, or a cucumber and yogurt dip.

350 g (12 oz) minced lamb
1 onion, chopped finely
1 garlic clove, crushed
2 teaspoons ground cumin
½ teaspoon dried mint
450 g (1 lb) frozen chopped spinach, thawed and well drained
125 g (4½ oz) ricotta cheese
grated nutmeg
4 teaspoons low-fat spread, melted
375 g packet of frozen filo pastry, thawed
salt and freshly ground black pepper

1. Cook the lamb in a non-stick frying-pan, stirring to break up any lumps of meat and to brown the mince evenly. Add the onion and cook for a further 5 minutes.
2. Add the garlic, cumin and mint and simmer for 5 minutes. Remove from the heat and stir in the spinach and ricotta cheese. Season well with salt, pepper and a little grated nutmeg.
3. Preheat the oven to Gas Mark 5/190°C/375°F. Brush the base and sides of a 30 × 23 cm (12 × 9 inch) baking dish with a little melted low-fat spread.
4. Line the dish with half the filo pastry sheets, letting the short ends overhang at either end. Spread the lamb and spinach mixture over the pastry and then cover with the remaining sheets, brushing the melted spread between each sheet.
5. Trim any overhanging sheets of pastry and tuck neatly in around the edges. With a sharp knife, cut through the layers to the base of the dish, to mark out 16 squares.
6. Bake for 30 minutes, until golden brown and crisp. Leave for 10 minutes before cutting out the squares.

Variation
Replace the minced lamb with 125 g (4½ oz) of feta cheese, crumbled. Save 1½ Points per serving.

Lamb and Root Vegetable Stew with Minty Dumplings

Points per serving: 10½
Total Points per recipe: 42
Serves: 4
Preparation time: 15 minutes
Cooking time: 1¼ hours
Freezing: recommended
Calories per serving: 530

Tender lamb chops hidden under a cloud of minty dumplings are a great family feast.

1 tablespoon sunflower oil
4 × 150 g (5½ oz) lamb loin chops, trimmed
2 leeks, sliced
2 celery sticks, chopped
2 carrots, sliced
175 g (6 oz) swede, cut into 2.5 cm (1-inch) chunks
1 tablespoon plain flour
450 ml (16 fl oz) lamb or vegetable stock
1 teaspoon dried thyme
½ teaspoon dried rosemary
salt and freshly ground black pepper

For the dumplings:
85 g (3 oz) self-raising flour
½ teaspoon dried mint
½ teaspoon dried parsley
2 tablespoons hard margarine
salt

1. Preheat the oven to Gas Mark 4/180°C/350°F. Heat the oil in a flameproof casserole and brown the chops on both sides. Remove and set aside.
2. Add the leeks, celery, carrots and swede and cook for 2–3 minutes. Sprinkle on the flour and cook for a further minute. Blend in the stock and herbs. Season with salt and pepper.
3. Return the chops to the casserole. Cover and transfer to the oven to cook for 45 minutes.
4. Meanwhile, make the dumplings: sift the flour and a pinch of salt into a bowl. Mix in the dried herbs and then rub in the margarine until the mixture resembles fine breadcrumbs. Add just enough water to make a soft, manageable dough. Shape into 8 small dumplings.
5. Add the dumplings to the casserole, cover and cook for a further 30 minutes, or until the meat is very tender and the dumplings are light and fluffy.
6. Serve one chop and two dumplings per portion, with some vegetables and gravy.

Variation
Replace the swede with turnip.
   Use pork instead of lamb (reduce by 1 Point per serving) and replace the rosemary with sage. Replace the mint with mixed herbs.

Cook's note
Dumplings can be frozen uncooked and simply defrosted and popped on top of various casseroles – they are a real comfort food. 1 dumpling = 2½ Points.

Tender Lamb with a Trio of Bastes

Points per serving: 3½
Total Points per recipe: 14
Serves: 4
Preparation and cooking time: 20 minutes
Freezing: not recommended
Calories per serving: 285

Lamb chops are good value and easy to prepare. Here are three different bastes to brush them with, prior to cooking. Serve with fresh vegetables.

4 medium-size lamb loin chops, trimmed (3 Points each)
fresh mint or rosemary sprigs, to serve

For the redcurrant and orange baste:
2 tablespoons redcurrant jelly, melted
grated zest and juice of 1 orange
1 tablespoon black peppercorns, crushed
¼ teaspoon dry mustard powder

For the mint, mustard and yogurt baste:
1 tablespoon mint jelly
1 teaspoon honey mustard or whole-grain mustard
4 tablespoons low-fat plain Bio-yogurt
salt and freshly ground black pepper

For the tomato and rosemary baste:
2 tablespoons tomato ketchup
1 teaspoon dried rosemary
1 shallot, chopped
chilli sauce

1. Mix together the ingredients for your chosen baste. Season with salt and pepper.
2. Preheat the grill. Brush the chops with the marinade and grill for 6–8 minutes on each side for the loin or chump chops or 4–6 minutes each side for the cutlets. Baste frequently during cooking with the baste.
3. Serve the chops garnished with fresh mint or rosemary sprigs.

Cook's note
The bastes are delicious with pork and chicken, too.

Turkish Lamb

A welcoming stew on a cold day – you can use as many or as few vegetables as you like in this casserole. In Greece or Cyprus, pork would probably be used.

1 tablespoon sunflower or
    olive oil
2 onions, sliced
2 garlic cloves, chopped finely
450 g (1 lb) lean lamb, cubed
225 g (8 oz) okra
4 small courgettes, cut into thick
    slices, or 2 large courgettes,
    cut into chunks
400 g (14 oz) canned chopped
    tomatoes
1 tablespoon tomato purée
2 bay leaves
1 tablespoon chopped fresh
    oregano
1/2 teaspoon ground cinnamon
    or 1 cinnamon stick
about 300 ml (1/2 pint)
    vegetable or lamb stock
salt and freshly ground black
    pepper

1. Heat the oil in a large non-stick saucepan and fry the onions and garlic for 5 minutes, or until golden. Remove with a slotted spoon to a flameproof casserole.
2. Brown the meat in the pan, and add it to the onion and garlic.
3. Add the okra and courgettes to the pan and sauté briskly; then stir in the chopped tomatoes, tomato purée, bay leaves, oregano, cinnamon and half the stock. Pour over the lamb and onions. Season with salt and pepper.
4. Cover and simmer for 1 hour, stirring occasionally, until the meat is very tender. Add more stock, as necessary.
5. Adjust the seasoning, to taste. Serve with fresh vegetables.

Cook's note

Okra – also known as 'ladies' fingers' – is a starchy, green finger-shaped pod, frequently used in Middle-Eastern and Indian cookery. It naturally thickens stews and soups, so there is no need to add any additional starch.

Turkey Croquettes

This is good with a spicy chutney or tomato sauce, or with a spoonful of cranberry relish, and served with Crunchy Coleslaw (see page 91) or Mediterranean Vegetable Salad (see page 69).

600 g (1 lb 5 oz) potatoes, cubed
3 tablespoons skimmed milk
1/4 teaspoon grated nutmeg
150 g (51/2 oz) cooked turkey,
    minced
2 spring onions, chopped finely
1 egg, beaten
a little flour, for handling
salt and freshly ground black
    pepper
For the crumb coating:
25 g (1 oz) fine fresh
    breadcrumbs
25 g (1 oz) half-fat Cheddar
    cheese, grated finely

1. Cook the potatoes in salted, boiling water for 10–12 minutes, or until tender. Drain and mash thoroughly, with the milk, nutmeg and a little salt and pepper, to taste.
2. In a bowl, mix together the turkey, spring onions and warm potato. Add enough beaten egg to bind the mixture.
3. Divide the mixture into eight equal portions and shape each into a croquette, using lightly floured hands.
4. Mix together the breadcrumbs and cheese. Season with salt and pepper. Place in a shallow bowl and gently roll each croquette in the crumb mixture, pressing lightly.
5. Place on a non-stick baking sheet and cook for 35–40 minutes, turning half-way, until crisp and browned. Serve.

Variation

Replace the turkey with ham or smoked salmon trimmings. Don't forget to check the Points.

Cook's note

In the absence of leftover cooked turkey, buy some fresh minced turkey or a turkey escalope. Cook, cool and mince finely.

118

Sweet and Sour Turkey

Points per serving: 4
Total Points per recipe: 16
Serves: 4
Preparation and cooking time:
25 minutes
Freezing: not recommended
Calories per serving: 195

Buy a turkey breast fillet or a pack of stir-fry strips of turkey for this speedy mid-week meal. Serve with noodles, rice or a jacket potato.

2 teaspoons sunflower oil
350 g (12 oz) turkey breast,
    cut into strips
2 spring onions, cut into 2.5 cm
    (1-inch) lengths
1 red pepper, de-seeded and
    sliced
1 yellow pepper, de-seeded and
    sliced
227 g can of water chestnuts,
    drained
350 g jar of Light Stir-fry Pour
    Over Sauce
115 g (4 oz) canned pineapple
    pieces in natural juice,
    drained
salt and freshly ground black
    pepper

1. Heat the oil in a large, non-stick frying-pan or wok. Add the turkey and stir-fry briskly for 2–3 minutes, until sealed.
2. Add the spring onions, peppers and water chestnuts and stir-fry for a further 3–4 minutes.
3. Pour on the sauce and add the pineapple. Mix well, bring to the boil, reduce the heat and simmer for 3–4 minutes. Season to taste and serve.

Variation
Replace the turkey with Quorn, for a vegetarian alternative. Add 2 Points per serving.

Turkey, Leek and Apricot Casserole with a Herb Crumble

Points per serving: 7
Total Points per recipe: 28
Serves: 4
Preparation time: 20 minutes
Cooking time: 25 minutes
Freezing: recommended
Calories per serving: 410

The addition of sesame seeds (you can also use chopped sunflower seeds), makes a lovely, crunchy crumble topping to this fruity casserole. Serve with carrots and green beans.

For the filling:
2 teaspoons sunflower oil
350 g (12 oz) turkey, cubed
2 large leeks, sliced
2 tablespoons plain flour
300 ml (1/2 pint) vegetable stock
150 ml (1/4 pint) cider
10 ready-to-eat dried apricots,
    halved
1/2 teaspoon dried thyme
salt and freshly ground black
    pepper
For the crumble:
85 g (3 oz) plain flour
2 tablespoons sesame seeds,
    toasted
40 g (11/2 oz) hard margarine
1/2 teaspoon dried thyme or
    1 teaspoon chopped fresh
    thyme
1/2 teaspoon dried sage or
    1 teaspoon chopped
    fresh sage
1 teaspoon snipped fresh chives

1. Preheat the oven to Gas Mark 5/190°C/375°F. Heat the oil in a saucepan, add the turkey and fry for 3–4 minutes, stirring, until the meat is sealed. Transfer to a plate.
2. Add the leeks to the saucepan and sauté gently for 10 minutes, until softened. Return the turkey to the saucepan. Sprinkle on the flour and cook gently for 1 minute. Gradually blend in the stock and cider, stirring continuously, until the sauce thickens.
3. Stir in the apricots and thyme. Season with salt and pepper. Spoon into a 1.2 litre (2 pint) casserole dish.
4. To make the crumble topping, sift the flour into a large mixing bowl. Add the sesame seeds and a pinch of salt. Rub in the margarine, until the mixture resembles breadcrumbs. Mix in the herbs.
5. Sprinkle the crumble topping evenly over the turkey. Cook for 20–25 minutes, or until golden brown.

Variation
Replace the apricots with ready-to-eat prunes or 1 large cooking apple, chopped. The Points remain the same.

Turkey, Pepper and Pasta Bake

Points per serving: 6½
Total Points per recipe: 13

Serves: 2
Preparation time: 20 minutes
Cooking time: 30 minutes
Freezing: recommended
Calories per serving: 415

Pasta bakes are a popular family favourite, so double up the quantities, if required.

225 g (8 oz) minced turkey
1 small onion, chopped
1 garlic clove, crushed
1 small red or green pepper, de-seeded and chopped
2 teaspoons sunflower oil
400 g (14 oz) canned chopped tomatoes
100 ml (3½ fl oz) stock or water
85 g (3 oz) pasta shapes, e.g. shells, farfalle or penne
½ teaspoon dried oregano or marjoram
salt and freshly ground black pepper
25 g (1 oz) half-fat Cheddar cheese, grated, to serve

1. Heat the oven to Gas Mark 4/180°C/350°F. Heat a non-stick frying-pan until hot and then dry-fry the minced turkey, stirring well, for 7–8 minutes, or until cooked and crumbly.
2. Add the onion, garlic, pepper and oil. Mix well, cover and cook for 5 minutes, until the vegetables have softened.
3. Stir in the tomatoes, stock or water, pasta shapes, herbs and seasoning. Bring to the boil and simmer for 2 minutes.
4. Spoon the mixture into a small casserole dish. Cover and bake for 30 minutes.
5. Uncover and serve hot, sprinkled with the grated cheese.

Devilled Turkey Escalopes

Points per serving: 4½
Total Points per recipe: 9

Serves: 2
Preparation and cooking time:
25 minutes
Freezing: not recommended
Calories per serving: 245

Turkey has become a very popular meat to enjoy throughout the year – not just at Christmas. It offers good value and is very low in fat. Look out for turkey mince, stir-fries and joints, as well as tender, 'quick-to-cook' escalopes.

2 teaspoons olive oil
1 carrot, cut into thin strips
1 courgette, cut into thin strips
1 tablespoon plain flour
½–1 teaspoon mild chilli powder
½ teaspoon ground turmeric
2 × 125 g (4½ oz) turkey escalopes
125 g (4 oz) button mushrooms, sliced
1 tablespoon Worcestershire sauce
salt and freshly ground black pepper
1 tablespoon chopped fresh parsley, to garnish

1. Heat the oil in a non-stick frying-pan and stir-fry the carrot and courgette for 2 minutes, until tinged golden brown. Using a slotted spoon, remove and set aside.
2. Pop the flour, chilli and turmeric in a food bag, with a little salt and pepper. Add the escalopes and shake the bag to coat the turkey lightly.
3. Cook the turkey in the hot frying-pan for 2 minutes on each side. Add the mushrooms, Worcestershire sauce, seasoning and 150 ml (¼ pint) of boiling water. Cover and cook for 5 minutes.
4. Return the carrot and courgette to the frying-pan and simmer for a further 5 minutes, until the vegetables are tender and the sauce has thickened.
5. Adjust the seasoning, to taste. Serve, garnished with chopped parsley.

Liver and Onions in a Whole-grain Mustard Sauce

Points per serving: 3½
Total Points per recipe: 14

Serves: 4
Preparation and cooking time:
20 minutes
Freezing: not recommended
Calories per serving: 170

Serve this quick dish with mashed potato and carrots.

1 teaspoon sunflower oil
1 onion, sliced finely
350 g (12 oz) lamb's liver, cut into bite-size pieces
3 tablespoons dry sherry
1 teaspoon cornflour
2 teaspoons whole-grain mustard
salt and freshly ground black pepper

1. Toss the oil and onion together. Heat a non-stick frying-pan, and when hot, add the onion mixture. Stir-fry for 5 minutes, until golden and softened.
2. Add the liver and cook for 1 minute, on one side, until browned; then turn over and cook for a further minute.
3. Blend the sherry with the cornflour, add to the frying-pan, with the mustard and 200 ml (7 fl oz) of water. Briskly bring to the boil, stirring, until the sauce has thickened slightly. Season to taste, and serve immediately.

Variation
Replace the lamb's liver with chicken livers.

Cook's note
Most offal needs the minimum amount of cooking time, although this depends on personal preferences. Liver tends to toughen if it is overcooked.

Kidneys Provençal

Points per serving: 3
Total Points per recipe: 6

Serves: 2
Preparation and cooking time:
30 minutes
Freezing: not recommended
Calories per serving: 270

Nutritious and quick to prepare, these kidneys taste great with mashed potato or freshly cooked pasta and courgettes.

2 teaspoons sunflower oil
1 onion, sliced
1 garlic clove, crushed
6 medium-size lamb's kidneys, halved and skinned
2 teaspoons plain flour
4 tomatoes, skinned, de-seeded and cut into strips
1 tablespoon tomato purée
¼ teaspoon chopped fresh thyme
4 tablespoons white or red wine
4 fresh basil leaves, torn
salt and freshly ground black pepper

1. Heat a non-stick saucepan and add the oil, onion and garlic. Cook gently for 5 minutes, or until softened and golden.
2. Meanwhile, using scissors, snip out the white core from the kidneys. Wash and pat dry with kitchen paper. Add to the onions and cook, stirring, until browned all over. Sprinkle on the flour and cook for a further minute.
3. Add the tomatoes, tomato purée, thyme and wine. Stir well and season with salt and pepper. Cover and simmer for 15 minutes. Stir in the fresh basil just before serving.

Variation
Replace the kidneys with 2 medium-size slices of lamb's liver, cut into strips. Simmer for just 10 minutes. Points remain the same.

Add ½ red pepper, de-seeded and cut into strips at step 3.

Liver, Bacon and Cherry Tomato Brochettes with Creamy Onion Sauce

Points per serving: 6½
Total Points per recipe: 13

Serves: 2
Preparation and cooking time:
25 minutes
Freezing: not recommended
Calories per serving: 395

Serve these brochettes with fresh green beans or courgettes and new potatoes.

1 onion, halved and sliced finely

2 medium-size slices of lamb's or calves' liver, each cut into 6 equal pieces

3 rashers of rindless streaky bacon

2 teaspoons Dijon or whole-grain mustard

6 cherry tomatoes

6 button mushrooms

2 teaspoons plain flour

150 ml (¼ pint) skimmed milk

2 teaspoons sunflower oil

1 tablespoon half-fat crème fraîche

salt and freshly ground black pepper

1. Place the onion in a small saucepan, with just enough cold water to cover. Bring to the boil, then reduce the heat, cover and simmer gently for 5 minutes, or until softened.

2. Meanwhile, wash the liver and pat dry. Using the back of a knife, stretch the bacon out on a board, until very thin. Spread with a thin layer of mustard and then cut each into four equal pieces. Wrap one strip around each piece of liver and thread on to a wooden or metal skewer, alternating with a cherry tomato and a button mushroom.

3. Remove the cover from the onions and boil them until all but a couple of teaspoons of water has completely evaporated. Remove from the heat. Sprinkle on the flour and mix to a paste. Place back over the heat and cook for 1 minute. Gradually blend in the milk and bring to the boil, stirring until the sauce is smooth and has thickened. Cover and remove from the heat.

4. Meanwhile, preheat the grill to a medium-hot setting. Brush the tomatoes and mushrooms with a little oil and season with salt and pepper. Grill the brochettes for 8–10 minutes, turning and brushing with the oil, until the bacon is crisp and the tomatoes are cooked. Keep warm under the grill.

5. Stir the crème fraîche into the onion sauce. Season with salt and pepper and gently warm through. Arrange the brochettes on a plate and spoon some sauce alongside.

Variation

Replace the lamb's liver with chicken livers, washed and trimmed.

Cook's note

The streaky bacon will keep the liver succulent and protect it from overcooking and drying out.

Fish and Shellfish

· ·

There are few foods quite as nutritious, quick to prepare or cook and as readily accepted in different diets as fish. It is today's convenience food and, thankfully, there are still good local fishmongers on hand, as well as wet-fish counters in your supermarket, to help you select and understand the varieties and the best methods of cooking fish.

No longer are we only partnering fish with mild sauces or breadcrumbs. There are now lively, exotic tastes working wonders on the various textures and fishy flavours. Try Thai Mackerel (see page 140) or Indian Fish Patties with Cucumber and Tomato Relish (see page 136), for starters!

Few can deny the pleasure of tucking into a plate of fish and chips – whether at home or the local chippie. With **1,2,3 Success Plus**, you can still have takeaway fish and chips or enjoy fat free chips (see page 84) with fish. Look out for the prepared breaded fish and chips in handy single portions and clearly labelled with nutritional information and oven-cooking instructions, so you can calculate your Points and enjoy the occasional treat.

Canned fish, too, is a very convenient and tasty addition to sandwich fillings, risottos and pasta bakes (see Tuna, Pasta and Cauliflower Gratin, page 127). A good stock in the larder means you should always be able to rustle up a satisfying meal. Just remember to buy fish canned in brine or spring water, or a tomato sauce. Fish in oil adds unnecessary Points.

While recipes in this chapter recommend a good mainstream fish, in many instances, you can swap different varieties around, but do try and use fish from the same or a similar species; for example, cod can be replaced with hake or coley. Recipes using an oily fish like mackerel will work well with trout or salmon too. Times and methods for cooking will then be consistent and give good results.

Don't forget to enjoy the simplicity of fresh-grilled fish, with just a squeeze of lemon or a sprinkling of fresh snipped herbs.

If you haven't previously cast your net further afield, the *1,2,3 Success Plus Cookbook* will certainly offer some tasty bait – while helping you lose weight at the same time!

chapter 6

1

2

3

4

5

7

8

9

Rollmop Herrings with Apple, Cucumber and Chive Relish

Points per serving: 9
Total Points per recipe: 18

Serves: 2
Preparation time: 10 minutes
Freezing: not recommended
Calories per serving: 315

Several days spent rolled up with a piece of pickled cucumber in a spiced vinegar marinade transform herrings into rollmops! They are delicious, traditionally eaten with dark rye bread.

4 rollmop herrings
For the relish:
1 crisp green apple, e.g. Golden Delicious or Granny Smith
2 teaspoons lemon juice
2.5 cm (1-inch) piece of cucumber, chopped
1 tablespoon snipped fresh chives
2 tablespoons low-fat plain fromage frais
salt and freshly ground black pepper
fresh watercress sprigs, to garnish
1 medium-size slice, per serving, of German-style (rye) or brown bread, quartered, to serve

1. Quarter and core the apple. Thinly slice two quarters. Toss in the lemon juice and then drain on a piece of kitchen paper, reserving the juice.
2. Peel and coarsely grate the remaining apple. Mix with the remaining lemon juice, the cucumber, chives and fromage frais. Season well with salt and pepper.
3. Arrange the rollmop herrings, sliced apple and some relish on individual serving plates. Garnish with fresh watercress and serve with the bread.

Cook's notes

Do not prepare the relish too far ahead of time, as the cucumber may leach water into the fromage frais.

Alternatively, sprinkle the diced cucumber with salt and leave for 10–15 minutes, to draw liquid out; then rinse and dry on kitchen paper.

Potato-Topped Cod and Broccoli Pie

Points per serving: 4
Total Points per recipe: 16

Serves: 4
Preparation time: 30 minutes
Cooking time: 30 minutes
Freezing: recommended
Calories per serving: 355

For a change, use canned tomatoes and a white sauce to make a creamy tomato sauce for this delicious fish pie.

For the potato topping:
750 g (1 lb 10 oz) potatoes, cubed
100 ml (3¹/₂ fl oz) skimmed milk
25 g (1 oz) half-fat Cheddar cheese, grated
For the filling:
225 g (8 oz) broccoli florets
1 teaspoon sunflower oil
1 small onion, chopped finely
210 g (7¹/₂ oz) canned chopped tomatoes with herbs
2 tablespoons chopped fresh parsley
450 g (1 lb) cod fillets, skinned and cubed
200 ml (7 fl oz) skimmed milk
4 teaspoons cornflour
1 teaspoon lemon juice
salt and freshly ground black pepper

1. Cook the potatoes in salted, boiling water, until tender. Mash with the milk and season, to taste, with salt and pepper. Put to one side.
2. Meanwhile, cook the broccoli in a little salted, boiling water, until just tender. Drain and refresh in cold water; then drain thoroughly.
3. Heat the oil in a saucepan and cook the onion for 5 minutes, until softened. Add the chopped tomatoes and parsley and simmer for 5 minutes.
4. Meanwhile, place the cod and milk in a small saucepan. Cover and poach for 4–5 minutes, until the cod is opaque and just cooked. Remove the cod with a slotted spoon and transfer to an ovenproof 900 ml (1¹/₂-pint) dish. Add the broccoli florets.
5. Drain the milk into a jug. Blend the cornflour with a tablespoon of water and whisk into the milk. Return to the saucepan and heat, stirring constantly, until the sauce thickens.
6. Preheat the oven to Gas Mark 6/200°C/400°F. Mix the tomato sauce with the white sauce. Season with salt, pepper and lemon juice. Pour over the fish and broccoli. Top with the mashed potato. Sprinkle on the cheese.
7. Bake for 30 minutes, or until the potato topping is golden.

Variation
Replace the broccoli with cauliflower or sliced leeks or a combination of vegetables.

Tuna and Potato Rissoles with a Speedy Tomato Sauce

A little leftover mash can go a long way. Serve these tasty rissoles with mashed celeriac and peas, or a mixed salad.

185 g (6¹/₂ oz) canned tuna in brine, drained
125 g (4¹/₂ oz) cold mashed potato
1 shallot or 1 small onion, chopped finely
1 tablespoon chopped fresh parsley
1 tablespoon chopped fresh dill
anchovy essence
3 tablespoons dried 'natural-colour' breadcrumbs
salt and freshly ground black pepper
For the sauce:
295 g (10¹/₂ oz) canned half-fat tomato soup, e.g. Campbells
chilli or Worcestershire sauce
1 tablespoon finely chopped mixed fresh herbs, e.g. parsley, dill, chives and basil

1. Preheat the oven to Gas Mark 4/180°C/350°F.
2. In a bowl, mix together the tuna, potato, shallot or onion, herbs and a few drops of anchovy essence. Season, to taste, with salt and pepper.
3. Divide into four and lightly form into round or sausage-shaped rissoles. Gently press or roll in the dried crumbs, to give a light, even coating. (You can make ahead of time and chill at this step, until required.)
4. Cook on a non-stick baking tray for 10 minutes; then flip over and cook for a further 8–10 minutes, until golden.
5. Gently heat the soup, until smooth and hot. Do not boil. Add a little chilli or Worcestershire sauce, to taste, and stir in the herbs.
6. Serve the rissoles on a pool of sauce.

Variation

Replace the tuna with canned pink or red salmon. Add ¹/₂ Point per serving.

Salmon and Broccoli Pancakes

Use either salmon or tuna for this tasty bake. Serve with carrots or a mixed salad and crusty bread.

8 pancakes (see page 204)
225 g (8 oz) broccoli, broken into small florets
300 ml (¹/₂ pint) skimmed milk
2 tablespoons cornflour
1 teaspoon Dijon mustard
200 g (7 oz) canned salmon, roughly flaked
1 tablespoon snipped fresh chives or dill
salt and freshly ground black pepper

1. Preheat the oven to Gas Mark 5/190°C/375°F.
2. Cook the broccoli in lightly salted, boiling water, until just tender. Drain thoroughly.
3. Meanwhile, blend the milk and cornflour until smooth and then heat, stirring constantly, until smooth and thickened. Beat in the mustard and add the broccoli, salmon and herbs. Season, to taste, with salt and pepper.
4. Divide the filling between the centre of the pancakes. Roll up and arrange, seam down, in an ovenproof dish. Cover with foil and cook for 15–20 minutes, until heated through. Serve.

Variation

Replace the salmon with four hard-boiled eggs, chopped. Sprinkle on 25 g (1 oz) of Cheddar cheese before cooking, uncovered. Don't forget to add 1 Point per serving.

125

Fisherman's Cobbler

Fresh cod and vegetables in a creamy tomato sauce, topped with herb scones are delicious!

4 × 125 g (4¹/₂ oz) cod fillets
For the sauce:
1 small red onion, chopped
1 small celery stick, sliced
1 garlic clove, crushed
2 small courgettes, sliced thinly
*400 g (14 oz) canned chopped
    tomatoes with herbs*
2 tablespoons tomato purée
2 tablespoons white wine
*salt and freshly ground black
    pepper*
For the herb scones:
175 g (6 oz) self-raising flour
50 g (1¹/₄ oz) low-fat spread
*2 tablespoons chopped fresh
    parsley*
*1 tablespoon chopped fresh dill
    or chives*
*about 3 tablespoons skimmed
    milk*
plain flour

1. Preheat the oven to Gas Mark 6/200°C/400°F. Heat a non-stick frying-pan and add the onion, celery, garlic and courgettes, stirring constantly. Stir-fry for 3–4 minutes or until just softening.

2. Pour on the chopped tomatoes and tomato purée. Bring to the boil and then simmer, covered, for 10 minutes. Stir in the wine. Season to taste with salt and pepper.
3. Meanwhile, make the herb scones. In a bowl, sift together the flour and a little salt. Rub in the low-fat spread, until the mixture resembles breadcrumbs. (A food processor will do this in seconds!)
4. Stir in the herbs and bind with enough milk to form a soft dough.
5. Turn out on to a lightly floured surface and press the dough out to about 2 cm (³/₄-inch) thick. Cut into 8 rounds with a 5 cm (2-inch) plain cutter. Dust lightly with flour.
6. Arrange the cod in the base of a 1.5-litre (2³/₄-pint) round casserole dish. Pour on the sauce.
7. Overlap the scones around the edge of the dish. Immediately cook for 25 minutes, or until the scones are golden brown and risen.

Cook's note

If you want to prepare the cobbler in advance, leave the tomato sauce to cool before pouring it over the fish. Place the scones on it at the last minute.

Weight Watchers note

Look out for the Light/Reduced Fat Cook-in-Sauces. They are great for speed and convenience and adding instant variety. A tomato or mushroom sauce would work well in this recipe.

Cod Steaks with Honey and Mustard

Brush this marinade on to your favourite fish to liven it up instantly. It's delicious on tuna or salmon steaks too. Serve with fresh green vegetables or a salad and jacket potatoes.

2 × 175 g (6 oz) cod steaks
For the marinade:
2 teaspoons clear honey
*1 tablespoon whole-grain
    mustard*
2 tablespoons white wine
2 teaspoons olive oil

1. Preheat the grill to a moderate setting. Line the grill rack with a piece of kitchen foil. Mix the marinade ingredients together.
2. Brush the cod steaks with the marinade and cook for 5–6 minutes on each side, basting them frequently.

Variation

Use a barbecue- or salsa-flavoured mustard.

Cook's note

If you bulk-buy fresh fish to freeze for later use, this is a recipe that you can quickly prepare – coating the fish with the marinade – and then freeze.

Tuna, Pasta and Cauliflower Gratin

Points per serving: 3½
Total Points per recipe: 14
Serves: 4
Preparation time: 20 minutes
Cooking time: 30 minutes
Freezing: recommended
Calories per serving: 375

This savoury supper dish can be made a couple of days in advance, to cook and serve mid week.

1 small cauliflower, broken into florets
125 g (4½ oz) macaroni or shell pasta shapes
2 teaspoons sunflower margarine
1 onion, chopped
25 g (1 oz) plain flour
600 ml (1 pint) skimmed milk
100 g (3½ oz) half-fat Cheddar cheese, grated finely
1 tablespoon chopped fresh chives or dill
1 teaspoon lemon juice
200 g (7 oz) canned tuna in brine or spring water, drained
2 tomatoes, sliced
salt and freshly ground black pepper

1. Cook the cauliflower in lightly salted, boiling water, until just tender. Drain thoroughly. Preheat the oven to Gas Mark 5/190°C/375°F.
2. Cook the pasta in salted, boiling water according to pack instructions. Drain.
3. Melt the margarine in a medium saucepan and cook the onion for 3–4 minutes. Sprinkle on the flour and cook, stirring, for 1 minute.
4. Gradually, blend in the milk, stirring continuously, until the sauce becomes smooth and thickened. Fold in the pasta, 55 g (2 oz) of the cheese, the fresh herbs and lemon juice. Now add the tuna and cauliflower. Season, to taste, with salt and pepper.
5. Spoon the gratin into a 1.3-litre (2½-pint) ovenproof dish. Top with the tomatoes and sprinkle on the remaining cheese.
6. Bake in the oven for 25–30 minutes, until bubbling and golden. Serve.

Variation

Use broccoli and salmon instead of cauliflower and tuna. Fresh fish fillets work well too, but may dilute the sauce a little in cooking. Add 1 Point per serving.

Salmon and Tomato Soufflé Omelette

Points per serving: 6
Total Points per recipe: 6
Serves: 1
Preparation and cooking time: 10 minutes
Freezing: not recommended
Calories per serving: 370

A quick, nutritious supper – serve with green beans or courgettes.

100 g (3½ oz) canned pink or red salmon, drained
1 teaspoon horseradish sauce
2 eggs, separated
½ teaspoon sunflower oil
2 teaspoons snipped fresh chives
2 tomatoes, sliced thinly
salt and freshly ground black pepper

1. Mash the salmon with the horseradish and egg yolks, until smooth. Season with salt and pepper.
2. Whisk the egg whites in a clean, grease-free bowl, with a rotary or balloon whisk, until they form soft peaks.
3. Heat a non-stick omelette pan until very hot. Add the oil and quickly wipe around the pan with kitchen paper.
4. Quickly and lightly fold the egg whites into the salmon mixture, with the chives, and pour into the hot pan.
5. Turn down the heat to medium and cook for 2–3 minutes, until the base is set and the top is still moist. Arrange the tomato slices over one half of the omelette, slide this half on to a warmed plate and draw the pan over, to fold the omelette over the tomatoes. Serve immediately.

Variation

Use canned tuna or crab as an alternative to salmon in this tasty supper dish. Save ½ Point or 1½ Points respectively.

Crusted Cod Steaks with Cherry Tomato Sauce *(page 131)*

Smoked Haddock and Mushroom Gougère

A choux pastry puff, filled with smoked haddock in a mushroom sauce.

For the choux pastry:

100 g (3½ oz) plain flour,
  preferably strong flour
½ teaspoon salt
50 g (1¾ oz) sunflower
  margarine
2 eggs, beaten well

For the filling:

225 g (8 oz) smoked haddock
  fillet
300 ml (½ pint) milk
1 onion, chopped finely
1 carrot, chopped finely
225 g (8 oz) button mushrooms,
  chopped roughly
25 g (1 oz) cornflour
2 teaspoons chopped fresh parsley
2 teaspoons chopped fresh chives
salt and freshly ground black
  pepper

1. Preheat the oven to Gas Mark 6/200°C/400°F. Sift the flour and salt on to a sheet of greaseproof paper.

2. Place the margarine and 175 ml (6 fl oz) of water in a medium-size saucepan and heat slowly, until it comes to the boil. Shoot in the flour and beat hard with a wooden spoon, until the mixture comes away from the sides of the saucepan.

3. Cool slightly and then beat in the eggs, until you have a smooth, glossy and stiff paste. You may not need all the egg. Set aside while you make the filling.

4. Place the haddock, milk, onion and carrot in a saucepan. Bring to a gentle simmer; then cover and cook for 7–8 minutes or until the fish flakes easily. Lift the fish out on to a board and flake the pieces, discarding the skin and any bones.

5. Add the mushrooms to the milk, cover and cook for a further 2 minutes. Blend the cornflour with a drop of water, then mix into the sauce. Stir continuously, until the mixture comes to the boil and thickens. Add the parsley and chives and fold in the haddock flakes. Season with salt, to taste and plenty of pepper.

6. Spoon the choux pastry around the edge of a round, shallow, ovenproof dish. Spoon the filling into the centre.

7. Bake for 35–40 minutes, until well risen and golden brown.

Variation

Replace the fish with cooked chicken or cooked ham.

For a vegetarian alternative, omit the haddock and add cooked broccoli and sweetcorn to the mushroom sauce. Deduct ½ Point per serving.

Cheesy Baked Cod

Enjoy this delicious fish bake without worrying about too many Calories, thanks to the fat-reduced ingredients.

2 × 125 g (4½ oz) cod fillets,
  skinned and boned
2 tomatoes, sliced
a pinch of dried mixed herbs
125 g (4½ oz) low-fat plain
  fromage frais
2 spring onions, chopped
75 g (2¾ oz) half-fat Cheddar
  cheese, grated
salt and freshly ground black
  pepper
2 lemon twists, to garnish

1. Preheat the oven to Gas Mark 4/180°C/350°F. Arrange the fish fillets, side by side, in a shallow ovenproof dish. Arrange the tomato slices over the fish. Season well with salt and pepper and sprinkle on the herbs.

2. Mix together the fromage frais, spring onions and all but a tablespoon of cheese. Season, to taste. Spoon over the tomatoes and then sprinkle the remaining cheese on top.

3. Bake for 20 minutes, or until golden. Garnish with a lemon twist and serve immediately.

Variations

Replace the Cheddar with Double Gloucester cheese, adding 2 Points per serving.

Give the fish the Italian theme, by replacing the cheese with diced half-fat mozzarella cheese and replacing the mixed herbs with chopped fresh basil. Deduct ½ Point per serving.

Cook's note

This recipe can simply be multiplied to serve more – and is ideal, too, as a single serving.

Quick Creamy Kedgeree

This is a cheat's version, but who would know – or tell?! Serve with a green or tomato salad.

175 g (6 oz) smoked haddock
*   fillet, skinned*
395 g (14 oz) canned
*   microwaveable long-grain*
*   rice (plain or Indian-style)*
1/2 × 450 g jar of low-in-fat
*   creamy curry sauce*
2 tablespoons frozen peas
100 g (3 1/2 oz) cooked, peeled
*   prawns, thawed if frozen*
1 spring onion, chopped
1 tomato, sliced, to garnish

1. Place the fish in a shallow dish, with a tablespoon of water. Cover and microwave on a medium setting (800W output/CAT. E oven) for 4–5 minutes. Leave to stand.
2. Cook the rice, according to the pack instructions.
3. Gently heat the curry sauce in a non-stick saucepan, add the peas and simmer for 3 minutes.
4. Stir in the flaked haddock, cooked rice, prawns and spring onion. Heat through for 2–3 minutes.
5. Spoon on to two warm plates. Garnish with slices of tomato and serve immediately.

Baked Plaice Fillets with Orange and a Tarragon Sauce

Pop it into the oven just before seating guests; this delicious recipe for cooking plaice leaves you unflappable and the house free of fishy smells! Serve with baby new potatoes and courgettes or green beans.

1 tablespoon half-fat butter
8 small plaice fillets, rinsed
grated zest and juice of 1 lemon
2 oranges
150 ml (1/4 pint) white wine or
*   dry cider*
salt and coarsely ground black
*   pepper*
For the sauce:
1 tablespoon chopped fresh
*   tarragon*
1 tablespoon chopped fresh
*   parsley*
4 tablespoons low-fat plain
*   fromage frais*
fresh watercress, to garnish

1. Preheat the oven to Gas Mark 6/200°C/400°F. Lightly butter a shallow roasting tray and arrange the fillets in the bottom. Dot with the remaining butter.
2. Sprinkle the fillets with the lemon zest, half the juice, salt and plenty of black pepper, to taste.
3. Using a small sharp knife, cut the bottom off the oranges, sit on a board and cut away strips of the peel and pith. Cut each orange into thin, circular slices. Arrange these over the fillets.
4. Pour the wine or cider around the fish. Bake for 10–15 minutes (depending on the thickness of the fillets). Use a fish slice to transfer the fish to warmed serving plates.
5. Place the roasting tin on the hob, over a high heat, and briskly whisk in the remaining lemon juice, herbs and fromage frais. Season with salt and pepper. Spoon alongside the plaice.
6. Serve immediately, garnished with fresh watercress sprigs.

Variation

Instead of the plaice, use four halibut fillets. Save 1 Point per serving.

Crusted Cod Steaks with Cherry Tomato Sauce

Points per serving: 3½
Total Points per recipe: 7

Serves: 2
Preparation time: 10 minutes
Cooking time: 20 minutes
Freezing: not recommended
Calories per serving: 205

Serve these delicious crusty cod steaks with green beans or courgettes.

2 × 175 g (6 oz) cod steaks
grated zest and juice of ½ lemon
15 g (½ oz) fresh breadcrumbs
2 tablespoons chopped fresh
    herbs, e.g. parsley, thyme,
    tarragon and oregano
salt and freshly ground black
    pepper

For the tomato sauce:
1 teaspoon sunflower oil
1 shallot or small onion,
    chopped finely
250 g (9 oz) cherry tomatoes,
    halved
2 tablespoons dry white wine

1. Make the sauce first. Heat the oil in a small saucepan and gently cook the shallot or onion, until softened but not coloured. Add the tomatoes, wine and salt and pepper. Cover and simmer for 10 minutes. Transfer to a liquidiser or food processor and blend until smooth. Adjust the seasoning, to taste. Return to the rinsed saucepan and reheat gently.
2. Place the cod steaks in a shallow, flameproof dish and sprinkle on the lemon juice. Lightly season with salt and pepper. Cook under a preheated grill for 6 minutes.
3. Meanwhile, mix together the lemon zest, breadcrumbs and herbs. Season with some black pepper.
4. Turn the steaks over and spoon on the crumb topping. Grill for a further 5 minutes, until the steaks are cooked through and the topping is golden. Place the cod on a pool of the tomato sauce.

Variation

Replace the cod with salmon steaks. Add 2½ Points per serving.

Parmesan-Glazed Sole Fillets with Grilled Herb Tomatoes

Points per serving: 4
Total Points per recipe: 8

Serves: 2
Preparation and cooking time:
15 minutes
Freezing: not recommended
Calories per serving: 240

Wonderful fresh flavours – very simply cooked. Serve with mangetout or broccoli.

4 ripe plum tomatoes, halved
1 small shallot, chopped finely
3 teaspoons olive oil
½ teaspoon caster sugar
2 sole fillets, each weighing
    about 150 g (5½ oz),
    rinsed and patted dry
1 tablespoon lemon juice
1 teaspoon chopped fresh
    parsley
15 g (½ oz) grated parmesan
    cheese
1 teaspoon chopped fresh
    oregano or marjoram
1 teaspoon chopped fresh basil
salt and freshly ground black
    pepper

1. Preheat the grill to medium. Arrange the tomatoes in the centre of the grill pan, cut-side up, and sprinkle each with some shallot, ¼ teaspoon of olive oil and a pinch of sugar. Season well with salt and pepper. Grill for 3 minutes.
2. Lay the sole fillets on either side of the tomatoes. Season with salt and pepper. In a basin, mix together the lemon juice, 1 teaspoon of olive oil and the parsley. Brush on the fillets.
3. Grill the sole and tomatoes for 5 minutes. Baste the fish with the remaining lemon mixture. Sprinkle over the grated parmesan cheese. Turn the grill up to high.
4. Top the tomatoes with the oregano or marjoram and basil.
5. Pop the grill pan back under the grill for 1–2 minutes, just to melt the parmesan and wilt the herbs. Serve at once.

Variation

Top each tomato with a teaspoon of pesto sauce, instead of the olive oil and onion mix. You will then only require 1 teaspoon of oil for the recipe. Deduct ½ Point per serving.

Brochettes of Monkfish wrapped in Parma Ham

Points per serving: 4
Total Points per recipe: 16

Serves: 4

Preparation and cooking time:
10 minutes + 1–2 hours marinating

Freezing: not recommended

Calories per serving: 185

Served on a fan of refreshing melon, these kebabs will make a memorable meal – and with little effort.

450 g (1 lb) monkfish
70 g packet of Parma ham
1 small honeydew melon,
    halved and de-seeded
For the marinade:
1 shallot, chopped finely
1 garlic clove, crushed
3 teaspoons olive oil
3 teaspoons chilli sauce or
    1 teaspoon prepared chilli
    paste
1 teaspoon whole-grain mustard
juice of 1/2 lemon
salt and freshly ground black
    pepper
fresh flat-leaf parsley sprigs,
    to garnish

1. Cut the monkfish into 2.5 cm (1-inch) chunks, allowing 4–5 chunks per person. Cut the Parma ham into strips and fold them around the fish. Arrange in a shallow dish.
2. Mix together all the ingredients for the marinade and pour over the fish. Cover and refrigerate for 1–2 hours, turning occasionally.
3. Thread the fish parcels on to 4 skewers. Cook under a hot grill for 8–10 minutes, basting with the marinade and turning occasionally, until the monkfish is cooked and the ham is crisp and brown.
4. Meanwhile, cut each melon half into 8–12 thin slices. Cut away the rind. Arrange the slices on the serving plates and lay a cooked kebab on top.
5. Serve immediately, garnished with parsley.

Cook's note

Monkfish has a supreme flavour, reminiscent of lobster, and a meaty texture. The tail end is filleted and widely available. The other end is very ugly!

Warm Minted Plaice with Asparagus and Potato Salad

Points per serving: 5 1/2
Total Points per recipe: 22

Serves: 4

Preparation and cooking time:
20 minutes

Calories per serving: 230

Freezing: not recommended

Mint is not often associated with fish, which is a shame as it works well – particularly in this warm summer salad. Serve as a light lunch, accompanied with baby carrots or a mixed salad.

8 medium-size plaice fillets,
    skinned
2 tablespoons chopped fresh mint
300 g (10 1/2 oz) new potatoes
300 ml (1/2 pint) dry white
    wine
125 g (4 1/2 oz) extra-fine
    asparagus tips
4 tablespoons low-fat plain
    Bio-yogurt
salt and freshly ground black
    pepper

1. Season the plaice fillets and sprinkle with half the chopped mint. Roll the fillets up and secure each with a cocktail stick.
2. Place the potatoes in one layer in a saucepan. Pour on the wine. Cover and bring to the boil. Simmer for 8 minutes, until almost tender.
3. Lay the fish rolls and asparagus on top of the potatoes, so they will steam whilst the potatoes finish cooking. Continue to simmer, covered, for 5 minutes, or until the potatoes and asparagus are tender and the fish is opaque and firm.
4. Carefully transfer the cooked fish, asparagus and potatoes to a serving plate, using a slotted spoon.
5. Quickly reduce the cooking juice over a high heat until there are about 2–3 tablespoons left. Remove from heat and stir in the yogurt and remaining mint. Season well with salt and pepper and drizzle over the fish and vegetables. Serve at once.

Variation

Replace the mint with chives and garnish with lemon or lime wedges.

Weight Watchers note

For a special occasion, replace the yogurt with half-fat cream. Add 1/2 Point per serving.

Rainbow Trout with Cucumber, on a Seabed of Noodles

Points per serving: 6½
Total Points per recipe: 13
Serves: 2
Preparation and cooking time: 8 minutes
Freezing: not recommended
Calories per serving: 500

Not quite a stir-fry, but definitely as easy! Serve these strips of trout (or you could use salmon) and cucumber on a bed of rice as an alternative to noodles.

2 teaspoons sunflower margarine
¼ cucumber, peeled, de-seeded and cut into matchsticks
250 g (9 oz) rainbow trout fillets, cut into thin strips
2 tablespoons dry white wine
3 tablespoons half-fat crème fraîche
½ teaspoon Dijon mustard
2 teaspoons chopped fresh chives
salt and freshly ground black pepper

125 g (4½ oz) fine egg-noodles, to serve

1. Start to prepare the noodles, according to the pack instructions.
2. Melt the margarine in a non-stick frying-pan and stir-fry the cucumber for 30 seconds. Add the trout and stir-fry for a further 1½–2 minutes.
3. Add the wine and cook rapidly, until it has nearly evaporated.
4. Remove the frying-pan from the heat. Mix the crème fraîche, mustard and chives together and add to the frying-pan. Place over a low heat and gently heat through. Season to taste.
5. Serve the fish and cucumber on a bed of hot noodles.

Variation

Use horseradish sauce instead of mustard. Use other firm fish, such as salmon or sole, instead of trout. Add 1½ Points per serving.

Seared Halibut with a Leek and Mustard Crust

Points per serving: 3
Total Points per recipe: 12
Serves: 4
Preparation and cooking time: 25 minutes
Freezing: not recommended
Calories per serving: 160

Serve these crumble-topped fish steaks with fresh vegetables or Roasted Tomato Salad with Red Onion and Spinach (see page 91).

3 teaspoons olive oil
4 × 115 g (4 oz) halibut steaks
juice of ½ lemon
1 leek, shredded finely
4 tablespoons fresh white breadcrumbs
2 teaspoons whole-grain mustard
1 teaspoon chopped fresh parsley
1 teaspoon chopped fresh tarragon or chives
salt and freshly ground black pepper
4 lemon wedges, to serve

1. Preheat the grill to a moderate heat. Heat a non-stick frying-pan and add 2 teaspoons of olive oil. Season the fish with a little lemon juice, salt and pepper. When the oil is smoking, 'sear' the fish steaks, pressing them down with a spatula. They will only need 30–40 seconds on each side, to seal and give a nice golden brown appearance. Transfer to the grill rack.
2. Reduce the heat and add the remaining teaspoon of olive oil and the leek to the frying-pan. Cook for 3–4 minutes, until softened and golden. Add the breadcrumbs and mustard and continue to cook, stirring frequently, until the mixture becomes quite dry.
3. Stir in the fresh herbs, and season well with salt and pepper.
4. Grill one side of the fish for 3–4 minutes. Turn it over carefully and spoon on the crumble mixture. Grill for 2–3 minutes, or until the crumble is golden.
5. Serve immediately, with lemon wedges.

Variation

Use any firm-fleshed fish steaks for this recipe. Salmon (add 1 Point per serving) and cod (save ½ Point per serving) are ideal.

Filo-Wrapped Salmon with Lemon and Dill Sauce

Points per serving: 8½
Total Points per recipe: 17

Serves: 2
Preparation and cooking time:
30 minutes
Freezing: not recommended
Calories per serving: 490

Wrapping the fish in a pastry parcel helps it to remain succulent. Enjoy the aroma as you cut into the parcel – and it tastes even better!

4 sheets of filo pastry, thawed
    if frozen
2 teaspoons sunflower oil
2 teaspoons chopped fresh
    parsley
1 teaspoon chopped fresh chives
2 × 150 g (5½ oz) salmon
    fillets, skinned
juice of 1 lemon
salt and freshly ground black
    pepper

For the sauce:
1 teaspoon finely grated
    lemon zest
4 tablespoons Greek-style
    natural yogurt
1 tablespoon chopped fresh dill
½ teaspoon caster sugar
1 teaspoon Dijon mustard

1. Preheat the oven to Gas Mark 6/200°C/400°F. Place two sheets of filo pastry side by side on a work surface and brush with some of the oil. Cover each sheet with a second sheet.
2. Sprinkle the chopped parsley and chives over the centre of the pastry. Lay the salmon on top. Drizzle on the lemon juice. Season with salt and pepper.
3. Bring up the pastry and fold over, to form a neat parcel. Place, seam-down, on a non-stick baking sheet. Brush with the remaining oil. Bake for 12–15 minutes, until golden.
4. Meanwhile, make the sauce. In a small basin, mix together all the ingredients. Place the basin in a saucepan of simmering water to warm through. Season with salt and pepper.
5. Serve the salmon parcels with the sauce.

Variation
Replace the Dijon mustard with tarragon mustard.

Indian Fish Patties with Cucumber and Tomato Relish

Points per serving: 1½
Total Points per recipe: 6

Serves: 4
Preparation and cooking time:
25 minutes
Freezing: not recommended
Calories per serving: 110

It's all too easy to be traditional when it comes to cooking fish – so try these spicy 'fishburgers'. Serve with plain, boiled rice and some green beans.

300 g (10½ oz) white fish
    fillets, skinned, e.g. cod
    or haddock
100 g (3½ oz) cooked, peeled
    prawns, thawed if frozen
2 garlic cloves, chopped
1 large fresh green chilli,
    de-seeded and chopped
1 teaspoon mild curry powder
½ teaspoon salt
1 teaspoon vegetable oil

For the relish:
½ cucumber, de-seeded and
    chopped finely
2 spring onions, trimmed and
    chopped finely
2 tomatoes, de-seeded and
    chopped finely
juice of ½ lemon
1 tablespoon chopped fresh
    coriander, parsley or mint
salt and freshly ground black
    pepper

1. Check the fish for any bones. Chop roughly and place in a food processor, with the prawns, garlic, chilli, curry powder and salt. Blend to a smooth paste.
2. Divide the mixture into eight and, wetting your hands (to prevent the mixture from sticking), form into patties.
3. Make the relish. Mix together all the ingredients and spoon into a small bowl for serving.
4. Heat a large, non-stick frying-pan and, when it is quite hot, add the vegetable oil.
5. Cook the patties for about 3–4 minutes on each side, until nicely browned and just firm. Serve with the relish.

Weight Watchers note
If you have some low-fat cooking spray, use it to coat the hot pan before cooking the patties.

Warm Lemon Couscous with Cod and Mushrooms

175 g (6 oz) couscous
finely grated zest and juice of
    1 lemon
1 small onion, chopped finely
250 g (9 oz) cod fillet
175 g (6 oz) button mushrooms,
    sliced
175 g (6 oz) fine green beans,
    cut into 2.5 cm (1-inch)
    lengths
4 teaspoons extra-virgin olive oil
2 tablespoons chopped fresh
    flat-leaf parsley
salt and freshly ground black
    pepper

1. Put the couscous in a colander or steamer. Pour some boiling water through the couscous, breaking up the lumpy grains with a fork. Drain. Stir in half the lemon zest.
2. Put the onion, cod fillet, mushrooms and green beans in a large saucepan. Add enough hot water just to cover the fish. Set the steamer or colander over the saucepan and slowly bring to the boil. Then reduce the heat and simmer for 5–6 minutes, or until the fish begins to flake.
3. Meanwhile, mix together the olive oil, remaining lemon zest and juice, half the parsley, salt and pepper.
4. Lift the steamer or colander off the saucepan. Carefully transfer the fish to a chopping board and skin and flake it gently.
5. Drain the vegetables and stir into the couscous, with half the dressing. Arrange the couscous on four plates, divide the fish evenly between the couscous and drizzle on the remaining dressing.
6. Garnish with parsley and serve.

Variation
Replace the green beans with frozen peas and sweetcorn. Add 1 Point per serving.

Cook's note
Couscous is a wheat-based semolina product, available from supermarkets. It only needs soaking for 30 minutes to swell the grains, although you can take a short cut and steam it for 8–10 minutes.

Hot and Sour Smoked Mackerel with Rice and Pineapple

Try this fresh new way of serving smoked mackerel – similar to a risotto, but with a touch of the Orient.

400 ml (14 fl oz) fish stock
100 g (3¹/₂ oz) basmati rice
1 lemon-grass stalk, halved
1 garlic clove, sliced
2.5 cm (1-inch) piece of fresh
    root ginger, peeled and
    chopped
¹/₂ large fresh red chilli, de-seeded
    and chopped finely
grated zest and juice of
    1 small lime
75 g (2³/₄ oz) dwarf green
    beans, halved
2 pineapple rings canned in
    natural juice, drained and
    cut into 8
2 × 150 g (5¹/₂ oz) peppered
    smoked mackerel fillets,
    skinned and cut into chunks
2 spring onions, chopped
2 teaspoons brown sugar
2 teaspoons fish sauce
    (optional, see Cook's note)
salt and freshly ground black
    pepper
1 tablespoon chopped fresh
    coriander, to garnish

1. Pour the stock into a large, non-stick frying-pan and bring to the boil. Stir in the rice, a little salt (not necessary if a stock cube is used), the lemon grass, garlic, ginger, chilli and lime zest. Bring back to a steady boil; then simmer for 5 minutes.
2. Stir in the green beans and simmer for a further 5 minutes or until nearly all the stock has been absorbed.
3. Fold in the pineapple, mackerel pieces and spring onions. Gently heat through for 2–3 minutes.
4. Finally, stir in the lime juice, brown sugar and fish sauce, to taste, if using. Add a little more salt, to taste, and some pepper. Serve at once, garnished with chopped coriander.

Variation
Replace the mackerel with firm, white fish fillets (such as halibut or cod), cubed and added at step 2. Cod will be 7¹/₂ Points per serving and halibut will be 8 Points per serving.

Cook's note
An indispensable ingredient in Thai cooking, fish sauce is prepared from fermented salted fish or shrimps. It gives a subtle savouriness in a similar way that soy sauce enhances Chinese cooking. The closest Western substitute is anchovy sauce.

Chilli Prawn Stir-Fry

Points per serving: 6
Total Points per recipe: 6

Serves: 1
Preparation and cooking time:
12 minutes
Freezing: not recommended
Calories per serving: 465

1 small carrot, cut into thin
    strips
1/4 red pepper, de-seeded and
    sliced
1 teaspoon sunflower oil
1 garlic clove, crushed
1 small fresh green chilli,
    de-seeded and sliced thinly
55 g (2 oz) egg-noodles
2 tablespoons light soy sauce
1 tablespoon dry sherry
1 teaspoon sesame oil
a pinch of sugar
115 g (4 oz) cooked, peeled
    prawns, thawed if frozen
salt and freshly ground black
    pepper

1. Heat a non-stick wok until hot, then stir in the carrot, pepper, sunflower oil, garlic and chilli. Cook briskly, stirring and tossing, for 2 minutes.
2. Meanwhile, soak the egg-noodles in boiling water, according to the pack instructions. Drain and pile on to a warm plate.
3. Mix the soy sauce, sherry, sesame oil and sugar into the vegetables. Cook for a minute; then add the prawns.
4. Stir-fry for 1–2 minutes, or until piping hot. Season to taste and serve with the noodles.

Cook's note

Remember to wash your hands thoroughly after handling fresh chillies.

Spicy Fish Creole with Coconut and Lime Rice

Points per serving: 6
Total Points per serving: 24

Serves: 4
Preparation time: 10 minutes
Cooking time: 25 minutes
Freezing: recommended
Calories per serving: 375

No need to use exotic tropical fish for this spicy dish. It's an ideal recipe for cod – or for a more special occasion, use a combination of prawns and monkfish.

2 teaspoons sunflower oil
1 onion, chopped
1 garlic clove, crushed
1 teaspoon grated fresh root
    ginger
2 teaspoons garam masala
1/2 teaspoon chilli powder
1/2 teaspoon ground allspice
400 g (14 oz) canned choppd
    tomatoes with chilli
2 tablespoons tomato purée
1 teaspoon treacle or molasses
    sugar
225 g (8 oz) canned pineapple
    chunks in natural juice
450 g (1 lb) thick cod fillets,
    skinned and cut into chunks
a pinch of cayenne pepper
For the rice:
175 g (6 oz) long-grain rice
grated zest and juice of 1 lime
4 teaspoons desiccated coconut
2 teaspoons finely chopped fresh
    parsley or coriander
salt and freshly ground black
    pepper

1. Heat the oil in a non-stick shallow saucepan. Add the onion, garlic and ginger and cook gently for 3–4 minutes until softened. Add the garam masala, chilli powder and allspice and cook for a further minute.
2. Add the tomatoes, tomato purée and treacle or sugar. Drain the juice from the pineapple into a measuring jug and top up to 150 ml (1/4 pint) with cold water. Add to the saucepan. Simmer, uncovered, for 10 minutes.
3. Stir in the pineapple and fish. Season with salt and cayenne and simmer, covered, for a further 8–10 minutes.
4. Meanwhile, cook the rice in salted, boiling water for 10 minutes. Stir in the lime zest and juice and coconut and continue cooking for 2 minutes, or until the rice is tender. Stir in the chopped parsley or coriander. Season well with salt and pepper.
5. Serve the rice on warmed plates, accompanied by the Creole fish.

Cook's note

Garnish with fresh lime slices and sprigs of coriander, if you like.

Weight Watchers note

In the absence of treacle, use sugar or honey. Remember that all sugars contain 1/2 Point per heaped teaspoon.

Quick Paella

Points per serving: 5½
Total Points per recipe: 22

Serves: 4
Preparation and cooking time:
30 minutes
Freezing: not recommended
Calories per serving: 400

Paella, to many of us, is reminiscent of holidays in Spain – where vast pans of this delicious rice dish are cooked over hot charcoals. Linger over this quick version – accompanied with a big salad and, maybe, a glass of red wine!

1 large onion, chopped
2 garlic cloves, crushed
1 small green or red pepper,
    de-seeded and sliced
1 tablespoon vegetable oil or
    olive oil
250 g (9 oz) arborio (risotto) rice
400 g (14 oz) canned chopped
    tomatoes with herbs
500 ml (18 fl oz) chicken stock
2 teaspoons paprika
75 g (2¾ oz) cooked, boneless,
    skinless chicken breast,
    chopped
200 g (7 oz) cooked, peeled
    prawns, thawed if frozen
115 (4 oz) frozen peas, thawed
salt and freshly ground black
    pepper

1. Heat a large, non-stick frying-pan and, when hot, stir in the onion, garlic, green or red pepper and oil. Cook for 5 minutes, stirring, until softened.
2. Add the rice, tomatoes, stock, paprika, chicken and seasoning. Bring to the boil; then cover and simmer for 15 minutes.
3. Uncover and stir in the prawns and peas. Check the seasoning and reheat until piping hot. Serve immediately.

Cook's note

If you do not have a lid for your frying-pan, use a large, heatproof chopping board to cover it.

Couscous with Spicy Prawns served with a Coriander Sauce

Points per serving: 8
Total Points per recipe: 16

Serves: 2 as a light lunch
Preparation and cooking time:
15 minutes
Freezing: not recommended
Calories per serving: 500

Tantalisingly full of flavours, this salad is best freshly prepared and accompanied with a pitta bread or crisp green or tomato salad.

For the couscous.
125 g (4½ oz) couscous
grated zest and juice of 1 lime
2 spring onions, chopped
½ teaspoon ground coriander

For the prawns:
175 g (6 oz) cooked, peeled king
    prawns, thawed if frozen
juice of 1 lime
2 teaspoons clear honey
1 teaspoon black peppercorns,
    crushed
1 small fresh red chilli, de-seeded
    and chopped finely
½ medium-size avocado, sliced
5 cm (2-inch) piece of
    cucumber, halved, de-seeded
    and sliced diagonally

For the yogurt sauce:
3 tablespoons Greek-style
    natural yogurt
2 tablespoons mango chutney
½ garlic clove
a small handful of fresh
    coriander leaves
salt and freshly ground black
    pepper

1. Place the couscous in a bowl and soak it in 300 ml (½ pint) of warm water, for 5 minutes. Stir in the lime zest and juice, spring onions and ground coriander. Season to taste and divide between two serving plates.
2. Place the prawns in a bowl, add the lime juice, honey, peppercorns and chilli. Season well and then fold the prawns through the ingredients, to coat and mix thoroughly.
3. Prepare the sauce: place all the ingredients in a liquidiser and blend until smooth. Season to taste.
4. Arrange the avocado and cucumber on the couscous and spoon over the prawns. Serve with a spoonful of the coriander sauce.

Cook's note

Serve the couscous at room temperature, not chilled.

Thai Mackerel

Ask your fishmonger to let you know when he next has fresh mackerel. Its flavour is wonderful freshly caught – the oily fish is succulent and perfect for grilling.

4 medium-size mackerel fillets
For the marinade:
125 ml (4 fl oz) rice wine or
    dry sherry
2 tablespoons dark soy sauce
2 tablespoons mango chutney
1 red chilli, de-seeded and
    sliced thinly
2 spring onions, chopped
grated zest and juice of 1 lime

1. Bring a pan of water to the boil. Set a steamer on or insert a colander in it. Lay the fillets in the steamer, cover and cook for 3 minutes. Transfer to a shallow dish to cool.
2. Place the rice wine or sherry, soy sauce and chutney in a small saucepan and gently heat, stirring, until melted and smooth. Remove from the heat, allow to cool, then stir in the chilli, spring onions and lime juice and zest.
3. Pour the marinade over the fish. Cover and chill for 2 hours – ideally overnight.
4. To cook the mackerel, transfer the fillets from the marinade and place, skin-side up, under a preheated grill. Cook for 5 minutes. Heat the remaining marinade in a small saucepan, bringing to the boil for 1 minute.
5. Spoon the hot marinade over the cooked fillets and serve.

Variation
Chill the cooked mackerel and serve cold with plain-cooked rice, stir-fried vegetables or Chinese Leaf Salad with an Oriental Dressing (see page 93).

Cook's note
Make this up as far as step 3 the night before you plan to cook the mackerel.

Arabian Baked Trout

A lifetime ally of dieters, trout is a very economical and nutritious fish, readily available and easy to prepare. But you can have too much of a good thing, so here is a real change for our loyal friend. Serve with a green salad or cucumber raita (see page 58) and a jacket potato.

2 trout fillets
1 teaspoon ground cumin
1 teaspoon ground coriander
a pinch of cayenne pepper
2 tablespoons chopped fresh
    parsley
2 tablespoons chopped fresh
    coriander
1 garlic clove, crushed
2 tablespoons low-fat plain yogurt
juice of 2 limes
2 teaspoons olive oil
salt

1. Place the trout in a shallow, ovenproof dish.
2. In a non-stick frying-pan, dry-fry the cumin, coriander and a pinch of cayenne over a low heat for 1 minute. Stir frequently. Allow to cool.
3. Mix the spices with the herbs, garlic, yogurt, lime juice and olive oil. Season with a little salt and then spread over the trout.
4. Cover and leave to marinate for 30 minutes. Preheat the oven to Gas Mark 4/180°C/350°F.
5. Brush the fish with marinade again; then cover with foil, transfer to the oven and bake for 25 minutes.
6. Serve the cooked fish with its cooking juices spooned over.

140

Hoisin Prawns with Cucumber and Onion Salad

Treat yourself to some ready-cooked tiger prawns from the fish counter. Succulent and so quick to re-heat – equally as fast to disappear! Serve with crusty fresh bread.

12 raw, shelled tiger prawns, rinsed and dried
1 tablespoon hoisin sauce
2 teaspoons sesame oil
1 teaspoon cumin seeds
assorted salad leaves, to serve

For the salsa:

1/4 cucumber, de-seeded and chopped finely
2 spring onions, chopped
2 tablespoons light soy sauce
2 tablespoons lemon juice
2 tablespoons chopped fresh coriander
2 teaspoons sugar
freshly ground black pepper

1. Marinate the prawns in the hoisin sauce, for 30 minutes.
2. Meanwhile, mix together the ingredients for the salsa and spoon into a small bowl for serving.
3. Heat a large, non-stick frying-pan. Add the sesame oil and cumin seeds and sauté for 20 seconds. Then add the tiger prawns and the marinade. Toss briskly, cooking for about 2–3 minutes.
4. Divide the prawns between the plates and garnish with assorted salad leaves.

Variation

Replace the tiger prawns with 250 g (9 oz) of monkfish tail, cut into chunks, or a thick fillet of salmon, cubed. Add 1 or 2 Points per serving, respectively.

Spaghetti with Seafood Sauce

Serve with spaghetti or tagliatelle – and wear a bib in anticipation of stubborn tomatoey stains!

2 teaspoons olive oil
1 small onion, chopped
1 garlic clove, crushed
1/2 teaspoon chilli powder
1/2 green pepper, de-seeded and chopped
200 g (7 oz) canned chopped tomatoes
2 tablespoons dry white wine
1/2 teaspoon dried oregano
115 g (4 oz) spaghetti
100 g (3 1/2 oz) cooked peeled prawns, thawed if frozen
100 g (3 1/2 oz) canned tuna in brine, drained
50 g (1 3/4 oz) frozen cooked mussels, thawed
salt and freshly ground black pepper
1 tablespoon chopped fresh parsley, to garnish

1. Heat the oil in a small saucepan. Add the onion and garlic and cook for 2 minutes. Stir in the chilli powder and green pepper and cook for a further minute.
2. Add the tomatoes, wine and oregano. Simmer, covered, for 10 minutes.
3. Meanwhile, cook the spaghetti in plenty of salted, boiling water for 8–10 minutes or until just *al dente*.
4. Season the tomato sauce with salt and pepper. Stir in the prawns, tuna and mussels and gently heat through, uncovered, for 6 minutes.
5. Drain the cooked spaghetti and divide between two bowls. Spoon on the sauce and top with chopped parsley. Serve at once.

Variation

Replace the tuna, mussels and prawns with 250 g (9 oz) of seafood cocktail, thawed if frozen. Check the packet for Points.

Seafood Lasagne

Look out for packs of assorted seafood in the chilled fish counter. Alternatively, make up your own favourite combination.

1 teaspoon vegetable oil
1 garlic clove, crushed
1 small onion, finely chopped
400 g (14 oz) canned chopped
    tomatoes
50 g (1¾ oz) button
    mushrooms, quartered
1 teaspoon tomato purée
1 teaspoon dried basil or
    1 tablespoon chopped
    fresh basil
400 g (14 oz) mixed, cooked
    seafood, e.g. mussels, prawns,
    squid rings, thawed if frozen
6 sheets of ready-to-cook lasagne

For the topping:
250 g (9 oz) low-fat plain
    fromage frais
1 egg, beaten
15 g (½ oz) grated parmesan
    cheese
a pinch of grated nutmeg
salt and freshly ground black
    pepper

1. Preheat the oven to Gas Mark 5/190°C/375°F. Heat the oil in a non-stick saucepan and then cook the garlic and onion, until softened but not coloured.
2. Add the chopped tomatoes, mushrooms, tomato purée and basil. Season, to taste, and then simmer, covered, for 10 minutes. Stir in the seafood.
3. Spoon half the seafood sauce into the base of a shallow, rectangular ovenproof dish. Cover with three sheets of lasagne. Spoon over the remaining sauce and cover with the rest of the lasagne.
4. Make the topping. Mix together the fromage frais and egg. Season with a little salt, pepper and grated nutmeg. Pour over the lasagne. Sprinkle on the parmesan. Cook for 35–40 minutes, until the topping is golden brown.

Variation:
Replace the mixed seafood with a combination of 350 g (12 oz) of smoked haddock and cooked broccoli. Deduct a ½ Point per serving.

Italian Seafood Pasta

Use all prawns, or cubes of smoked fish (haddock or cod) if you prefer. This speedy supper is delicious served with green beans or courgettes.

125 g (4½ oz) pasta shells
2 teaspoons olive oil
1 onion, chopped
1 garlic clove, crushed
1 red pepper, de-seeded and
    sliced
75 g (2¾ oz) button mushrooms,
    sliced
125 g (4½ oz) low-fat soft cheese
    with garlic and herbs
100 ml (3½ fl oz) skimmed
    milk
350 g (12 oz) mixed cooked
    seafood, e.g. mussels, prawns,
    squid rings, thawed if frozen
8 fresh basil leaves, torn
salt and freshly ground black
    pepper

1. Cook the pasta in lightly salted, boiling water for 8–10 minutes, or until *al dente*. Drain.
2. Meanwhile, heat the oil in a shallow, non-stick saucepan and cook the onion, garlic, pepper and mushrooms for 3–4 minutes.
3. Reduce the heat and add the cheese and milk to the softened vegetables. Blend to a smooth consistency. Stir in the fish. Season with salt and pepper. Cover and gently heat through for 7–8 minutes.
4. Stir in the pasta and basil. Season with plenty of pepper and serve on warm plates.

Cook's note

This seafood pasta can be served cold, too. Make up the creamy cheese sauce to step 3 – but do not add the seafood. This and the pasta should both be added cold. (Don't forget, the seafood is already cooked!)

Rice, Beans, Grains and Pasta

Although they are naturally low in fat, rice, beans and pasta are often served with sauces which are high in fat. But here you'll find delicious, healthy sauces to help keep the Points low and satisfaction high! Tagliatelle in Peanut Butter Sauce (see page 163) is just one tasty example.

Once you have made up one or two sauces, you will soon be adapting and matching them to other ideas. The combinations become endless. Moreover, with half-fat cheeses and other low-calorie dairy foods, you can still make classic sauces – all you lose is unwanted fat and not the taste! Try Courgette and Lentil Moussaka (see page 151) or Couscous and Ratatouille Gratin (see page 157).

Many of the recipes in this chapter are high in fibre. You can increase the fibre even further by replacing white rice or egg pasta with brown rice or wholewheat pasta. This will make your dish much more filling – it will take longer to eat and, hence, give greater satisfaction.

One or two of the recipes in this chapter include meat, but in smaller quantities, to show how both meat and its vegetarian equivalent can be combined to offer really exciting meals – Minced Beef, Lentil and Pea Kheema (see page 154), or a Spicy Sausage and Bean Cassoulet (see page 150), for example, will perhaps overtake the familiar chilli con carne as a healthy compromise between meat and pulses or beans.

Whether it is just a light meal such as Felafels with Pitta and Raita (see page 156), or hearty Cabbage Parcels with a Spicy Rice and Mushroom Filling (see page 144), the whole family can enjoy satisfying, easy-to-cook meals – and discover wonderful new flavours and spicy aromas hidden in many of these super recipes.

chapter 7

And for times when you want more traditional food, there's comforting Ham and Vegetable Pasta Gratin or a Bean and Vegetable Charlotte with a Cheesy Herb Crust (see pages 160 and 150). Delicious, tailor-made recipes to tempt you and make following *1,2,3 Success Plus* an enjoyable new experience!

Cabbage Parcels with a Spicy Rice and Mushroom Filling

For the parcels:

8 large cabbage leaves
1 teaspoon sunflower oil
1 small onion, chopped finely
75 g (2³/₄ oz) mushrooms,
    chopped finely
¹/₂ teaspoon ground allspice
125 g (4¹/₂ oz) cooked rice
300 ml (¹/₂ pint) vegetable stock
salt and freshly ground black
    pepper

For the tomato sauce:

1 small onion, grated
1 garlic clove, crushed
400 g (14 oz) canned chopped
    tomatoes
1 teaspoon dried oregano
a pinch of sugar

1. Blanch the cabbage leaves in salted, boiling water for 1 minute, then drain and refresh under cold running water. Set aside on kitchen paper whilst you prepare the filling.
2. Heat the oil in a saucepan and gently cook the onion, until soft. Add the mushrooms and cook for 3–4 minutes. Stir in the allspice and rice. Season, to taste. Spoon equal amounts of the filling on to each leaf and roll them up, tucking in the ends to form neat parcels.
3. Place the parcels in the base of a large saucepan and pour over the stock. Cover and simmer gently for 20 minutes.
4. Meanwhile, prepare the quick tomato sauce. Put all the ingredients in a small pan and simmer, for 15 minutes. Season, to taste.
5. To serve, remove the hot parcels with a slotted spoon and arrange two on each plate, with a little tomato sauce spooned alongside.

ⓥ

Tuna, Leek and Rice Gratin

Here is a recipe that is quickly put together. Serve with fresh vegetables.

1 teaspoon sunflower oil
1 large leek, sliced finely
400 g (14 oz) canned tuna in
    brine, drained and flaked
175 g (6 oz) cooked long-grain
    rice
295 g (10¹/₂ oz) canned half-fat
    condensed mushroom soup
4 tablespoons skimmed milk
25 g (1 oz) fresh breadcrumbs
25 g (1 oz) half-fat Cheddar
    cheese, grated finely
salt and freshly ground black
    pepper

1. Preheat the oven to Gas Mark 4/180°C/350°F.
2. Heat the oil in a frying-pan and sauté the leek for 2–3 minutes. Stir in the tuna and rice. Mix together the soup and milk and fold into the tuna mixture. Season, to taste.
3. Spoon the tuna mixture into a gratin dish. Mix together the breadcrumbs and cheese and sprinkle over the tuna.
4. Bake for 25 minutes.

Courgette and Rice Tian

A Mediterranean 'bake' with an unusual, but tasty, combination of low-calorie ingredients. Serve with a crisp green salad.

2 medium-size slices of white
    bread, crusts removed
300 ml (½ pint) skimmed milk
125 g (4½ oz) long-grain rice
2 eggs, beaten
4 teaspoons olive oil
1 garlic clove, chopped
25 g (1 oz) half-fat Cheddar
    cheese, grated finely
450 g (1 lb) small courgettes,
    thinly sliced
225 g (8 oz) tomatoes, peeled,
    de-seeded and sliced
1 tablespoon chopped fresh
    parsley or thyme
2 teaspoons grated parmesan
    cheese
salt and freshly ground black
    pepper

1. Tear the bread into small pieces and place in a bowl, with the milk. Leave to soak. Preheat the oven to Gas Mark 6/200°C/400°F.
2. Cook the rice in salted, boiling water for 10–12 minutes, until tender. Drain well.
3. Beat together the eggs and oil and add to the bread and milk, with the garlic and half the cheese. Season well with salt and pepper.
4. Carefully fold the cooked rice, courgettes, tomatoes and herbs into the bread mixture. Pour into a shallow gratin dish. Sprinkle with the remaining Cheddar and the parmesan cheese.
5. Bake for 35–40 minutes, until golden brown and firm to the touch. Serve warm or cold.

Ⓥ if using free-range eggs and vegetarian cheeses

Nutty Mushroom Pilaff

Buy quick-cook brown rice, to speed up cooking this nutty, nutritious supper. Serve with a green salad.

2 teaspoons olive oil
150 g (5½ oz) quick-cook,
    long-grain brown rice
a pinch of ground turmeric
1 onion, sliced
350 ml (12 fl oz) hot vegetable
    stock
225 g (8 oz) open cup
    mushrooms, sliced
25 g (1 oz) pine kernels
2 tablespoons mixed chopped
    fresh herbs, e.g. chives,
    parsley and thyme
salt and freshly ground black
    pepper

1. Heat 1 teaspoon of olive oil in a non-stick saucepan, stir in the rice, a good pinch of turmeric and the onion and cook gently for 3 minutes, stirring constantly.
2. Add the hot stock, bring to the boil, cover and simmer over a gentle heat for 25 minutes.
3. Meanwhile, heat a non-stick frying-pan and, when hot, add the remaining teaspoon of oil and the mushrooms. Stir-fry for 3–4 minutes, then add the pine kernels and continue to stir-fry, until the mushrooms have softened and the nuts turn golden. Season, to taste. Stir in the herbs.
4. When the rice is tender and has absorbed all the stock, season to taste, and fork in the hot mushrooms and nuts. Serve immediately.

Cook's note
Fresh herbs are an excellent source of vitamins and minerals and freeze well. When using them instead of dried herbs, remember to double the amount.

Ⓥ

Chilli Bean Risotto *(opposite)*
Stuffed Peppers with Mushrooms and
Yellow Rice *(opposite)*

Stuffed Peppers with Mushrooms and Yellow Rice

Points per serving: 2½
Total Points per recipe: 10
Serves: 4
Preparation time: 25 minutes
Cooking time: 20 minutes
Freezing: not recommended
Calories per serving: 185

4 medium-size peppers, green,
red, yellow or a mixture
100 g (3½ oz) Thai-style or
basmati rice
1 medium-size leek, sliced
1 carrot, grated coarsely
115 g (4 oz) button mushrooms,
sliced
300 ml (½ pint) vegetable or
chicken stock
1 teaspoon ground turmeric
55 g (2 oz) half-fat Cheddar
cheese, grated
salt and freshly ground black
pepper

To serve:
4 tablespoons low-fat plain
yogurt
2 tablespoons chopped fresh
parsley

1. Preheat the oven to Gas Mark 5/190°C/375°F. Halve the peppers lengthways. Retain the stalks but remove the core and seeds. Blanch the shells in boiling water for 3 minutes; then drain, upside down.
2. Meanwhile, put the rice, leek, carrot, mushrooms, stock, turmeric and seasoning into a pan. Bring to the boil, cover and simmer gently for 10 minutes, without lifting the lid.
3. Remove from the heat and allow to stand for 5 minutes; then stir in the cheese. Check the seasoning.
4. Spoon the filling into the pepper shells and place in an ovenproof dish.
5. Cover with foil and bake for about 20 minutes, or until the peppers are tender.
6. Serve hot, topped with the plain yogurt and sprinkled with the parsley.

Cook's notes

These peppers are delicious eaten cold, too. Replace the plain yogurt with 4 tablespoons of low-calorie vinaigrette dressing or mayonnaise.

Ⓥ if using vegetable stock and vegetarian cheese

Chilli Bean Risotto

Points per serving: 5½
Total Points per recipe: 11
Serves: 2
Preparation and cooking time:
30 minutes
Freezing: recommended
Calories per serving: 355

1 onion, chopped
2 garlic cloves, crushed
2 teaspoons olive oil
115 g (4 oz) arborio (risotto)
rice
600 ml (1 pint) hot vegetable
stock
2 tomatoes, skinned and
chopped
200 g (7 oz) canned red kidney
beans in chilli sauce
a good pinch of dried oregano
salt and freshly ground black
pepper

To serve:
15 g (½ oz) parmesan cheese,
freshly grated
1 tablespoon chopped fresh
parsley

1. Heat a large, non-stick frying-pan until hot and then toss in the onion, garlic and oil. Sauté for 5 minutes, until softened.
2. Add the rice and cook, stirring, for 1 minute, until opaque.
3. Stir in a quarter of the stock and cook gently until it has all been absorbed. Stir occasionally.
4. Add the remaining stock in three or four steps, stirring frequently and ensuring all the stock has been absorbed each time before you add any more. This will take about 15 minutes.
5. When the rice is softening and nearly all the stock has been absorbed, stir in the tomatoes, kidney beans in chilli sauce, oregano and seasoning.
6. Serve at once, sprinkled with parmesan cheese and parsley.

Variation

If you do not have kidney beans in chilli sauce, use plain canned red kidney beans and add 1 teaspoon of mild chilli powder at step 2.

Cook's note

A true risotto uses arborio rice, which gives a creamy texture and unique flavour. It is readily available in most supermarkets.

Ⓥ if using vegetarian cheese

Chinese-Style Rice with Baby Sweetcorn Cobs

Points per serving: 8
Total Points per recipe: 16

Serves: 2
Preparation time: 10 minutes
Cooking time: 10 minutes
Freezing: not recommended
Calories per serving: 265

A versatile rice dish – enjoy it on its own, or with some cooked prawns or as a side dish with grilled duck.

2 teaspoons sunflower oil
1 cm ($\frac{1}{2}$ inch) piece of fresh root ginger, peeled and chopped
1 garlic clove, crushed
1 carrot, chopped
50 g ($1\frac{3}{4}$ oz) button mushrooms, sliced
100 g ($3\frac{1}{2}$ oz) baby sweetcorn cobs, sliced lengthways
2 tablespoons frozen peas
227 g canned water chestnuts, drained and sliced
225 g (8 oz) canned cooked Thai-style or long-grain white rice
2 teaspoons soy sauce
salt and freshly ground black pepper

1. Heat the oil in a large frying-pan or wok, and gently fry the ginger and garlic for a minute. Add the carrot, mushrooms, sweetcorn, peas and water chestnuts and stir-fry for a further 2–3 minutes.
2. Stir in the rice and then the soy sauce, reduce the heat and continue to cook until the rice is thoroughly heated through.
3. Season, to taste, with salt and pepper. Serve.

Variations

This serves 4 as an accompaniment. Points per serving will be 4. Calories per serving will be 130. A teaspoon of sesame oil added at step 2 adds a superb flavour. Don't forget to add 1 Point to the total Points per recipe!

Serve this as a complete meal for two, topped with strips of omelette. Beat 2 eggs with a finely chopped spring onion and a drop of water. Season. Pour into a 20 cm (8-inch) non-stick frying-pan and cook until set. Turn out on to a board and cut into 2.5 cm (1-inch) strips. Arrange on the hot rice and serve. Add 1½ Points per serving.

Weight Watchers note

Use canned spray cooking oil when stir-frying vegetables in a non-stick pan. You will be amazed at how many Points you will save.

Rice 'n' Beans

Points per serving: 3
Total Points per recipe: 12

Serves: 4 as an accompaniment
Preparation and cooking time:
25 minutes
Freezing: recommended
Calories per serving: 170

Based on a Jamaican favourite, this tasty rice dish is delicious on its own with a tomato sauce, or with Jerk Chicken with a Pineapple Salsa or Devilled Turkey Escalopes (see pages 109 and 120).

2 teaspoons low-fat spread
1 small onion, finely chopped
1 garlic clove, crushed
125 g ($4\frac{1}{4}$ oz) long-grain rice
$\frac{1}{2}$ teaspoon dried thyme
1 bay leaf
1 cinnamon stick
1 tablespoon desiccated coconut
300 ml ($\frac{1}{2}$ pint) vegetable or chicken stock
210 g ($7\frac{1}{2}$ oz) canned red kidney beans, drained and rinsed
salt and freshly ground black pepper

1. Melt the spread in a saucepan and cook the onion over a gentle heat for 5 minutes. Stir in the garlic and rice and cook for a further 2 minutes.
2. Add the thyme, bay leaf, cinnamon and coconut. Stir in the stock, bring to the boil, reduce the heat, cover and simmer for 8–10 minutes.
3. Stir in the kidney beans and cook for a further 5 minutes, until the rice has absorbed the stock and is tender. Season, to taste. Serve.

Variation

Add 1 small chopped fresh green chilli at step 2.

Ⓥ if using vegetable stock

Mushroom Rice with Parmesan and Basil

Points per serving: 6
Total Points per recipe: 12

Serves: 2
Preparation and cooking time: 35 minutes
Freezing: recommended
Calories per serving: 420

Serve this rice dish on its own, with parmesan cheese, or as an accompaniment to lamb chops or Pork and Leek Roulades with a Mushroom Sauce (see page 103).

2 teaspoons olive oil
1 onion, chopped
1 garlic clove, crushed
175 g (6 oz) fresh dark-gilled
    mushrooms, chopped into
    1 cm (1/2-inch) chunks
175 g (6 oz) long-grain rice
425 ml (3/4 pint) vegetable stock
1 tablespoon sherry or Madeira
    wine
1 sprig of fresh thyme
salt and freshly ground black
    pepper

To serve:
8 fresh basil leaves, torn
25 g (1 oz) fresh parmesan
    cheese, grated or shaved

1. Mix together the oil, onion and garlic. Heat a non-stick pan and cook the onion and garlic until softened but not coloured. Add the mushrooms, cover and continue to cook over a low heat for 10 minutes, to let the mushrooms 'sweat' gently and release their juices.
2. Stir in the rice, 300 ml (1/2 pint) of vegetable stock, sherry, thyme and salt and pepper, to taste.
3. Bring to the boil, cover and then simmer for 15 minutes, adding a little more stock, if necessary. (This depends on how much moisture the mushrooms have released.)
4. Fork the cooked rice through, discarding the thyme. Adjust the seasoning to taste.
5. Sprinkle on the basil and parmesan cheese. Serve.

Variation
This serves 4 as an accompaniment. Points per serving will be 3. Calories per serving will be 210.

Cook's note
If you are going to serve this rice cold, leave to cool, then cover and chill until required. Sprinkle with the basil and parmesan just before serving, with 2 tablespoons low-fat vinaigrette dressing.

Weight Watchers note
Omit the parmesan cheese and save 2 1/2 Points in total.

Ⓥ if using vegetarian cheese

Mixed Bean Casserole in a Mustard and Lemon Sauce

Points per serving: 7
Total Points per recipe: 14

Serves: 2
Preparation and cooking time: 15 minutes
Freezing: not recommended
Calories per serving: 335

Substantial as a meal on its own, with pitta bread or a jacket potato and salad; or serve it as an accompaniment for plain-grilled fish or chicken.

2 teaspoons sunflower oil
1 onion, thinly sliced
125 g (4 1/2 oz) button
    mushrooms, sliced
grated zest of 1 small lemon
1 teaspoon light muscovado
    sugar
2 teaspoons whole-grain mustard
2 teaspoons chopped fresh
    tarragon or 1/2 teaspoon
    dried tarragon
1 teaspoon snipped fresh chives
150 ml (1/4 pint) tub Greek-
    style natural yogurt
400 g (14 oz) canned red
    kidney beans, rinsed and
    drained
225 g (8 oz) canned flageolet
    beans, rinsed and drained
salt and freshly ground black
    pepper

1. Heat the oil in a non-stick saucepan, add the onion and cook for 5 minutes, until softened but not coloured. Add the mushrooms and continue to cook for 3 minutes.
2. Stir in the lemon zest, sugar, mustard, tarragon, chives and yogurt. Heat through; do not allow the sauce to boil. Season to taste.
3. Add the beans. Cover and heat through gently for 2–3 minutes. Serve hot.

Variation
This serves 4 as an accompaniment. Points per serving will be 3 1/2 and Calories per serving will be 165.

Ⓥ

Bean and Vegetable Charlotte with a Cheesy Herb Crust

Points per serving: 5
Total Points per recipe: 20

Serves: 4
Preparation time: 10 minutes
Cooking time: 45 minutes
+ 5 minutes grilling
Freezing: recommended at end of step 2
Calories per serving: 305

Crispy bread slices top this hearty vegetable and bean feast. Serve with extra Worcestershire sauce and fresh green beans or broccoli.

1 tablespoon vegetable oil
450 g (1 lb) assorted vegetables, e.g. carrots, leeks, courgette, mushrooms, fennel, cut in bite-size pieces
400 g (14 oz) canned mixed beans, drained and rinsed
400 g (14 oz) canned chopped tomatoes with herbs or garlic
1 teaspoon Worcestershire sauce
4 tablespoons red or white wine
2 fresh thyme sprigs
salt and freshly ground black pepper

For the topping:
3 medium-size slices of white bread, crusts removed
3 teaspoons whole-grain mustard
1 tablespoon mixed chopped fresh herbs, e.g. parsley, chives and rosemary
50 g (1³/4 oz) mature Cheddar cheese, grated finely

1. Preheat the oven to Gas Mark 4/180°C/350°F. Heat the oil in a saucepan and sweat the vegetables for 10 minutes or until slightly softened.
2. Add the beans, tomatoes, Worcestershire sauce, wine and thyme. Season well with salt and pepper. Transfer to an ovenproof, lidded casserole dish. Cover tightly and cook for 45 minutes, until the vegetables are tender.
3. Preheat the grill. Lightly toast the bread slices. Spread with the mustard and then cut each slice into quarters. Sprinkle on the mixed herbs and cheese.
4. Remove the casserole from the oven. Arrange the bread squares, in an overlapping fashion, on top of the vegetables. Place the dish under a hot grill for 4–5 minutes, until the cheese is golden brown and bubbling.

Cook's note
Replace the mustard with a scraping of garlic purée.

Spicy Sausage and Bean Cassoulet

Points per serving: 6¹/2
Total Points per recipe: 13

Serves: 2
Preparation and cooking time: 30 minutes
Freezing: recommended at step 4
Calories per serving: 435

A little spicy pepperoni or garlic sausage goes a long way in this tasty cassoulet. Serve with a green salad.

1 teaspoon cooking oil
1 small onion, sliced
¹/2 red or green pepper, de-seeded and sliced
1 garlic clove, crushed
125 g (4¹/2 oz) garlic or pepperoni sausage sliced
200 g (7 oz) canned chopped tomatoes with chilli
2 teaspoons tomato purée
6 tablespoons cider
¹/2 teaspoon dried rosemary
¹/2 teaspoon dried thyme
3 juniper berries, crushed (optional)
300 g (10¹/2 oz) canned haricot or cannellini beans, rinsed and drained
salt and freshly ground black pepper
2 teaspoons chopped fresh parsley, to garnish
25 g (1 oz) 'hot' tortilla chips, coarsely crushed, to serve

1. Heat the oil in a non-stick frying-pan, add the onion and cook until softened. Add the pepper, garlic and sausage and cook for a further 3–4 minutes.
2. Add the tomatoes, tomato purée, cider, rosemary, thyme and juniper berries. Season with salt and pepper. Cover, bring to the boil; then simmer for 10 minutes.
3. Stir in the beans and simmer, uncovered, for a further 10 minutes. Adjust the seasoning, to taste.
4. Divide the cassoulet between warmed bowls. Garnish with chopped parsley and top with crushed tortilla chips. Serve immediately.

Variation
Add 225 g (8 oz) of lean cubed pork, instead of the spicy sausage. Simmer for 40 minutes at step 2. The Points remain the same.

Cook's note
Add ¹/2 teaspoon of hot chilli powder at step 1, if you like it extra-hot!

150

Ⓥ if using vegetarian cheese

Spicy Stuffed Aubergines

These stuffed aubergines make a nutritious lunch or evening meal. Serve with a mixed, green-leaf salad.

1 aubergine, halved lengthways
2 teaspoons olive oil
1 shallot, chopped
1 garlic clove, chopped
¹/₂ teaspoon ground cumin
¹/₂ teaspoon ground coriander
¹/₂ teaspoon chilli powder
2 tablespoons red lentils
¹/₂ red pepper, de-seeded and
   chopped
200 g (7 oz) canned chopped
   tomatoes with herbs
1 tablespoon tomato purée
1 tablespoon mixed chopped
   fresh herbs, e.g. oregano,
   chives and parsley
2 teaspoons grated parmesan
   cheese
2 tablespoons fresh brown
   breadcrumbs
salt and freshly ground black
   pepper

1. Scoop out the flesh from the aubergine and chop the flesh finely. Set aside. Blanch the aubergine shells in a saucepan of boiling water for 1–2 minutes. Drain thoroughly and place in a shallow ovenproof dish.
2. Heat the oil in a saucepan. Add the shallot and garlic and cook for 5 minutes. Add the cumin, coriander and chilli and cook for a further minute.
3. Add the aubergine flesh, lentils and red pepper and cook for a further 3–4 minutes. Stir in the chopped tomatoes, tomato purée and herbs. Season with salt and pepper. Cover and simmer for 5–8 minutes, until the lentils have swollen.
4. Preheat the oven to Gas Mark 4/180°C/350°F. Pile the tomato and aubergine mixture into the shells. Mix the cheese and breadcrumbs together and sprinkle over each stuffed aubergine.
5. Bake for 25–30 minutes or until the aubergines are tender. Serve at once.

Variation

Replace the aubergine with 2 courgettes, halved lengthways.

Ⓥ if using vegetarian cheese

Courgette and Lentil Moussaka

Lentils have recently become very fashionable, despite their presence for hundreds of years! They are particularly popular in Middle-Eastern and Indian cookery, but try them in this version of moussaka. Serve with fresh vegetables or a mixed salad.

1 onion, chopped
2 garlic cloves, crushed
2 teaspoons vegetable or olive oil
75 g (2³/₄ oz) red lentils
2 courgettes, chopped
600 ml (1 pint) vegetable stock
2 tablespoons light soy sauce
¹/₄ teaspoon dried thyme
2 medium-size potatoes, peeled
   and sliced thinly
450 ml (16 fl oz) skimmed milk
2 tablespoons plain flour
1 tablespoon low-fat spread
a pinch of grated nutmeg
2 tablespoons dried natural-
   colour breadcrumbs
salt and freshly ground black
   pepper

1. Heat a non-stick saucepan until hot; then stir in the onion, garlic and oil. Cook for about 5 minutes or until softened.
2. Mix in the lentils, courgettes, stock, soy sauce, thyme and salt and pepper, to taste. Bring to the boil, then cover and simmer for 15 minutes, until the lentils have thickened.
3. Preheat the oven to Gas Mark 5/190°C/375°F. Pour the lentil mixture into a shallow casserole dish and arrange the potatoes on top, overlapping.
4. Place the milk, flour, low-fat spread, nutmeg and seasoning in a small saucepan. Slowly bring to the boil, stirring with a whisk, until the sauce thickens and is smooth.
5. Pour the sauce evenly over the potatoes, sprinkle over the breadcrumbs and bake for 30 minutes or until the potatoes have softened and the surface is golden brown. Allow to stand for 10 minutes before serving.

Weight Watchers note

Lentils are a rich source of protein and are one of the few pulses that do not need soaking before cooking. 1 heaped tablespoon of cooked lentils (about 35 g) = ¹/₂ Point.

Ⓥ if using vegetarian low-fat spread

Spiced Chick-Peas with Courgettes

A very quick dish to prepare. Serve it with plain, boiled rice or a jacket potato, and a tablespoon of low-fat plain yogurt.

2 teaspoons sunflower oil
1 large onion, sliced
1 garlic clove, crushed
1 teaspoon ground cumin
1 teaspoon hot curry paste
6 small courgettes, sliced
juice of 1 lemon
400 g (14 oz) canned chick-
*   peas, rinsed and drained*
2 tablespoons sultanas
salt and freshly ground black
*   pepper*

1. Heat a non-stick frying-pan, add the oil, onion and garlic and sauté for 3–4 minutes, until just beginning to soften.
2. Add the cumin and curry paste and cook for 1 minute. Toss in the courgettes, coating them thoroughly with the spices. Cover and cook for 5 minutes.
3. Add the lemon juice, chick-peas and sultanas and simmer, covered, for a further 5 minutes. Season well with salt and pepper. Serve hot.

Variation

Stir in 210 g (7 oz) canned chopped tomatoes at step 2, or serve with Coriander Sauce (see page 156).

Cook's note

Try out various blends of curry paste for a different taste – and heat!

Minced Beef, Lentil and Pea Kheema

A 'kheema' is an Indian dish that uses minced beef or lamb. It tends to be fragrant rather than hot – thanks to the Persian influences. Excuse all the ingredients – they are worth measuring out! Serve with freshly cooked spinach or green beans and boiled rice.

2 teaspoons sunflower oil
1 teaspoon cumin seeds
1 large onion, chopped
1 cm (¹/₂-inch) piece of fresh
*   root ginger, grated*
2 garlic cloves, crushed
2 teaspoons ground coriander
1 teaspoon ground cinnamon
1 teaspoon ground mixed spice
¹/₂ teaspoon ground turmeric
¹/₂ teaspoon grated nutmeg
¹/₂ teaspoon chilli powder
300 g (10¹/₂ oz) extra-lean
*   minced beef*
400 g (14 oz) canned chopped
*   tomatoes*
2 tablespoons red lentils
2 tablespoons frozen peas
2 tablespoons low-fat plain
*   yogurt*
2 tablespoons chopped fresh
*   coriander*
salt and freshly ground black
*   pepper*

1. Heat the oil in a saucepan, add the cumin seeds and fry until they pop. Add the onion, ginger and garlic and cook for 7–8 minutes, or until golden brown.
2. Add the coriander, cinnamon, mixed spice, turmeric, nutmeg and chilli powder. Stir-fry over a low heat for 2 minutes.
3. Add the minced beef and continue stir-frying until the meat has browned and is crumbly.
4. Add the chopped tomatoes, lentils and 150 ml (¹/₄ pint) of water. Cover and simmer for 15 minutes.
5. Add the peas and simmer for 5 minutes. Stir in the yogurt and fresh coriander. Heat gently – do not boil! Season, to taste, with salt and pepper.

Variations

Replace the lentils with 400 g (14 oz) canned chick-peas, rinsed and drained and added at step 5. Omit the water. Add 1 Point per serving. If you use minced lamb, add 2 Points per serving.

ⓥ

Spaghetti with a Red Lentil Sauce

Points per serving: 4¹/₂
Total Points per recipe: 9

Serves: 2
Preparation and cooking time:
30 minutes
Freezing: recommended for sauce only
Calories per serving: 385

Spaghetti derives its name from the Italian word 'spago', meaning 'string'. You can use tagliatelle or pasta spirals instead.

2 teaspoons olive oil
1 leek, sliced
1 garlic clove, crushed
1 carrot, grated
¹/₂ teaspoon ground allspice
¹/₂ teaspoon ground cumin
2 tablespoons red lentils
*200 g (7 oz) canned chopped
    tomatoes*
1 tablespoon red wine
300 ml (¹/₂ pint) vegetable stock
*1 teaspoon chopped fresh
    marjoram or ¹/₂ teaspoon
    dried majoram*
*1 teaspoon snipped fresh chives
    or ¹/₂ teaspoon dried chives*
125 g (4¹/₂ oz) spaghetti
*salt and freshly ground black
    pepper*
*1 tablespoon chopped fresh
    parsley, to garnish*

1. Heat the oil in a saucepan, add the leek and garlic and cook for 5 minutes, until softened. Stir in the carrot, allspice and cumin and cook for a further minute.
2. Add the lentils, tomatoes, wine and stock. Bring to the boil; then simmer for 10 minutes. Add the marjoram and chives. Season to taste with salt and pepper. Simmer for a further 5 minutes.
3. Meanwhile, cook the pasta according to the pack instructions. Drain thoroughly.
4. To serve, divide the spaghetti between two bowls, spoon on the hot sauce and garnish with chopped parsley. Serve at once.

Variation

Add 1 tablespoon of sultanas at step 2. Add ¹/₂ Point per serving.

Weight Watchers note

Red lentils need no soaking, so they are quick to prepare. They add instant bulk and texture to sauces and are bursting with protein. A good alternative to meat.

Potato, Spinach and Chick-Pea Curry

Points per serving: 4¹/₂
Total Points per recipe: 18

Serves: 4
Preparation time: 10 minutes
Cooking time: 30 minutes
Freezing: recommended
Calories per serving: 250

A complete vegetable dish, nutritious enough eaten on its own with a little mango chutney or as a spicy accompaniment to grilled fish or poultry.

2 teaspoons sunflower oil
1 large onion, sliced
2 garlic cloves, crushed
1 teaspoon cumin seeds
1 large carrot, chopped
*400 g (14 oz) potatoes, cut into
    2.5 cm (1-inch) chunks*
3 tablespoons mild curry paste
*400 g (14 oz) canned chick-
    peas, drained and rinsed*
*200 g (7 oz) canned chopped
    tomatoes*
300 ml (¹/₂ pint) vegetable stock
*225 g (8 oz) young spinach
    leaves, torn*
*salt and freshly ground black
    pepper*
*1 tablespoon chopped fresh
    coriander, to garnish*

1. Heat the oil in a saucepan and gently cook the onion and garlic, until golden brown.
2. Add the cumin seeds, carrot and potatoes and cook for 1–2 minutes. Stir in the curry paste and cook for a further minute.
3. Mix in the chick-peas, chopped tomatoes and vegetable stock. Cover and simmer for 20 minutes or until the potatoes are tender. (Add an extra tablespoon of vegetable stock, if required.)
4. Stir in the spinach, cover and continue to cook for 10 minutes. Season with salt and pepper before serving, garnished with chopped coriander.

Weight Watchers note

Serve this tasty vegetable dish with 1 tablespoon of low-fat plain yogurt, mixed with a teaspoon of lime pickle per serving. This adds ¹/₂ Point per serving.

ⓥ   ⓥ

Flageolet Beans and Fusilli in a Coriander Sauce

Soaking beans and pulses overnight and then cooking does give them a better taste and texture, but it takes time we often do not have! So, stock up on canned beans – a good standby and very nutritious.

350 g (12 oz) pasta shapes, e.g. fusilli (twists)
400 g (14 oz) canned flageolet beans, rinsed and drained
For the sauce:
2 teaspoons sunflower oil
1 large onion, sliced
1 garlic clove, crushed
25 g (1 oz) plain flour
600 ml (1 pint) skimmed milk
2 tablespoons chopped fresh coriander
1 teaspoon lime juice
salt and freshly ground black pepper
fresh coriander sprigs, to garnish
2 tomatoes, de-seeded and chopped, to serve

1. Cook the pasta in plenty of salted, boiling water for 8–10 minutes, or until just *al dente*.
2. Meanwhile, heat the oil in a non-stick saucepan, add the onion and garlic and cook gently for 5 minutes, to soften but not colour. Sprinkle on the flour and cook for 1 minute. Remove from the heat and add the milk gradually. Bring to the boil, stirring constantly, until the sauce is smooth and thickened. Stir in the coriander, lime juice and salt and pepper, to taste.
3. Tip the beans into the boiling pasta for the last minute, just to heat through. Drain thoroughly. Stir into the sauce. Serve, hot, garnished with chopped tomatoes and fresh coriander sprigs.

Variation

Reduce the pasta by 100 g (3½ oz) and add 100 g (3½ oz) chopped cooked chicken breast or poached salmon flakes to the coriander sauce. The Points will remain the same.

Cook's note

When describing pasta as *al dente*, this literally means 'to the tooth' – with some bite or texture still remaining in the pasta.

Felafels with Pitta and Raita

The Middle-Eastern equivalent of our burgers – these chick-pea patties are a popular 'take away' sold by street vendors. Try this delicious version for a satisfying snack.

400 g (14 oz) canned chick-peas, drained
1 garlic clove, crushed
1–2 tablespoons plain flour
1 teaspoon ground coriander
½ teaspoon ground cumin
1 tablespoon chopped fresh mint or coriander or 1 teaspoon dried mint
1 teaspoon salt
a good pinch of dried dill
1 tablespoon sunflower oil
For the raita:
¼ cucumber, halved and de-seeded
1 spring onion, chopped finely
1 tablespoon chopped fresh mint or coriander
150 ml (¼ pint) low-fat plain yogurt
a good pinch of ground cumin
salt and freshly ground black pepper
To serve:
4 mini pitta breads
2 tomatoes, sliced

1. Pat the chick-peas dry with kitchen paper, then purée in a food processor with the garlic, flour, spices, mint, salt and dill.
2. When the mixture has a soft mashed consistency, transfer to a bowl and form into eight patties, using slightly wet hands (this helps prevent the mixture from sticking to you!). Chill for an hour.
3. For the raita, coarsely grate or chop the cucumber and mix with the spring onion, mint or coriander, yogurt and cumin. Season to taste with salt and pepper.
4. Heat the oil in a non-stick frying-pan and, when hot, brown the felafels for 3–4 minutes on each side, carefully turning them with a fish slice. Remove and keep warm.
5. Warm the pitta breads in the oven or under the grill. Split and fill each with a felafel. Spoon in the raita and top with slices of tomato. Serve immediately.

Potato Cakes with a Cheesy Bean and Mushroom Topping

Points per serving: 3½
Total Points per recipe: 14

Serves: 4
Preparation time: 10 minutes
Cooking time: 30 minutes
Freezing: not recommended
Calories per serving: 270

An economical supper to suit all the family. Serve with crusty bread or a mixed salad.

700 g (1 lb 9 oz) potatoes, cut into chunks
150 ml (¼ pint) skimmed milk
4 spring onions, chopped finely
420 g can of Weight Watchers from Heinz baked beans
75 g (2¾ oz) mushrooms, wiped and chopped
50 g (1¾ oz) half-fat Cheddar cheese, grated finely
salt and freshly ground black pepper

1. Cook the potatoes in salted, boiling water, until tender. Drain and return to the saucepan. Add the milk, and mash until smooth. Season with salt and pepper. Mix in the spring onions and then leave until cool enough to handle.
2. Preheat the grill to a moderately hot setting. Divide the potato into four and shape into potato cakes, about 10 cm (4 inches) in diameter. Transfer to a lightly greased baking sheet and grill for 4–5 minutes.
3. Meanwhile, in a small saucepan, heat together the baked beans and mushrooms. Stir in half the grated cheese. Season, to taste. Spoon equally over each potato cake and top with the remaining cheese.
4. Return to the grill for a further 2–3 minutes, until the cheese is golden brown. Use a fish slice to transfer the potato cakes to a serving plate.

 if using vegetarian cheese

Mex-Veg Tacos

Points per serving: 4
Total Points per recipe: 16

Serves: 4
Preparation and cooking time: 20 minutes
Freezing: not recommended
Calories per serving: 235

An informal and sociable light lunch or supper – Mexican-style tacos are fun to eat. Here, the recipe uses lentils instead of minced beef.

2 garlic cloves, crushed
1 teaspoon olive oil
400 g (14 oz) canned green lentils, drained
115 g (4 oz) mushrooms, chopped
½ teaspoon ground cumin
1 teaspoon ground coriander
1 teaspoon dried oregano
1 teaspoon mild chilli powder
salt and freshly ground black pepper

To serve:
8 taco shells
½ iceberg lettuce, shredded finely
2 tomatoes, chopped
55 g (2 oz) half-fat Cheddar cheese, grated
4 pickled jalapeño chillies (optional), halved lengthways
8 teaspoons low-fat plain fromage frais

1. Lightly cook the garlic in the oil for a minute; then stir in the lentils, mushrooms, cumin, coriander, oregano, chilli powder and, finally, salt and pepper, to taste.
2. Simmer for 5 minutes, until thickened. Set aside.
3. Meanwhile, heat the taco shells in a warm oven for 5 minutes. Stand them up in a shallow dish and spoon in the lentil mixture.
4. Top with shredded lettuce, tomatoes and cheese. Finish with a jalapeño chilli and a small dollop of the fromage frais.
5. Eat as soon as possible with your fingers – and plenty of paper napkins to hand!

Variation

Serve Guacamole (see page 30) divided between four taco shells and layered with lots of crunchy 'free' salad. Allow ½ Point for each taco shell.

Cook's note

Taco shells are tortillas (a Mexican pancake) that are deep-fried in the shape of a horseshoe.

Couscous and Ratatouille Gratin

If you don't know what to do with a glut of frozen ratatouille, here's a recipe that is different and perfect to impress your vegetarian friends with. Serve with crusty bread and a green salad.

400 g (14 oz) ratatouille
2 tablespoons tomato purée
1 tablespoon chopped fresh mixed herbs, e.g. parsley, basil and oregano
225 g (8 oz) couscous
450 ml (16 fl oz) hot vegetable stock
400 ml (14 fl oz) low-fat plain yogurt
100 g (3 1/2 oz) half-fat Cheddar cheese
1 egg, beaten
1/2 teaspoon ground cumin
salt and freshly ground black pepper

1. Preheat the oven to Gas Mark 5/190°C/375°F. Place the ratatouille in a 1.5-litre (2³/4-pint) deep ovenproof dish (a soufflé dish would be ideal). Mix the tomato purée with 4 tablespoons of water and the fresh herbs and stir this in to the ratatouille.
2. Place the couscous, with a little salt, in a bowl. Pour over the hot stock. Cover and leave for 10 minutes, to absorb the stock and swell up. Spoon over the ratatouille.
3. Mix together the yogurt, cheese, egg, cumin and a little salt and pepper, to taste. Pour over the couscous. Bake for 35 minutes, or until the topping is golden and set. Leave to stand for 5 minutes before serving.

Variation

Replace the ratatouille with Moroccan Vegetable Stew (see page 73). Points will remain the same.

Cook's note

You can buy canned ratatouille which works well in this baked gratin. Otherwise, make up your favourite recipe for the classic French stew – it's easier to make in a large quantity, so you can freeze some and be ready to make this delicious gratin.

Cracked Wheat Salad with Mint and Peas

Also known as cracked wheat, bulgar wheat is popular in the Middle East. This salad is a variation on the Lebanese dish, tabbouleh. Best eaten warm or at room temperature.

225 g (8 oz) bulgar wheat
4 tablespoons frozen peas
4 spring onions, chopped
4 tomatoes, skinned, de-seeded and sliced
2 tablespoons chopped fresh mint
2 tablespoons chopped fresh parsley
6 tablespoons lemon juice
150 ml (1/4 pint) low-fat plain yogurt
salt and freshly ground black pepper

1. Soak the bulgar wheat in 600 ml (1 pint) of lukewarm water for 30 minutes.
2. Cook the peas until just tender. Drain.
3. Meanwhile, place the spring onions, tomatoes, mint and parsley in a large bowl.
4. Drain the bulgar wheat in a sieve, then tip out on to a clean tea towel, gather up the edges and wring out any excess moisture.
5. Mix the bulgar wheat with the spring onions, tomato and herbs. Stir in the lemon juice.
6. Add the peas and yogurt and fork through to mix well. Adjust the seasoning to taste. Serve.

Cook's note

This is delicious accompanying grilled lamb chops and served with a spoonful of tzatziki; it's good with poached salmon, too.

(v) if using vegetarian cheese

(v)

Mex-Veg Tacos *(page 157)*

Fruity Couscous

1. Soak the couscous in the hot stock for 7–8 minutes.
2. Make the dressing by whisking all the ingredients together in a small bowl or jug.
3. Stir the apricots, raisins and nuts into the couscous. Stir in the dressing and chopped herbs. Season to taste.

Here's a fruity way with couscous – a cereal made from semolina that appears in many North-African dishes. Serve it at room temperature, to really taste the flavours.

125 g (4¹/₂ oz) couscous
300 ml (¹/₂ pint) hot vegetable stock
5 ready-to-eat dried apricots, chopped
1 heaped tablespoon raisins
15 g (¹/₂ oz) flaked almonds, toasted
1 tablespoon chopped fresh tarragon or parsley
1 tablespoon chopped fresh chives
For the dressing:
100 ml (3¹/₂ fl oz) orange juice
2 teaspoons mango chutney or spicy lime pickle
a pinch of ground cinnamon
¹/₂ teaspoon garlic purée (optional)
salt and freshly ground black pepper

Cook's note

Serve couscous with the Roasted Vegetables with Toasted Greek Cheese (see page 77) or Grilled Vegetable Kebabs with a Hot Tomato Glaze (page 77). Also good with grilled chops, fish or on its own, with a salad.

Ham and Vegetable Pasta Gratin

1. Cook the pasta in lightly salted, boiling water for 6–8 minutes or until just tender. Drain thoroughly.
2. Meanwhile, melt the butter in a non-stick saucepan. Add the leek and courgettes and sauté for 4–5 minutes. Add the tomatoes, mushrooms and herbs and cook for a further 4–5 minutes.
3. Preheat the grill to high. In a small bowl, mix together the yogurt, crème fraîche and milk.
4. Add the drained hot pasta to the cooked vegetables, with the ham. Season, to taste, with salt and pepper. Stir in the yogurt mixture. Mix well and then spoon into a shallow dish.
5. Sprinkle the crisps and cheese over the top. Grill for 5 minutes, to melt the cheese. Serve.

Serve this quick supper dish with a crisp green salad.

125 g (4¹/₂ oz) pasta shapes, e.g. fusilli tricolore (three-colour twists)
15 g (¹/₂ oz) butter
1 leek, sliced finely
2 courgettes, sliced
2 large tomatoes, skinned, de-seeded and chopped
100 g (3¹/₂ oz) button mushrooms
1 teaspoon dried mixed herbs (optional)
3 tablespoons low-fat plain yogurt
2 tablespoons half-fat crème fraîche
2 tablespoons skimmed milk
125 g (4¹/₂ oz) lean ham, chopped
25 g packet low-fat plain crinkle crisps, crushed coarsely
25 g (1 oz) half-fat Cheddar cheese, grated
salt and freshly ground black pepper

ⓥ

Rigatoni with Smoked Mackerel and Leek in a Horseradish Sauce

Points per serving: 9
Total Points per recipe: 18

Serves: 2
Preparation and cooking time:
20 minutes
Freezing: not recommended
Calories per serving: 615

Smoked mackerel has quite a strong, rich flavour, making it ideal to eat with pasta.

2 teaspoons margarine
1 leek, sliced finely
1 tablespoon cornflour
300 ml (½ pint) skimmed milk
2 teaspoons horseradish sauce
1 tablespoon chopped fresh
 chives or parsley
1 medium-size smoked mackerel
 fillet, skinned and flaked
125 g (4½ oz) pasta shapes,
 e.g. rigatoni or quills
salt and freshly ground black
 pepper

1. Melt the margarine in a saucepan and gently cook the leek for 10 minutes, until softened.
2. Blend the cornflour with 2 tablespoons of the milk and then stir into the remaining milk. Add to the leek, stirring continuously, until the sauce thickens and is smooth.
3. Stir in the horseradish and herbs, and season with salt and pepper. Add the flaked mackerel. Keep warm.
4. Meanwhile, cook the pasta in plenty of salted, boiling water for 8–10 minutes or until al dente. Drain thoroughly and divide between two warm bowls.
5. Spoon the mackerel and leek sauce over the pasta. Serve immediately.

Variation
Replace the horseradish with a mild mustard.

Mushroom, Leek and Broccoli Lasagne

Points per serving: 5½
Total Points per recipe: 22

Serves: 4
Preparation time: 15 minutes
Cooking time: 35 minutes
Freezing: recommended
Calories per serving: 305

A great family favourite; alternatively, divide into four portions and freeze ready for an instant and satisfying supper.

25 g (1 oz) low fat spread
1 large leek, sliced
125 g (4½ oz) mushrooms,
 sliced
25 g (1 oz) plain flour
300 ml (½ pint) skimmed milk
225 g (8 oz) broccoli florets,
 cooked
6 sheets of ready-to-cook lasagne
grated nutmeg
salt and freshly ground black
 pepper
For the topping:
1 egg, beaten
150 ml (5½ fl oz) Greek-style
 natural yogurt
50 g (1¾ oz) red Leicester
 cheese, grated

1. Melt the low-fat spread and gently cook the leek and mushrooms for 3–4 minutes. Sprinkle on the flour and continue cooking for a further minute. Remove from the heat.
2. Gradually, blend in the milk, then return to a low heat and continue to stir until the sauce thickens. Season to taste, with salt and pepper and a little grated nutmeg. Fold in the broccoli florets.
3. Place half the sauce in a rectangular shallow dish, cover with 3 sheets of lasagne. Pour over the remaining sauce and vegetables and top with the remaining lasagne sheets.
4. Whisk together the egg and yogurt. Lightly season. Spread over the lasagne. Sprinkle over the grated cheese.
5. Bake at Gas Mark 5/190°C/375°F for 35 minutes. Serve with a fresh green salad and crusty bread.

Variation
Replace the broccoli with cooked celeriac and carrots.

Cook's note
Choose brown (chestnut) mushrooms for a more flavoursome mushroom.

V if using free-range egg and vegetarian cheese

Mushroom, Leek and Broccoli Lasagne *(page 161)*

Tropical Pasta Salad with Orange and

Passion Fruit Dressing *(opposite)*

Tagliatelle in Peanut Butter Sauce

Peanuts are packed full of goodness and Calories, so they must be used sparingly! Try them in this surprisingly good sauce. Serve with tagliatelle or spaghetti and a fresh green salad.

350 g (12 oz) tagliatelle
2 tablespoons smooth peanut
*   butter*
25 g (1 oz) plain flour
¹/₂ teaspoon mild chilli powder
425 ml (³/₄ pint) skimmed milk
2 teaspoons chopped fresh
*   thyme or oregano*
1 tablespoon tomato purée
a dash of chilli sauce
salt and freshly ground black
*   pepper*

1. Cook the tagliatelle in plenty of salted, boiling water for 7–10 minutes or until *al dente*. Refer to the pack instructions.
2. Meanwhile, make the sauce. Heat the peanut butter in a non-stick saucepan: it will separate and become quite oily. Blend in the flour and chilli powder and cook for 1 minute.
3. Gradually add the milk and bring to the boil, stirring constantly, until the sauce thickens and becomes smooth. Stir in the thyme or oregano and tomato purée. Season to taste, with salt, pepper and a dash of chilli sauce.
4. Drain the cooked pasta and divide between four warmed bowls. Spoon the sauce over the top. Serve immediately.

Cook's note

Do take care if serving this to guests or children. Some people have a serious allergic reaction to peanuts.

Tropical Pasta Salad with Orange and Passion Fruit Dressing

Choose whatever fruits you like best. Vary the textures though, to give some crunch amidst the juicy fruits.

125 g (4¹/₂ oz) small pasta
*   shapes, e.g. shells, macaroni*
1 orange, segmented
5 cm (2-inch) piece of
*   cucumber, peeled, de-seeded*
*   and chopped*
50 g (1³/₄ oz) seedless green
*   grapes, halved*
1 small kiwi fruit, peeled,
*   halved and sliced*
¹/₄ red pepper, de-seeded and cut
*   into small strips*
¹/₂ papaya, peeled, de-seeded
*   and chopped*
1 small fresh red chilli, de-seeded
*   and chopped finely*
For the dressing:
1 passion fruit, halved
2 tablespoons low-fat plain
*   yogurt*
2 teaspoons clear honey
1 teaspoon finely grated
*   orange zest*
juice of 1 orange
1 teaspoon sherry or white-wine
*   vinegar*
2 teaspoons chopped fresh dill,
*   mint or chives*
freshly ground black pepper

1. Cook the pasta according to the pack instructions or until just *al dente*. Refresh in cold water. Drain thoroughly. Place in a large bowl.
2. Add the orange segments, cucumber, grapes, kiwi fruit, red pepper, papaya and chilli. Fold together gently.
3. Prepare the dressing. Using a teaspoon, scoop the seeds and juicy pulp from the passion fruit into a bowl. Add the remaining ingredients and mix together well. Season with a little pepper.
4. Fold the dressing into the pasta salad. Cover and chill for 15 minutes before serving.

Variation

This serves 4 as an accompaniment. Points per serving will be 2¹/₂ and Calories per serving will be 170. This is a delicious fruity recipe for pasta. If you want to add a savoury note, prawns, chicken and ham are delicious stirred in. Also, a little curry paste, to taste, adds a touch of spice to the dressing. Calculate the extra Points.

Ⓥ   Ⓥ

Lentil and Carrot Cannelloni with Creamy Tomato Sauce

Serves: 4
Preparation time: 30 minutes
Cooking time: 25 minutes
Freezing: recommended
Calories per serving: 400

For the filling:

2 teaspoons olive oil

1 onion, chopped

1 garlic clove, crushed

2 carrots, chopped

½ teaspoon chilli powder

115 g (4 oz) red or green lentils

1 tablespoon tomato purée

*1 tablespoon chopped fresh
    parsley*

*1 tablespoon chopped fresh
    oregano*

225 g (8 oz) cannelloni tubes

For the sauce:

1 onion, grated

*425 g (15 oz) canned chopped
    tomatoes with herbs*

1 tablespoon tomato purée

*150 g (5½ oz) very-low-fat
    plain fromage frais*

*55 g (2 oz) parmesan cheese,
    grated*

*salt and freshly ground black
    pepper*

1. Prepare the filling. Heat the oil in a non-stick frying-pan, add the onion and garlic and sauté for 2–3 minutes. Add the carrots, cover and continue to cook for 2–3 minutes.

2. Stir in the chilli powder and lentils. Cook for 1 minute. Add the tomato purée, fresh herbs and 300 ml (½ pint) of water. Stir, cover and cook for 20–25 minutes, stirring occasionally. Remove the lid for the last 3–4 minutes, to reduce and thicken the sauce. Season well with salt and pepper.

3. Meanwhile, cook the cannelloni tubes in a large saucepan of salted, boiling water for 10–12 minutes, until just tender. Check with the pack instructions. Drain.

4. Make the tomato sauce for the topping: place the onion, chopped tomatoes and tomato purée in a saucepan. Cover and simmer for 10 minutes; then continue to cook, uncovered, for 4–5 minutes. Stir in the fromage frais. Season with salt and pepper.

5. Preheat the oven to Gas Mark 5/190°C/375°F. Fill the pasta tubes with the carrot and lentil mixture. Lightly grease a shallow ovenproof dish and then arrange the cannelloni in one layer.

6. Pour the tomato sauce over the cannelloni. Sprinkle with the parmesan. Bake for 20–25 minutes, or until bubbling and golden.

164

Desserts

* *

1,2,3 Success Plus lets you follow a well balanced diet and enjoy all the foods you like most of all. The secret is the quantity, the way the food is prepared and the choice of ingredients. Knowing how to adapt some of your favourite recipes to give a healthier ingredients list means you can treat not only your family and friends to delicious puddings and creamy desserts – but also yourself.

Start off by browsing through this chapter – preferably not on an empty stomach! There are over thirty, fruity, creamy, chocolaty, scrumptious recipes to suit every occasion. A light and fluffy Lemon Soufflé Omelette (see page 166), for example, is not only a delicious satisfying sweet, but a nutritious snack. So too, is a slice of moist Fruit Bread with Spiced Apples (see page 166). If you miss lunch, or get home late and crave something sweet, one of these is a far healthier and more substantial snack than a chocolate bar that disappears in less time than it takes to unwrap it!

If you want a traditional pudding, try Tangy Bread and Butter Pudding (see page 170), with a low-fat custard – a great way to finish off the family lunch. Or, for a more impressive dessert to tempt your guests, how about the Jamaican Meringue Gâteau (see page 178) – crisp meringue with a pineapple and ginger filling. It's hard to believe such an indulgent recipe has been trimmed down to fit into your diet.

Try to buy low-fat alternatives to yogurts, creams and custards, so you can still have that finishing touch without adding too many Points. It's good to feel only indulgence and not an expanding waistline!

And on the days you don't have time to make your own dessert, do look for other healthy alternatives our supermarkets are now selling – silky chocolate mousses, creamy yogurt-based fools and desserts, as well as ready-prepared fresh fruit salads and compotes. The *1,2,3 Success Plus Cookbook* is designed to work around the unexpected – so you won't lose heart, or sight of that Goal Weight!

Lemon Soufflé Omelette

Points per serving: 3
Total Points per recipe: 3

Serves: 1
Preparation and cooking time:
10 minutes
Freezing: not recommended
Calories per serving: 155

1 egg, separated
2 heaped teaspoons lemon curd
1 teaspoon half-fat butter or
low-fat spread
¹/₂ teaspoon icing sugar, to serve

1. Preheat the grill to a medium setting. In a small bowl, whisk together the egg yolk and lemon curd, until pale and creamy.
2. In a grease-free small bowl, whisk the egg white until it forms soft peaks. Gently fold both mixtures together with a metal spoon.
3. Heat a small non-stick omelette pan until hot, then add the spread and, when melted and sizzling, add the egg mixture. Gently and quickly spread evenly.
4. Cook gently for about 2 minutes; then place under the grill for a further 1–2 minutes or until the surface looks puffy and golden and is firm to the touch.
5. Fold the omelette in half and serve immediately, sprinkled with a little sieved icing sugar.

Variation
Use 1 teaspoon of finely grated lemon zest and 1 teaspoon caster sugar instead of lemon curd.

Weight Watchers note
This is delicious eaten with a 55 g (2 oz) scoop of low-fat ice cream (add 1 Point per serving), or 2 tablespoons of low-fat plain fromage frais, sweetened with 1 teaspoon honey (add 2¹/₂ Points per serving).

Ⓥ if using free-range egg and vegetarian low-fat spread

Fruit Bread with Spiced Apples

Points per serving: 2
Total Points per recipe: 4

Serves: 2
Preparation and cooking time:
5 minutes
Freezing: not recommended
Calories per serving: 170

Here's a fruity number to relish. An ideal brunch, snack or pudding.

2 small slices of currant bread
2 tablespoons greek-style
natural yogurt
¹/₂ dessert apple, sliced thinly
1 teaspoon icing sugar, sifted
¹/₄ teaspoon ground allspice or
cinnamon

1. Preheat the grill to its highest setting. Toast the currant bread.
2. Spread the Greek yogurt over each slice, arrange the apple slices on top and sprinkle with the sieved icing sugar and allspice.
3. Replace under the grill and cook for 2–3 minutes or until lightly caramelised.

Variation
Replace the apple with a small banana (add ¹/₂ Point for 1 serving) or 3 apricot halves.

Weight Watchers note
Moist currant bread is a temptation – so slice and freeze the bread and remove 1 or 2 slices when required.
Ⓥ

Lemon Surprise Pudding

Points per serving: 4¹/₂
Total Points per recipe: 18

Serves: 4
Preparation time: 15 minutes
Cooking time: 40 minutes
Freezing: not recommended
Calories per serving: 240

50 g (1³/₄ oz) hard margarine
finely grated zest and juice of
1 lemon
75 g (2³/₄ oz) caster sugar
2 eggs, separated
25 g (1 oz) plain flour, sifted
175 ml (6 fl oz) skimmed milk

1. Preheat the oven to Gas Mark 4/180°C/350°F. Place a lightly sprayed 600 ml (1-pint), shallow, ovenproof dish in a roasting pan containing 2.5 cm (1 inch) of water.
2. Cream together the margarine, lemon zest and caster sugar, until light and fluffy. Beat in the egg yolks, flour and lemon juice; then gradually whisk in the milk.
3. Whisk the egg whites in a clean, grease-free bowl, until very stiff. Carefully fold them into the mixture. Using a spatula, pour the mixture into the dish.
4. Bake for 40 minutes. Serve immediately, making sure everyone has a fair share of the tangy lemon sauce that forms underneath!

Ⓥ if using free-range eggs and vegetarian margarine

Chocolate Fondue with Fresh Fruit Dippers

Here is a dessert to satisfy any chocoholics!

For the chocolate sauce:

3 teaspoons cornflour
4 teaspoons cocoa powder
300 ml (¹/₂ pint) skimmed milk
artificial sweetener, to taste
a few drops of vanilla essence
2 tablespoons half-fat single
*   cream*

For the fruit dippers, to serve:

2 small bananas, cut into chunks
8 strawberries, halved
1 pear, cut into wedges
2 fresh pineapple rings, cut
*   into chunks*
8 cherries
a little lemon juice
fresh mint leaves, to garnish

1. Blend the cornflour, cocoa and a little milk in a heatproof jug to give a smooth paste. Heat the remaining milk until boiling and pour on to the paste, whisking all the time to prevent any lumps from forming.

2. Return the mixture to the pan and gently bring to the boil, stirring, until the sauce is thick and smooth. Sweeten with artificial sweetener, to taste, and add a few drops of vanilla essence. Keep warm over a low heat.

3. Meanwhile, prepare the fresh fruits. Sprinkle the bananas and pear with a little lemon juice.

4. Place a small heatproof bowl in the centre of a large plate and arrange four sections of the assorted fruits. Decorate with mint leaves.

5. Pour the chocolate sauce into the dish and swirl in the cream. Serve immediately.

Variation

Replace the cream with a scoop of soft vanilla ice cream, leaving it to melt into the warm sauce. Add ¹/₂ Point per serving.

Cook's note

Remember to add a few drops of vanilla essence to bring out the chocolaty flavour in puddings and desserts.

Upside-down Plum and Cinnamon Bake

This is a dual-purpose recipe – great as a pudding and delicious as a cake. It freezes well, too, so make a batch and freeze one half for up to 3 months.

For the base:

4 tablespoons low-calorie
*   raspberry or plum jam*
450 g (1 lb) Victoria plums,
*   stoned and quartered*

For the sponge:

3 eggs
75 g (2³/₄ oz) caster sugar
70 g (2¹/₂ oz) plain flour
¹/₂ teaspoon ground cinnamon
40 g (1¹/₂ oz) butter, melted

1. Preheat the oven to Gas Mark 4/180°C/350°F. Line the base of a 28 × 18 cm (11 × 7-inch) tin with non-stick baking parchment.

2. Gently melt the jam with a tablespoon of water either in a small saucepan or in the microwave oven (using a medium-low setting) and pour evenly over the base of the tin. Arrange the plum quarters in rows on top.

3. Using an electric whisk, cream together the eggs and caster sugar until the mixture is pale and very thick and holds a trail for 2–3 seconds. Sift and fold in the flour and cinnamon; then fold in the melted butter.

4. Pour the mixture over the top of the plums. Bake for 25–30 minutes or until the sponge is golden and springy to the touch.

5. While still warm, carefully run a knife around the edge of the tin, place a cooling rack over the top of the tin, invert and remove the tin. Use a large palette knife to remove the paper carefully.

6. Slice into 12 portions. Serve.

Variations

For an apple and cinnamon bake, replace the plums with 450 g (1 lb) dessert apples, e.g. Cox's, and use blackberry or raspberry jam.

For an apricot and almond bake, replace the plums with fresh apricots, stoned and quartered. Use apricot jam and replace the cinnamon with almond essence, to taste.

Replace the cinnamon with 1 teaspoon of ground ginger.

Ⓥ if using free-range eggs

Banana and Cinnamon Pancakes

Frozen ready-made pancakes are a handy standby for a quick pudding.

4 pancakes (see page 204)
2 medium-size ripe bananas,
*   lightly mashed*
200 g (7 oz) very-low-fat plain
*   fromage frais*
1 teaspoon honey
To serve:
1 teaspoon icing sugar, sifted
1 teaspoon ground cinnamon

1. Wrap the pancakes in foil and warm them through under the grill or in a warm oven; or heat them through in the microwave for about 30–40 seconds.
2. Fold together the bananas, fromage frais and honey. Divide the mixture between the pancakes and gently roll up.
3. Dust the pancakes with sifted icing sugar and cinnamon. Serve at once.

Variation

Mix 4 teaspoons of chocolate-nut spread into the fromage frais and replace the cinnamon with cocoa powder. Add 1½ Points per serving.

Cook's note

Choose ripe, slightly soft bananas. The flavour and sweetness will be more intense.

Apricot Clafoutis

A traditional French pudding and a way of using up apples or cherries which are past their prime. You can use any firm fruit – bananas, pears or, in this recipe, apricots. Serve with low-fat plain yogurt.

450 g (1 lb) ripe apricots,
*   stoned and quartered*
3 tablespoons plain flour
a pinch of salt
3 eggs, beaten
4 tablespoons caster sugar
450 ml (16 fl oz) skimmed
*   milk*
25 g (1 oz) half-fat butter
1 teaspoon ground allspice or
*   cinnamon*

1. Preheat the oven to Gas Mark 7/220°C/425°F. Lightly spray a large, shallow, ovenproof dish. Scatter in the apricot quarters.
2. Sift the flour and salt into a bowl and then beat in the eggs and 3 tablespoons of sugar.
3. Heat the milk in a small saucepan until almost boiling and then beat into the egg mixture. Pour the batter over the apricots. Dot with small knobs of butter. Bake for 25–30 minutes or until the batter is set and golden brown.
4. Mix together the remaining sugar and spice and sprinkle over the top. Serve warm, with plain yogurt.

Variation

Replace the fresh apricots with 600 g (1 lb 4 oz) apricot halves in natural juice, drained and halved.

Cook's note

This pudding reheats well, although is best eaten fresh. If there are any leftovers, wrap in individual foil parcels and reheat in a hot oven for 10 minutes, opening the foil for the last few minutes.

Ⓥ if using free-range eggs

Chocolate Fondue with Fresh Fruit Dippers *(page 167)*

Baked Peaches with Ricotta and Almonds

Points per serving: 5
Total Points per recipe: 20

Serves: 4
Preparation time: 15 minutes
Cooking time: 20 minutes
Freezing: not recommended
Calories per serving: 250

Bring out the summer flavours. Peaches, nectarines or apricots are all ideal to use in this baked dessert, which should be served with ice cream or Greek-style plain yogurt.

2 egg whites
125 g (4¹/₂ oz) caster sugar
100 g (3¹/₂ oz) ricotta cheese
2 tablespoons ground almonds
1 tablespoon almond-flavoured
*   liqueur, e.g. Amaretto*
4 peaches, halved and stoned
25 g (1 oz) flaked almonds

1. Preheat the oven to Gas Mark 6/200°C/400°F.
2. Using electric beaters, whisk the egg whites in a large, grease-free bowl, until they form soft peaks. Whisk in the sugar, until stiff.
3. Place the cheese, ground almonds and liqueur in a bowl and whisk together, until smooth. Fold the meringue into the cheese mixture. Spoon into each peach half.
4. Scatter the flaked almonds on top and then arrange in a shallow, ovenproof dish and bake for 15–20 minutes, until the peaches are tender and the topping golden brown. Serve warm.

Variation
Replace the ground almonds with 10 small amaretti or macaroon biscuits, crushed. This will add 3 Points per serving.

Cook's notes
Serve with a raspberry or strawberry sauce, made simply by liquidising and sieving a drained can of the fruit in natural juice.
   Add artificial sweetener, to taste, and adjust the sauce consistency with a little of the natural juice.

Ⓥ if using free-range eggs and vegetarian cheese

Tangy Bread and Butter Pudding

Points per serving: 4
Total Points per recipe: 16

Serves: 4
Preparation time: 10 minutes
Cooking time: 25 minutes
Freezing: not recommended
Calories per serving: 220

A traditional family favourite and so simple to make. Use bread that is a day old.

8 × 2.5 cm (1-inch) slices of
*   French bread*
4 teaspoons low-fat spread
4 heaped teaspoons chunky-cut
*   marmalade*
300 ml (¹/₂ pint) skimmed milk
2 eggs
2 tablespoons caster sugar

1. Preheat the oven to Gas Mark 4/180°C/350°F.
2. Evenly spread both sides of the bread slices with a thin coat of low-fat spread. Sandwich the bread with the marmalade; then cut the 4 sandwiches in half. Arrange in a shallow ovenproof dish (about 1-litre/1³/₄-pint capacity).
3. Whisk together the milk, eggs and sugar. Pour over and around the sandwiches. Leave to stand for 15 minutes, so the milk can soak into the bread.
4. Bake for 25–30 minutes or until golden and the custard is slightly set.

Variation
For a more traditional pudding, replace the marmalade with 2 tablespoons of currants or sultanas.

Cook's note
For individual bread and butter puddings, divide the sandwiches and custard between four ramekin dishes. Reduce the cooking time to about 15 minutes.

Weight Watchers note
This is delicious eaten with Weight Watchers from Heinz Iced Dessert. Serve 1 scoop (60 g) of the vanilla flavour, and add 1¹/₂ Points per serving.

Ⓥ if using free-range eggs and vegetarian low-fat spread

Blackberry and Apple Meringue Pie

6 sheets of filo pastry, each
about 25 × 23 cm (10 × 9
inches), thawed if frozen
4 teaspoons low-fat spread or
half-fat butter, melted
450 g (1 lb) Bramley cooking
apples, peeled, cored and
sliced
2 eggs, separated
artificial sweetener, to taste
280 g (10 oz) canned
blackberries in apple juice,
drained
125 g (4½ oz) caster sugar

1. Preheat the oven to Gas
Mark 5/190°C/375°F. Place
a 20 cm (8-inch) pie dish or
spring-release flan tin on a
baking tray. Line the dish with
one sheet of pastry, brush with
the melted low-fat spread and
then repeat with the remaining
sheets, off-setting each one so
that the corners do not overlap.
Crumple up any over-hanging
pastry for a rim. Brush with any
remaining spread. Bake for
10–15 minutes or until golden.
2. Meanwhile, lightly cook the
apples in a saucepan for 10
minutes or until softened. Beat
with a wooden spoon until
smooth. Beat in the egg yolks.

Sweeten to taste with a little
artificial sweetener.
3. Fold in the blackberries. Pour
the mixture into the flan case and
bake for 10 minutes.
4. Meanwhile, whisk the egg
whites in a clean, grease-free bowl,
until stiff. Gradually whisk in the
caster sugar, until the whites are
very glossy and hold their shape.
5. Remove the pie from the oven.
Pile on the meringue and then
return to the oven for 10 minutes
or until the meringue is firm and
golden. Serve the pie warm.

Variation

This is a great way of using
a glut of stewed fruit such as
gooseberries, blackcurrants,
blackberries and so on. The egg
yolk will lightly set the purée in
the pastry case.

ⓥ if using free-range eggs and
vegetarian low-fat spread

Caramelised Fruit Sabayon

Choose your favourite fresh
fruits for this grilled dessert.
Prepare in advance up until
step 3 and then finish off under
the grill at the last moment.

For the sabayon:

2 egg yolks, beaten
50 g (1¾ oz) caster sugar
grated zest of ½ lemon
150 ml (¼ pint) low-alcohol
white wine
4 tablespoons low-fat plain
fromage frais

To serve:

450 g (1 lb) assorted fruits,
e.g. raspberries, blueberries,
pitted cherries, peach and
apricot slices and grapes

1. Preheat the grill to its highest
setting.
2. Place the egg yolks, two-thirds
of the sugar, the lemon zest and
wine in a heatproof bowl, set
over a pan of simmering water.
Using an electric whisk, beat the
mixture until it is smooth and
thickened. Add the fromage
frais and continue whisking for
1 minute.
3. Arrange the fruit in a shallow,
ovenproof dish or on four
individual, heatproof dessert
plates. Pour over the sabayon,
sprinkle on the remaining sugar
and place under the hot grill, until
bubbling and golden. Do keep an
eye on the plate, as the sugar can
burn very quickly. Serve at once.

ⓥ if using free-range eggs

Pear and Banana Strudel

4 sheets of filo pastry, each about
*   31 × 18 cm (12¹/₂ × 7 inches),*
*   thawed if frozen*
15 g (¹/₂ oz) butter, melted
2 tablespoons low-calorie jam
*   or marmalade*
400 g (14 oz) canned pears
*   in natural juice, drained*
*   and chopped*
1 medium-size banana, sliced
*   thinly*
1 teaspoon lemon juice

1. Preheat the oven to Gas
Mark 5/190°C/375°F. Line a
baking sheet with greaseproof
paper.

2. Brushing every second sheet
lightly with butter, layer the filo
pastry, offsetting the sheets
slightly, to give a large area.
3. Spread the jam over the
pastry, to within 2.5 cm (1 inch) of
the edges, and 5 cm (2 inches)
from one end. Then scatter the
chopped pear over the jam. Toss
the banana in the lemon juice and
arrange over the pear.
4. Fold in the sides of the pastry
and then roll up the strudel from
one end. Place, seam underneath,
on the baking sheet. Brush with
the remaining butter. Bake for
20 minutes, until golden and crisp.

Variations

Use canned apricots, or canned
red cherries, instead of pears.
    Use 100 g (3¹/₂ oz) ready-to-eat
dried fruit chopped, in place of
canned fruits.
    Sprinkle 1 tablespoon of
ground almonds over the fruit.
Add ¹/₂ Point per serving.

Poached Orchard Fruits in Cider

Apples, pears and cider – the
flavours of an English orchard.
These small moulds are delicious
served warm or cold and are
ideal, too, for packed lunches.

150 ml (¹/₄ pint) medium-dry
*   cider*
75 g (2³/₄ oz) golden caster
*   sugar*
finely grated zest and juice of
*   1 small lemon*
3 dessert apples, e.g. Cox's, peeled,
*   cored and sliced thinly*
3 firm dessert pears, peeled, cored
*   and sliced thinly*
50 g (1³/₄ oz) preserved ginger,
*   chopped*

1. Place the cider, sugar and
lemon zest and juice in a pan and
heat gently, stirring, until the
sugar has dissolved. Bring to the
boil and boil for 5 minutes.
2. Place the apples and pears
in a single layer in a non-stick
frying-pan. Pour over the hot
syrup, cover and simmer gently
for 5 minutes.
3. Remove the cover. Using a
fish slice, turn the fruit over and
simmer, uncovered, for a further
5 minutes, until the syrup has
nearly all evaporated.
4. Add the ginger to the fruit.
Leave to cool. Divide the fruit
between six ramekin dishes.
Cover and refrigerate overnight.
5. To serve, turn the apple
mould out on to a plate. Serve
with yogurt or fromage frais,
remembering to add the extra
Points.

Rhubarb and Orange Crumble

Points per serving: 5
Total Points per recipe: 20
Serves: 4
Preparation time: 15 minutes
Cooking time: 35 minutes
Freezing: recommended
Calories per serving: 295

*500 g (1 lb 2 oz) young
    rhubarb, sliced*
25 g (1 oz) soft brown sugar
grated zest and juice of 1 orange
175 g (6 oz) plain flour
*85 g (3 oz) low-fat spread or
    half-fat butter*
25 g (1 oz) demerara sugar

1. Preheat the oven to Gas Mark 5/190°C/375°F.
2. Put the rhubarb, brown sugar and orange juice in a saucepan, cover and gently poach for 10 minutes, or until the rhubarb juices start to run. Transfer into a 1.2-litre (2-pint) ovenproof dish.
3. Meanwhile, place the flour, low-fat spread and sugar in a bowl and, using a fork, work the low-fat spread into the flour until the mixture resembles breadcrumbs. Stir in the orange zest.
4. Sprinkle the crumble mixture over the rhubarb. Bake for 35 minutes, until the top is crisp and golden. Serve hot.

(V) if using vegetarian low-fat spread

Christmas Pudding

Points per serving: 3½
Total Points per recipe: 28
Serves: 8
Preparation time: 30 minutes
+ overnight standing
Cooking time: 5 hours + 2 hours reheating
Freezing: recommended
Calories per serving: 210

The **1,2,3 Success Plus** diet means that there's no need to miss out on any Christmas treats – so round off the festive lunch with a traditional slice of pud!

*350 g (12 oz) mixed dried
    fruits*
1 pot of strong tea
*55 g (2 oz) soft dark brown
    sugar*
*100 ml (3½ fl oz) brandy or
    rum*
*finely grated zest and juice of
    1 orange*
*1 dessert apple, peeled and
    grated*
1 carrot, grated finely
*100 g (3½ oz) fresh wholemeal
    breadcrumbs*
2 tablespoons self-raising flour
1 teaspoon ground mixed spice
*½ teaspoon freshly grated
    nutmeg*
1 egg, beaten
½ teaspoon margarine

1. Place the dried fruits in a bowl and pour over the hot tea. (Use a strainer, if necessary.) Leave to stand for 15 minutes. Then drain the fruit and return to the bowl. (This helps to plump up the fruit.)
2. Place the drained, dried fruits, soft dark brown sugar and brandy or rum in the bowl. Cover and leave to stand for 6 hours or, preferably, overnight. (This produces a dark, rich basis for the pudding.)
3. Add the remaining ingredients, except for the margarine, mixing thoroughly.
4. Use the margarine to grease a 750 ml (1½-pint) pudding basin. Spoon in the mixture. Lay a well fitting disc of greaseproof paper on top of the mixture. Cover the top of the basin with a double layer of greaseproof paper or foil and secure tightly.
5. Place the pudding in a steamer set over a saucepan of simmering water and steam steadily for 5 hours, topping up the saucepan with extra boiling water, as required.
6. Allow the pudding to cool. Replace the greaseproof paper or foil lid with a fresh piece. Store in a cool, dark place.
7. To reheat, steam the pudding for 2 hours. Serve with All-in-One White Sauce (see page 205), flavoured with 1 tablespoon of rum or brandy.

Variation

Replace the orange zest and juice with lemon.

Cook's note

If you use a microwave oven to reheat the pudding, do take care. Although this pudding does not contain a lot of sugar, it is packed full of fruit and will benefit from reheating at a lower level of power for a longer time, until very hot.

(V) if using a free-range egg and vegetarian margarine

Hot Chocolate and Rum Soufflé

This hot soufflé will be a memorable ending to a dinner party with friends. It is delicious served with fresh raspberries or lightly poached pears.

4 eggs, separated
40 g (1½ oz) caster sugar
3 tablespoons plain flour
1 tablespoon cocoa powder
300 ml (½ pint) skimmed milk
1 tablespoon rum or brandy
sifted icing sugar, to decorate

1. Preheat the oven to Gas Mark 4/180°C/350°F. Lightly grease a 1.7-litre (3-pint) soufflé dish.
2. Whisk the egg yolks and caster sugar together until pale and thick. Sift the flour and cocoa powder together. Fold the flour and cocoa into the egg mixture, then pour over the milk and rum or brandy. Mix together until smooth.
3. Transfer to a saucepan and gently bring to just boiling. Reduce the heat and cook gently, stirring continuously, for 2 minutes, or until the custard thickens and is smooth. Pour into a large, clean bowl.
4. In another clean, greasefree bowl, whisk the egg whites until stiff; then fold into the warm chocolate custard. Carefully, pour into the prepared dish.
5. Bake for 45 minutes, until well risen and firm to the touch. (Do not be tempted to open the oven door until the cooking time is almost up.)
6. Dust with a little sifted icing sugar and then rush to the table and serve!

Fragrant Rice Pudding with Crushed Fruits

Rice pudding and a dollop of jam is a traditional warming winter pud! Here is a more exotic version, served at room temperature with juicy fresh fruits.

50 g (1¾ oz) basmati or
* Thai rice*
500 ml (18 fl oz) skimmed milk
1 lemon grass stalk or a bay leaf
3 cardamom pods, crushed
* lightly (optional)*
artificial sweetener, to taste
a small selection of ripe soft
* fruits, e.g. raspberries,*
* blueberries, strawberries*
* and peeled, cubed mango*

1. Bring the rice, milk, lemon grass or bay leaf and cardamom pods (if using) to the boil in a non-stick saucepan.
2. Stir well and then reduce the heat to a gentle simmer. Cook, uncovered, for about 20 minutes, until the mixture thickens and the rice is tender. Stir occasionally.
3. Remove the lemon grass or bay leaf and cardamom pods. Leave the rice to cool, then stir in some sweetener, to taste.
4. Meanwhile, lightly crush the selection of fruits with a fork. Serve the rice in small bowls with the crushed fruits spooned on top.

Cook's note

Both basmati and Thai (or jasmine) rice have their own flavour, which should be taken advantage of in sweet as well as savoury dishes.

Iced Lemon Meringues

Points per serving: 4
Total Points per recipe: 16

Serves: 4

Preparation time: 15 minutes + freezing

Freezing: recommended

Calories per serving: 210

Fresh and tangy, these easy desserts can be made well in advance.

200 g (7 oz) low-fat plain
fromage frais
125 g (4½ oz) lemon curd
1 teaspoon lemon zest (to taste)
2 teaspoons brandy or orange
liqueur, e.g. Cointreau
50 g (1¾ oz) meringue, broken

To serve:
fresh raspberries or blueberries
fresh mint leaves

1. In a large bowl, mix together the fromage frais and lemon curd. Add a little lemon zest, to taste. (It depends on how sharp the lemon curd is.) Stir in the liqueur.
2. Fold in the broken meringue, coating the pieces thoroughly with the lemon cream.
3. Transfer to four ramekin dishes or one small loaf tin, lined with clingfilm. Cover with freezer film. Freeze for 3–4 hours, or until firm.
4. Serve, decorated with a few raspberries or blueberries and fresh mint leaves.

Poached Pears and Prunes in Red Wine

Points per serving: 1½
Total Points per recipe: 6

Serves: 4

Preparation and cooking time:
20 minutes

Freezing: not recommended

Calories per serving: 95

Canned pears come to the rescue in providing a last minute dessert for those unexpected guests.

400 g (14 oz) canned pear
halves in natural juice
12 ready-to-eat prunes
150 ml (¼ pint) red wine
pared zest of ½ small lemon

1. Drain the pears, reserving 4 tablespoons of juice. Place the pears, juice, prunes, red wine and lemon zest in a saucepan.
2. Simmer, uncovered, for 10 minutes. Using a slotted spoon, remove the pears and prunes to a serving dish.
3. Allow the remaining juice to simmer for a few minutes, before pouring it over the fruit.
4. Serve warm or chilled, with ice cream, half-fat crème fraîche or yogurt, adding the Points. Serve with a crisp Almond Tuiles (see page 202).

Danish Apple Layer

Points per serving: 7½
Total Points per recipe: 15

Serves: 2

Preparation and cooking time:
10 minutes

Freezing: not recommended

Calories per serving: 250

Assemble this delicious pudding no more than half an hour before serving, to get maximum crunch!

115 g (4 oz) white breadcrumbs
25 g (1 oz) half-fat butter,
melted
25 g (1 oz) demerara sugar
2 heaped teaspoons cocoa
powder, sifted
225 g (8 oz) apple purée, chilled
150 ml (¼ pint) greek-style
natural yogurt
2 tablespoons half-fat crème
fraîche
ground cinnamon, to serve

1. Heat a non-stick frying-pan. Add the breadcrumbs and dry-fry, until the crumbs start to dry out and become crisp. Sprinkle on the melted butter and continue to stir-fry until the crumbs become golden and crisp.
2. Remove from the heat and stir in the demerara sugar and the cocoa powder, mixing well. Leave to cool.
3. Spoon a layer of the apple purée into the bottom of a 600 ml (1-pint) glass dish or four small, stemmed wine glasses.
4. Add a layer of chocolate crumbs. Repeat the layers, ending with the crumbs.
5. Mix the yogurt and crème fraîche together. Spoon on top of the chocolate crumbs. Dust with a little cinnamon. Serve.

Variation
Stir a few lightly stewed raspberries into the apple purée and, for a speedier 'creamy' topping, use 2 small tubs of very-low-fat raspberry yogurt. Add 1 Point per serving.

Cook's note
When there is a glut of cooking apples, purée and freeze in handy pack sizes, to suit your needs. Do not sweeten until thawed, just in case the apples are going into a savoury recipe. (Use artificial sweetener, if necessary.)

Jamaican Meringue Gâteau

Points per serving: 3
Total Points per recipe: 24

Serves: 8
Preparation time: 20 minutes
Cooking time: 45 minutes
Freezing: recommended
Calories per serving: 100

A special occasion dessert for entertaining: it can be prepared well in advance, so you can enjoy the occasion too!

4 egg whites
175 g (6 oz) light brown sugar
1 teaspoon cornflour
25 g (1 oz) toasted hazelnuts,
    chopped
200 g (7 oz) low-fat plain
    fromage frais, chilled
50 g (1³/₄ oz) preserved ginger,
    chopped finely, plus
    1 tablespoon ginger syrup
225 g (8 oz) fresh pineapple
    slices, chopped
1 tablespoon demerara sugar

1. Preheat the oven to Gas Mark 3/170°C/320°F. Line the bases of two 20 cm (8-inch) sandwich tins with non-stick baking parchment.
2. Using an electric whisk, whisk the egg whites in a grease-free bowl, until stiff. Add half the sugar and whisk again. Using a large metal spoon, fold in gently the remaining sugar, with the cornflour and hazelnuts.
3. Divide the meringue between the tins, spread evenly to the edges of the tin. Bake for 45 minutes. Turn off the oven and allow the meringue to cool in the oven.
4. Put the chilled fromage frais into a bowl. Fold in the ginger and the syrup. Fold in the chopped pineapple. Cover and chill until required.
5. Carefully peel off the parchment paper. Sandwich the two meringues with the pineapple and fromage frais. Sprinkle on the demerara sugar. Serve.

Variations

Replace the stem ginger and syrup with a tablespoon of rum and 2 teaspoons of icing sugar. Use 210 g (7 oz) canned pineapple in natural juice, drained and chopped, instead of the fresh pineapple.

Replace the pineapple with 3 medium-size bananas, sliced thinly. Add 1 Point per serving.

Crunchy Mallow Apples

Points per serving: 5¹/₂
Total Points per recipe: 22

Serves: 4
Preparation and cooking time:
20 minutes
Freezing: not recommended
Calories per serving: 390

I remember a similar pudding to this one at school – and always going back for seconds! Here is a much healthier alternative.

550 g (1 lb 5 oz) cooking
    apples, sliced
55 g (2 oz) light brown sugar
150 g (5¹/₂ oz) very-low-fat
    plain fromage frais
150 ml (¹/₄ pint) low-fat plain
    Bio-yogurt
1 tablespoon golden syrup
150 g (5¹/₂ oz) white
    marshmallows
115 g (4 oz) cornflakes

1. Gently cook the apples with the sugar and 2 tablespoons of water, until softened. Cool and beat until smooth. Pour into a 600 ml (1-pint) serving dish.
2. Mix together the fromage frais and yogurt and spread over the apples.
3. In a non-stick saucepan, gently melt together the syrup and marshmallows, stirring continuously, until the marshmallows have dissolved. Remove from the heat and stir in the cornflakes. Quickly spread over the fromage frais and yogurt.
4. Chill for 15 minutes before serving.

Variation

Replace the apples with 450 g (1 lb) of stewed gooseberries. Add ¹/₂ Point per serving.

178

Mango Sherbet with Passion Fruit

Points per serving: 2½
Total Points per recipe: 10
Serves: 4
Preparation time: 15 minutes
+ 4 hours freezing
Freezing: recommended
Calories per serving: 145

Mango has a perfumed flavour and a warm, tropical colour. Choose a ripe fruit with a rosy pink skin.

2 mangoes
2 tablespoons lime juice
150 ml (¼ pint) low-alcohol white wine
1 egg white
55 g (2 oz) caster sugar
2 passion-fruit, to serve

1. Peel the mangoes and, using a small sharp knife, cut away as much flesh as possible from the large stone. Purée the flesh with the lime juice and wine in a liquidiser or food processor.
2. In a clean, grease-free bowl, whisk the egg white until it forms soft peaks. Add the sugar and continue to whisk until stiff.
3. Fold the meringue mixture into the mango purée. Transfer to a rigid plastic container. Cover and freeze for 4 hours.
4. Transfer the mango sherbet to the refrigerator 10 minutes before serving, to allow it to soften slightly. Halve the passion-fruit and scoop out the sweet pulp and seeds.
5. Serve the mango sherbet in individual glass dishes, with a spoonful of passion-fruit drizzled over the top.

Ⓥ if using a free-range egg

Meringue Kisses

Points per serving: 1½
Total Points per recipe: 22½
Makes: 15
Preparation time: 15 minutes
Cooking time: 1½ hours
Freezing: not recommended
Calories per serving: 80

Light, crisp hazelnut meringue shells, with a fresh creamy filling: enjoy them as a dessert, with fresh raspberries or apricots, or as a tea-time treat.

For the meringues:

3 egg whites
125 g (4½ oz) caster sugar
25 g (1 oz) hazelnuts, roasted and ground
1 tablespoon cocoa powder, sifted

For the filling:

1 teaspoon instant coffee
3 tablespoons whipping cream
200 g (7 oz) low-fat plain fromage frais
2 teaspoons icing sugar, sifted

1. Line two baking sheets with non-stick baking parchment. Preheat the oven to Gas Mark 1/140°C/275°F.
2. Whisk the egg whites in a large, grease-free bowl, until stiff. Gradually whisk in the caster sugar, until the egg whites are stiff and glossy.
3. Gently fold in the hazelnuts and cocoa powder. Spoon the egg white into a piping bag fitted with a plain nozzle and pipe 30 small swirls on the baking sheets. (Alternatively, use two teaspoons to form small meringues.)
4. Cook for 1–1½ hours, until the meringues are dry and golden brown. Remove from the oven and leave to cool completely. Lift the meringues off the paper and transfer to an airtight container.
5. To make the filling, dissolve the coffee in 2 teaspoons of boiling water. Cool.
6. In a bowl, whisk together the whipping cream and fromage frais, until smooth and thickened. (Use an electric whisk to do this.) Whisk in the coffee and a little icing sugar, to sweeten. Chill until required.
7. Sandwich the meringues with the fromage frais filling. Pile up on a serving plate and dust with the remaining, sifted icing sugar.

Variation

Omit the coffee essence and replace the plain fromage frais with a raspberry- or apricot-flavoured fromage frais.

Cook's note

Use egg whites that are close to their best-before date; they will whisk up to a greater volume than very fresh egg whites.

Blackberry and Apple Meringue Pie *(page 171)*

Spicy Syllabub with a Honeycomb Crunch

A blend of spices, orange and sherry makes this an ideal dessert for Christmas, although it is delicious at any time of the year. Do not make it too far in advance.

2 tablespoons pale cream sherry
a pinch of ground cinnamon
a pinch of ground allspice
a pinch of ground cloves
grated zest and juice of 1 small
    orange
2 tablespoons caster sugar
    or honey
200 g (7 oz) very-low-fat plain
    fromage frais
150 ml (¼ pint) double cream
4 'fun-size' chocolate and
    honeycomb bars, e.g.
    Crunchies

1. Place the sherry, spices, orange zest and juice and sugar in a small bowl. Mix well, cover and leave to infuse for 1 hour.
2. In a bowl, whisk together the fromage frais and cream, until smooth. Gradually add the infused sherry and spice mixture and whisk until slightly thickened.
3. Roughly crush the chocolate and honeycomb bars and place half in the bases of four small, stemmed glasses. Spoon on some 'syllabub' and top with the remaining honeycomb crumbs. Serve as soon as possible.

Variation

Replace the sherry with 1 tablespoon of brandy or orange liqueur.

Cook's note

Use 2 whole cloves in place of the ground cloves, but do remove them at the end of step 1.

Gooseberry and Strawberry Yogurt Fool

My grandmother always used to make a gooseberry and strawberry pie – a wonderful combination of fruits. Try them in this creamy fool.

225 g (8 oz) gooseberries,
    topped and tailed
1 tablespoon clear honey
225 g (8 oz) strawberries,
    hulled
200 ml (7 fl oz) low-fat plain
    yogurt
artificial sweetener, to taste
a few drops of edible green food
    colouring (optional)
1 sachet of gelatine crystals
4 strawberries, to decorate

1. Place the gooseberries in a small saucepan, with 2–3 tablespoons of water, and simmer for 10 minutes or until the fruit has softened and most of the water has evaporated. Purée the gooseberries in a liquidiser or food processor. Sieve into a bowl. Stir in the honey.
2. Purée the strawberries; then sieve into another bowl.
3. Divide the yogurt between the two fruit purées and mix well. Sweeten the purées, to taste, with artificial sweetener and add a few drops of green colouring, if you like, to the gooseberry purée.
4. Put about 3 tablespoons of water in a cup. Sprinkle in the gelatine. Either stand the cup in a saucepan of simmering water or place it in the microwave on a defrost setting for 1–2 minutes. Once the gelatine has dissolved, stir for a few minutes, to cool it a little, and then whisk equal quantities into the 2 fruit purées. Leave to stand, until just beginning to set.
5. Divide half of the gooseberry fool between four stemmed wine glasses. Carefully, spoon on the strawberry purée. Use a cocktail stick to create a marbled effect between the two layers. Finally, spoon on the remaining gooseberry fool. Repeat the swirl effect.
6. Chill for 1 hour, until lightly set. Decorate each fool with a strawberry, thinly sliced and fanned out.

Ⓥ if using agar-agar instead of gelatine

Black Forest Sundae

Always a spectacular dessert and, if you have the Points to spare, crown it with a squirt of canned spray cream!

350 g (12 oz) canned pitted
    black cherries in syrup
1 teaspoon arrowroot
4 ready-made meringue nests,
    crushed coarsely
4 × 60 g (2 oz) scoops of Weight
    Watchers from Heinz
    Chocolate Swirl Iced
    Dessert

1. Strain the black cherries, reserving the syrup. In a small bowl, dissolve the arrowroot in a tablespoon of the syrup. Put the rest of the syrup in a small saucepan and bring to the boil. Pour on to the arrowroot, stirring constantly, and then return to the saucepan and simmer until the sauce has thickened and become clear.
2. Stir the cherries into the syrup. Leave to cool. Cover and chill until required.
3. Spoon some cherries into the bottom of four small sundae or glass dishes, followed by a layer of meringue. Spoon some ice cream on to the meringue and top with a final layer of sauce. Serve immediately.

Variation

For an alcoholic kick, add 2 teaspoons of kirsch or brandy at step 2. A pub measure of 25 ml is 1 Point.

Cranberry, Blueberry and Orange Terrine

4 medium-size oranges
150 g (5½ oz) fresh blueberries
1 sachet of gelatine crystals
300 ml (½ pint) cranberry
    juice

To decorate:

1 tablespoon blueberries
fresh mint leaves

1. Line a 450 g (1 lb) loaf tin with clingfilm.
2. Using a sharp knife, remove the peel and pith from the oranges. Slice them thinly. Layer the slices in the loaf tin, with the blueberries. Chill until required.
3. Put the gelatine into a heatproof jug and pour on a little of the cranberry juice. Bring the remaining cranberry juice to the boil in a small pan. Pour this on to the spongy gelatine, whisking continuously until the gelatine is completely dissolved.
4. Slowly, pour the cranberry juice over the layered fruit, gently shaking the tin once or twice to fill any air holes with juice. Refrigerate for 4–6 hours, or until the terrine has set.
5. To serve, place a plate over the loaf tin and invert. The terrine will fall out. Remove the clingfilm. Decorate the terrine with a cluster of blueberries and a sprig of fresh mint.

Variation

Replace the blueberries with strawberries or seedless green grapes, halved.

Ⓥ if using agar-agar instead of gelatine

Lime Cheesecake Pie

Serves: 10
Preparation time: 15 minutes
+ 2 hours chilling
Freezing: recommended
Calories per serving: 160

This cheesecake uses packet jellies to flavour and set the filling. Experiment with the various flavours available.

40 g (1½ oz) hard margarine
8 digestive biscuits, crushed
1½ packets sugar-free lime jellies
2 eggs, separated
150 ml (¼ pint) skimmed milk
grated zest and juice of 2 limes
350 g (12 oz) diet cottage cheese, sieved
150 ml (¼ pint) Greek-style natural yogurt
1 tablespoon caster sugar
To decorate:
1 lime twist
fresh mint sprigs

1. Melt the margarine over a low heat, add the biscuit crumbs and stir to coat evenly. Sprinkle them into a 23 cm (9-inch), shallow, open pie plate and press down, to form an even layer. Chill while you prepare the filling.
2. Using scissors, cut the jelly into cubes and gently heat, with 3 tablespoons of water, until dissolved. Do not boil.
3. In a bowl, beat the egg yolks and milk. Whisk in the jelly and return to the pan. Heat, stirring, for a few minutes. Remove from the heat and stir in the lime zest and juice. Cool, until just beginning to set.
4. Beat in the sieved cottage cheese and mix in the yogurt.
5. In a clean, grease-free bowl, whisk the egg whites until they form soft peaks. Add the sugar and whisk again. Whisk a tablespoon of the egg-white mixture into the cottage cheese mixture (this will slacken it). Fold in the remaining stiff egg whites.
6. Pour into the crumb case. Chill for 1–2 hours, or until set.
7. Decorate with a twist of fresh lime and fresh sprigs of mint.

Baked Austrian Cheesecake

Serves: 10
Preparation time: 15 minutes
Cooking time: 40 minutes
Freezing: recommended
Calories per serving: 185

Baked cheesecakes have a wonderful rich texture so you only need a small slice! This is an all-in-one method – quick to make and even quicker to disappear.

For the base:
40 g (1½ oz) hard margarine
6 digestive biscuits, crushed
For the filling:
400 g (14 oz) low-fat soft cheese
400 g (14 oz) very-low-fat plain fromage frais
3 eggs
grated zest and juice of 1 lemon
1 tablespoon plain flour
artificial sweetener, to taste
2 tablespoons sultanas
1 teaspoon ground cinnamon

1. Preheat the oven to Gas Mark 3/170°C/320°F. Line a 20 cm (8-inch), loose-bottomed cake tin with non-stick baking parchment or greaseproof paper.
2. Melt the margarine over a low heat, add the biscuit crumbs and stir to coat evenly. Sprinkle them into the cake tin and press down, to form an even layer. Chill whilst preparing the filling.
3. Place the soft cheese, fromage frais, eggs, grated lemon zest and juice and flour in a food processor and process until light and creamy. (Alternatively, use electric hand-held beaters.) Add artificial sweetener, to taste, and stir in the sultanas. Pour over the biscuit base. Bake for about 40 minutes.
4. Switch the oven off, open the door slightly and let the cheesecake cool completely.
5. Sieve the cinnamon over the surface just before serving.

Variation
For a chocolate cheesecake, replace the lemon zest and sultanas with 2 tablespoons of unsweetened cocoa powder, dissolved in 2 tablespoons of hot water.

Cook's note
An apricot or black-cherry sauce would be a delicious accompaniment. Drain and purée 410 g (14 oz) of canned fruits in natural juice. Add a little artificial sweetener, to taste.

Ⓥ if using free-range eggs

Poached Nectarines with Fromage Frais

Points per serving: 2
Total Points per recipe: 4

Serves: 2
Preparation time: 10 minutes + chilling
Freezing: not recommended
Calories per serving: 205

2 nectarines
1 tablespoon caster sugar
pared zest of 1/2 lemon
200 g (7 oz) low-fat plain
    fromage frais
fresh mint sprigs, to decorate

1. Place the nectarines in a bowl, cover with boiling water and leave for 1 minute. Drain, peel off the skins, halve and stone. Cut each half into 3 pieces. Reserve 2 segments for decoration.

2. Place the sugar, lemon zest and 100 ml (3½ fl oz) of water in a small pan. Bring to a rapid boil, stirring, until the sugar has dissolved and becomes syrupy. Add the nectarines and cook over a low heat for 5 minutes, shaking the pan occasionally.

3. Spoon 3 pieces of nectarine and some juice into the base of each sundae dish, cover with half the fromage frais, then top with the remaining fruit and juice and finish with the rest of the fromage frais.

4. Slice the reserved wedges and use to decorate. Top with mint sprigs. Serve well chilled.

Variation

Use 2 peaches or 6 fresh apricots, instead of nectarines.

Coffee Crème Caramels

Points per serving: 3
Total Points per recipe: 12

Serves: 4
Preparation time: 15 minutes
Cooking time: 35 minutes
Freezing: not recommended
Calories per serving: 170

Save up enough Points and indulge in a delicious pudding – a treat to look forward to at the end of the day, and perfect too, for entertaining.

100 g (3½ oz) granulated
    sugar
300 ml (1/2 pint) semi-skimmed
    milk
2 teaspoons instant-coffee
    granules
2 eggs, beaten
1 tablespoon brandy

1. Preheat the oven to Gas Mark 3/170°C/325°F.

2. Place 75 g (2¾ oz) of sugar in a small saucepan, with 100 ml (3½ fl oz) cold water. Heat gently, stirring, until the sugar has dissolved. Bring to a steady, gentle boil and allow the syrup to bubble. Do not stir, but watch the syrup turn a dark golden colour.

3. Carefully and quickly pour the caramel into the four ramekin dishes (about 125 ml/4 fl oz capacity). Stand the ramekin dishes in a shallow roasting tin.

4. Gently heat the milk and coffee in a small saucepan. In a bowl, whisk together the eggs, remaining sugar and brandy, until light and fluffy.

5. Pour the warm milk on to the egg mixture, whisking continuously. Strain the custard into a jug and then divide between the ramekin dishes. Cover each with a small piece of foil.

6. Pour enough hot water into the roasting dish to fill it to a depth of about 2.5 cm (1 inch). Carefully transfer the roasting dish to the oven.

7. Bake for 35 minutes, or until the custard is lightly set. Remove from the roasting dish to cool; then chill for several hours or, preferably, overnight before turning out on to individual dessert plates.

Variation

Replace the coffee and brandy with vanilla essence, to taste.

Ⓥ if using free range-eggs

Baked Austrian Cheesecake *(page 183)*
Cappuccino Floats *(page 186)*

Raspberry, Apple and Blueberry Pudding

A combination of raspberries, blueberries and apples makes a nice alternative to the traditional summer berries used in this traditional dessert. Use slightly stale bread for best results.

225 g (8 oz) blueberries
125 g (4¹/₂ oz) blackcurrants or
*   blackberries*
1 large Bramley apple, sliced
*   thinly*
75 g (2³/₄ oz) caster sugar
225 g (8 oz) raspberries
1 tablespoon crème de cassis
8 medium-size slices of white
*   bread, crusts removed*

1. Place the blueberries, blackcurrants or blackberries and apple in a heavy-based saucepan, with the sugar. Heat gently, stirring occasionally, for 5–10 minutes or until the fruits release their juices and the sugar has dissolved.
2. Add the raspberries and crème de cassis. Leave to cool.
3. Cut two circles of bread the same diameter as a 750 ml (1¹/₂-pint) pudding basin. Cut the remaining slices in half.
4. Line the bottom of the basin with one of the bread circles; then arrange the bread slices around the sides. Spoon the fruit in; then top with the second bread circle.
5. Cover with clingfilm and place a saucer small enough to fit inside the basin on top. Weigh down the saucer with tins from the storecupboard. Refrigerate overnight.
6. To serve, carefully unmould the pudding on to a deep serving plate.

Variation
Replace the blueberries and raspberries with blackberries and redcurrants.

Cook's note
Place the weighted basin on a tray or large plate, to catch any juices that overflow.

Cappuccino Floats

These instant puddings resemble frothy cappuccino coffees!

2 teaspoons instant-coffee
*   granules*
300 g (10¹/₂ oz) low-fat plain
*   fromage frais*
1 tablespoon icing sugar, sifted
75 g (2³/₄ oz) dark chocolate,
*   chilled*

1. Dissolve the coffee in 2 teaspoons of hot water. Mix with the fromage frais and icing sugar.
2. Using a potato peeler or coarse grater, shave off 25 g (1 oz) of chocolate curls. Put aside. Chop the remaining chocolate in a liquidiser or grate it finely.
3. Spoon half the fromage frais into four small ramekin dishes. Sprinkle over most of the chocolate. Add a final layer of fromage frais and sprinkle with the remaining chocolate.
4. Decorate with the chocolate curls. Chill until required.

Cakes and Bakes

1,2,3 Success Plus brings you a diet that's easy to follow and does not deprive you of those special treats we all find hard to resist, such as Double Chocolate Chip Cookies (see page 203) or Microwave Muesli Bars (see page 199).

All the delicious recipes in this chapter take advantage of the healthiest of ingredients, including reduced-calorie spreads, yogurts and creams. Enjoy them at their freshest and you will not need to add anything extra.

Traditional favourites are made with less sugar and fat than the standard recipes – who can say no to a slice of Banana and Honey Loaf? (see page 194).

Although low fat spreads do not work well in creamed sponge cake mixes, they are easier to incorporate into rubbed-in cakes, such as Pineapple and Coconut Loaf (see page 193). Frostings and creamy fillings are delicious made with low-fat plain fromage frais or low-fat soft cheese.

Lots of these recipes are ideal for the family's lunch boxes; a slice of Mixed Fruit Teabread or a Sticky Date and Oat Flapjack is a welcome accompaniment to the afternoon teabreak – and you know you are in control of the number of Points you are eating (see pages 193 and 202).

Children and adults will love the savoury and sweet muffins. Try a freshly baked Cranberry and Banana Muffin (see page 190) for breakfast, perhaps, or how about warm Welsh Griddle Cakes (see page 190) by the fireside on a cold winter's day?

Experiment once you have found a favourite recipe by changing the flavour: add some ground ginger or lemon zest to a tealoaf, perhaps, or substitute an alternative fruit.

For special occasions, try Strawberry Mousse Gâteau (see page 199), or adapt Strawberries and Cream Sponge (see page 198) to a swiss roll filled with low-sugar jam or fruit purée.

1

2

3

4

5

6

7

8

Chapter 9

Mushroom and Ham Muffins

Points per muffin: 2
Total Points per recipe: 24

Makes: 12
Preparation and cooking time:
30 minutes
Freezing: recommended
Calories per muffin: 140

Ideal for a brunch, the lunch box or teatime, these muffins will disappear very quickly!

350 g (12 oz) self-raising flour
1 teaspoon baking powder
1/2 teaspoon salt
50 g (1³/4 oz) low-fat spread or half-fat butter
85 g (3 oz) button mushrooms, chopped
50 g (1³/4 oz) ham, chopped
1 tablespoon chopped fresh chives or parsley
2 eggs
225 ml (8 fl oz) skimmed milk
salt and freshly ground black pepper

1. Preheat the oven to Gas Mark 6/200°C/400°F. Lightly spray 12 deep muffin tins, or line a patty tin with 12 muffin cases.
2. Put the flour, baking powder and salt in a bowl (or use a food processor). Rub the spread or butter in, until the mixture is crumbly. (Do not over-handle the soft spread – using a fork may help.)
3. Stir in the mushrooms, ham and chopped herbs. Season with salt and pepper.
4. Mix together the eggs and milk and pour on to the dry ingredients. Mix thoroughly.
5. Divide the mixture between the cases. Bake for 20 minutes, or until well risen, firm and golden.
6. Leave for 5 minutes before transferring to a wire rack to cool. These are best served warm.

Variation

Replace the ham with 50 g (1³/4 oz) of grated half-fat Cheddar or Edam cheese.

Cottage Cheese, Celery and Walnut Teabread

Points per slice: 3
Total Points per recipe: 30

Makes: 10 slices
Preparation time: 10 minutes
Cooking time: 1 hour
Freezing: recommended
Calories per slice: 170

An old-fashioned recipe, probably devised in the mid-nineteenth century, when breads relied on the newly acquired raising agents other than yeast to give them a lift. This is delicious served warm with Baked Tomatoes with Sweetcorn and Mozzarella (see page 43) or Grilled Asparagus, with Onion and Herb Dressing (see page 82) and salads. Good in the lunch box, with Marmite, and served with soups.

225 g (8 oz) plain cottage cheese
75 g (2³/4 oz) light brown soft sugar
3 eggs, beaten
225 g (8 oz) self-raising flour
1 teaspoon baking powder
2 celery sticks, chopped finely
9 walnut halves, chopped finely
salt

1. Preheat the oven to Gas Mark 4/180°C/350°F. Line a 900 g (2 lb) loaf tin with baking parchment or greaseproof paper.
2. Sieve the cottage cheese into a bowl. Add the sugar and eggs. Cream until light (use an electric hand-held whisk or rotary beaters to do this).
3. Sieve the flour, baking powder and a pinch of salt, on to the creamed mixture and fold in. Add the celery and walnuts.
4. Spoon into the prepared tin. Bake for 1 hour, until well risen and golden brown. Cool in the tin for 5 minutes before turning out on to a wire rack, to finish cooling. Slice and serve fresh.

Variation

For a less savoury bread, use cottage cheese with pineapple and omit the celery.

Cook's note

Speed up the method by using a food processor to chop the walnuts and cream the cheese, sugar and eggs.

Ⓥ if using free-range eggs

Herby Cheese Loaf

Points per serving: 4
Total Points per recipe: 24

Serves: 6
Preparation time: 10 minutes
+ 50 minutes proving
Cooking time: 20 minutes
Freezing: recommended at end of step 3
Calories per serving: 130

Similar to the Italian bread foccacia, this delicious bread can be eaten with soups or as an accompaniment to salads and starters. It is delicious eaten with a dip, too.

280 g (10 oz) bread or pizza-
*   base mix*
4 teaspoons olive oil
2 garlic cloves, crushed
1 teaspoon dried thyme
1 teaspoon dried rosemary or
*   oregano*
2 tablespoons chopped fresh
*   parsley and/or chives*
100 g (3¹/₂ oz) half-fat Cheddar
*   cheese, grated*
coarse sea salt (optional)

1. Lightly grease a large baking tray with low-fat cooking spray.
2. Make up the bread mix according to the pack directions, adding 2 teaspoons of olive oil, the garlic and the herbs with the liquid.
3. Knead to form a dough. Work in the grated cheese, just until the dough is smooth. Turn out on to a lightly floured surface and press out to a 20 cm (8-inch) circle. Transfer to the baking tray. Brush with the remaining olive oil. Prick the bread with a fork all over and then leave to 'prove', or rise, for 50 minutes. Preheat the oven to Gas Mark 7/220°C/425°F.
4. Just before baking, sprinkle a little coarse sea salt over the surface, if you like. Bake for 15–20 minutes until golden.
5. Cut into six wedges and eat freshly baked.

Variation
Try your own favourite mix of herbs, or add caraway seeds or a little chopped onion.

Cook's note
If cooking from frozen, allow 30 minutes at Gas Mark 6/200°C/400°F

Weight Watchers note
If you prefer, replace the half-fat Cheddar cheese with 55 g (2 oz) of extra-mature Cheddar cheese.

Ⓥ if using vegetarian cheese

Yogurt and Orange Scones

Points per scone: 3
Total Points per recipe: 24

Makes: 8
Preparation time: 10 minutes
Cooking time: 40 minutes
Freezing: recommended before baking
Calories per scone: 210

Cut into wedges and serve warm, with a thin spread of reduced-calorie strawberry jam. The yogurt helps keep the scone moist, so you won't need to spread butter on it!

450 g (1 lb) plain flour
2 teaspoons salt
1 teaspoon baking powder
¹/₄ teaspoon bicarbonate of soda
¹/₄ teaspoon ground cinnamon
2 teaspoons light brown soft
*   sugar*
finely grated zest of 1 orange
150 ml (¹/₄ pint) low-fat plain
*   Bio-yogurt*

1. Preheat the oven to Gas Mark 5/190°C/375°F. Line a baking sheet with non-stick baking parchment.
2. Sift the flour, salt, baking powder, bicarbonate of soda, cinnamon and sugar into a bowl. Stir in the orange zest, yogurt and about 150 ml (¹/₄ pint) of cold water, to bind to a smooth, soft, but manageable dough.
3. Knead the dough lightly on a floured surface and shape into a 15 cm (6-inch) round. Mark into 8 wedges.
4. Bake for 35–40 minutes or until the top is golden brown and the base sounds hollow when rapped with your knuckles.

Ⓥ

♦ **Savoury Breads, Scones and Muffins**

Welsh Griddle Cakes

Afternoon tea around the fire? These delicious cakes were originally cooked on bakestones or griddles over an open fire – a non-stick frying-pan is a good substitute.

225 g (8 oz) self-raising flour
a pinch of salt
40 g (1¹/₂ oz) caster sugar
¹/₄ teaspoon ground mixed spice
75 g (2³/₄ oz) sunflower
*   margarine*
85 g (3 oz) currants
1 egg, beaten

1. Sieve the flour, salt, sugar and spice into a bowl. Rub in the sunflower margarine, until the mixture resembles fine breadcrumbs.
2. Stir in the currants. Add the beaten egg and mix to a soft dough. (If it seems a little crumbly, add a few drops of water.)
3. Roll out on a lightly floured board to a thickness of 5 mm (¹/₄ inch). Use a plain 5 cm (2-inch) pastry cutter to cut out rounds. Re-roll any trimmings and cut out more rounds.
4. Dredge a heavy-based, flat frying-pan or griddle with flour. Heat the frying-pan and batch-cook the cakes on one side until golden brown. Turn over and continue cooking for 5–7 minutes, or until crisp and lightly browned. Serve warm, with reduced-calorie jam.

Ⓥ if using vegetarian margarine
and a free-range egg

Cranberry and Banana Muffins

What a treat for breakfast or a weekend tea – these light, moist muffins take no time at all to make – or to disappear!

50 g (1³/₄ oz) caster sugar
100 g (3¹/₂ oz) hard margarine
450 g (1 lb) ripe bananas,
*   mashed well*
2 eggs, beaten
225 g (8 oz) self-raising flour
1 teaspoon baking powder
150 g (5¹/₂ oz) fresh cranberries

1. Preheat the oven to Gas Mark 6/200°C/400°F. Line a patty-tin tray or bun tray with 12 paper muffin cases.
2. Using electric beaters, cream together the sugar and margarine, until light and fluffy. Add the bananas and eggs and whisk well.
3. Sift in the flour and baking powder and beat in quickly. Then fold in the cranberries.
4. Divide the mixture between the paper cases. Bake for 20–25 minutes or until well risen. Transfer to a wire rack, to cool.

Cook's note

Test to see whether cake and sponge mixtures are cooked – insert a skewer or sharp knife in the centre. It should come out clean and not wet.

Ⓥ if using vegetarian margarine
and free-range eggs

Hot Cross Buns

Serve these fresh at breakfast on Good Friday! Indeed, although they are traditionally eaten at Easter, there's no reason why you should not enjoy these spicy fruit buns throughout the year.

450 g (1 lb) strong white flour
1 teaspoon salt
1/2 teaspoon ground allspice
1/2 teaspoon ground cinnamon
1/2 teaspoon ground nutmeg
grated zest of 1 small lemon
1 sachet of easy-blend dried yeast
25 g (1 oz) sunflower
    margarine
300 ml (1/2 pint) tepid
    skimmed milk
2 tablespoons clear honey
1 egg, beaten
150 g (51/2 oz) mixed dried
    fruit, e.g. raisins, currants
    and mixed peel
1 teaspoon clear honey, to glaze

1. Sift the flour, salt, mixed spice, cinnamon and nutmeg into a large bowl. Stir in the lemon zest and yeast.
2. Whisk the margarine into the warm milk, until it melts. Add the honey and egg and beat together well.
3. Blend the tepid, milky mixture into the flour, with the dried fruits, mixing until you have a sticky dough. Turn this out on to a lightly floured surface and knead well, until the dough becomes smooth and elastic.
4. Place in a lightly floured bowl and cover with lightly oiled clingfilm. Leave in a warm place to 'prove' until it doubles in size, about 1 hour.
5. Lightly spray two baking sheets with canned spray cooking oil. Knock back the dough, divide into 12 equal pieces and knead each one for 2 minutes, before shaping into a bun. Space six buns on each sheet. Cover lightly with a piece of oiled clingfilm and leave in a draught-free area, to double in size again.
6. Preheat the oven to Gas Mark 6/200°C/400°F. Use a knife to cut a cross on each bun. Bake for 20–25 minutes, until well risen and golden.
7. Transfer to a wire cooling rack and glaze the hot cross buns by brushing a little warm clear honey over each one. Serve at once.

Variations

Add the grated zest of 1 orange instead of the lemon.

Replace the three individual spices with 2 teaspoons of ground mixed spice.

Cook's notes

Work in a warm kitchen with warm bowls and utensils. This will help speed up the dough preparation.

Make sure the milk is of a 'hand-hot' temperature, when added to the flour and yeast.

Weight Watchers notes

Serve these buns really fresh from the oven. There will be no need to add any butter or spread.

Prove at step 5, overnight in the refrigerator, so you can pop them straight into the oven to bake in time for breakfast!

Ⓥ if using vegetarian margarine and a free-range egg

Lemon and Raisin Drop Scones

125 g (41/2 oz) self-raising flour
a pinch of salt
a pinch of baking powder
1 tablespoon caster sugar
grated zest of 1 small lemon
1 egg, beaten
100 ml (31/2 fl oz) skimmed
    milk
55 g (2 oz) raisins

1. Sieve the flour, salt and baking powder into a bowl. Stir in the sugar and lemon zest. Beat in the egg and half the milk, to form a thick, creamy batter. Stir in the remaining milk and raisins.
2. Heat a large, heavy-based, non-stick frying-pan or griddle. Grease with spray-on oil.
3. Drop small rounds of scone mixture from a tablespoon into the pan. Cook over a moderate heat, until bubbles show on the scone surface. Carefully, turn over with a knife and cook for a further 1–2 minutes, or until the underside is golden.
4. Repeat until all the mixture is used up. Keep the scones warm in a clean, folded tea towel. Serve straight away.

Ⓥ if using a free-range egg

Apricot and Ginger Teabread

A good, basic fruit cake and one you can vary to suit. Try dried pears or apples, instead of apricots. Add a few walnuts – it is easy to calculate the Points.

280 g (10 oz) ready-to-eat dried apricots, chopped finely
300 ml (½ pint) strong tea
25 g (1 oz) preserved stem ginger, chopped
225 g (8 oz) plain flour
2 teaspoons baking powder
125 g (4½ oz) soft dark brown sugar
1 egg, beaten
1 teaspoon ground mixed spice

1. Place the apricots in a bowl and cover with the tea. Soak for 2 hours, stirring occasionally.
2. Line a 900 g (2 lb) loaf tin with baking parchment or greaseproof paper. Preheat the oven to Gas Mark 4/180°C/350°C.
3. Add all the remaining ingredients to the soaked apricots. Mix together well. Turn into the tin. Brush with 2 tablespoons water.
4. Cook for 1 hour, or until firm to the touch. An inserted knife should come out clean. (You may need to cover the cake with greaseproof paper after 40 minutes, to prevent further browning.)
5. Leave to cool in the tin for 10 minutes before transferring to a wire rack to cool completely. Store in an airtight container.

Cook's note

Use a fruit tea, such as mango or lemon verbena, to soak the apricots in.

Ⓥ if using a free-range egg

Pineapple and Coconut Loaf

175 g (6 oz) self-raising flour
½ teaspoon ground cinnamon or ground mixed spice
50 g (1¾ oz) low-fat spread
50 g (1¾ oz) caster sugar
125 g (4½ oz) canned pineapple pieces in natural juice
2 eggs, beaten
25 g (1 oz) desiccated coconut

1. Preheat the oven to Gas Mark 2/150°C/300°F. Line a 450 g (1 lb) loaf tin.
2. Sieve the flour and spice into a large bowl. Add the low-fat spread and rub it in, using a fork or cool fingertips, until the mixture resembles breadcrumbs. Stir in the sugar.
3. Drain the pineapple, reserving 1 tablespoon of the juice.
4. Beat the eggs into the flour mix, with the pineapple juice. Fold in the pineapple pieces and the coconut.
5. Spoon the mixture into the cake tin and bake for 40–45 minutes, or until well risen and firm to the touch.

Ⓥ if using vegetarian low-fat spread and free-range eggs

Mixed Fruit Teabread

This is very similar to malt bread – and improves with keeping. Serve sliced thinly, with a thin covering of low-fat spread or light cream cheese.

225 g (8 oz) mixed dried fruit
175 g (6 oz) soft brown sugar
300 ml (½ pint) strong cold tea
1 egg, beaten
300 g (10½ oz) self-raising flour

1. In a large bowl, mix together the fruit, sugar and tea. Cover and leave to stand in a cool place overnight.
2. Preheat the oven to Gas Mark 3/170°C/320°F. Line a 450 g (1 lb) loaf tin with baking parchment or greaseproof paper.
3. Beat the egg and flour into the soaked fruit, until thoroughly mixed. Pour into the loaf tin and bake for 1¼–1½ hours. Cool in the tin before removing.
4. Wrap the cake in greaseproof paper or foil and store in an airtight container for at least 2 days before slicing.

Ⓥ if using a free-range egg

Banana and Honey Loaf

Points per slice: 3½
Total Points per recipe: 28

Makes: 8 slices
Preparation time: 10 minutes
Cooking time: 1 hour
Freezing: recommended
Calories per slice: 215

Don't throw away those black bananas. Here's a recipe that will transform them into a moist, delicious, fat-free cake! It's delicious with a little low-fat greek-style natural yogurt.

225 g (8 oz) wholemeal flour
2 teaspoons baking powder
a pinch of salt
55 g (2 oz) dark molasses sugar
75 g (2¾ oz) clear honey
3 large, over-ripe bananas
75 g (2¾ oz) sultanas or
  raisins

1. Preheat the oven to Gas Mark 4/180°C/350°F. Line a 450 g (1 lb) loaf tin with greaseproof paper.
2. Sift the flour, baking powder and salt into a bowl.
3. Melt the sugar and honey together in a small saucepan. Leave to cool slightly.
4. Mash the bananas well. Mix all the ingredients together thoroughly (an electric mixer will make this effortless!).
5. Pour the mixture into the prepared tin. Bake for 1 hour, or until risen and firm to the touch and an inserted skewer comes out cleanly. Leave to cool in the tin.
6. When cold, store in an airtight container for up to a week. Serve warm or cold.

Spiced Apple Cake

Points per slice: 3½
Total Points per recipe: 56

Makes: 16 slices
Preparation time: 10 minutes
Cooking time: 1½ hours
Freezing: recommended
Calories per slice: 200

A moist spicy apple cake. Pop a slice into the lunch box or enjoy with a leisurely cup of tea!

350 g (12 oz) self-raising flour
1 teaspoon baking powder
2 teaspoons ground mixed spice
85 g (3 oz) low-fat spread
50 g (1¾ oz) butter
300 g (10½ oz) cooking apples,
  chopped
225 g (8 oz) sultanas
115 g (4 oz) light brown sugar
150 ml (¼ pint) skimmed milk
1 egg, beaten
1 tablespoon demerara sugar

1. Preheat the oven to Gas Mark 3/170°C/320°F. Line a 20 cm (8-inch) round cake tin with baking parchment or greaseproof paper.
2. Sieve the flour, baking powder and spice into a bowl. Rub in the low-fat spread and butter, until the mixture resembles fine breadcrumbs.
3. Fold in the apples, sultanas and brown sugar. Mix together the milk and egg and stir this into the cake mixture, to form a soft, dropping consistency.
4. Pour into the prepared cake tin. Sprinkle the surface with the demerara sugar. Bake for 1¼–1½ hours, until well risen and firm to the touch.
5. Leave to cool for a while in the tin, before transferring to a wire rack.

Cook's note
This cake improves if kept wrapped in foil for one day before serving.

Weight Watchers note
Slice and individually wrap the portions in freezer film and small polythene bags. Store in the freezer for up to one month – and take out a portion as required.

Ⓥ if using vegetarian low-fat spread and a free-range egg

Ⓥ

Lemon Drizzle Cake

Points per slice: 3½
Total Points per recipe: 42

Makes: 12 slices
Preparation time: 20 minutes
Cooking time: 1 hour
Freezing: recommended at end of step 3
Calories per slice: 195

Here's a moist citrussy cake – low in fat and absolutely scrumptious!

50 g (1¾ oz) butter
250 g (9 oz) caster sugar
grated zest of 1 lemon
250 g (9 oz) self-raising flour
1 teaspoon baking powder
1 egg
100 ml (3½ fl oz) skimmed
    milk
2 tablespoons low-fat plain
    yogurt
juice of 2 lemons

1. Preheat the oven to Gas Mark 4/180°C/350°F. Lightly grease and line the base of a 900 g (2 lb) loaf tin. In a bowl or food processor, whisk the butter and 200 g (7 oz) of sugar, until light and fluffy.
2. Add the lemon zest, the flour, baking powder, egg, milk and yogurt. Process until smooth. Spoon into the prepared tin and level out the top.
3. Bake for 55–60 minutes or until springy to the touch and browned. Cool in the tin for 10 minutes.
4. Place the juice of 2 lemons in a saucepan with the remaining sugar and 150 ml (¼ pint) of water. Bring to the boil, stirring until the sugar has dissolved; then leave to bubble for 4–5 minutes, until it becomes syrupy. Remove from the heat.
5. Pierce the cake in several places with a cocktail stick and then spoon the syrup over.

Variation
Replace the lemons with oranges, or make a St Clement's version, using one of each fruit!

Weight Watchers note
Remove temptation and freeze slices, until required. Wrap in freezer film and store in a rigid plastic box.

Passion Cake with an Orange Frosting

Points per slice: 5½
Total Points per recipe: 66

Makes: 12 slices
Preparation time:
Cooking time: 1¾ hours
Freezing: recommended for cake only
Calories per slice: 425

More commonly known as carrot cake, this moist, spicy cake has cut a few corners to save Points, without sacrificing flavour.

250 g (9 oz) wholemeal flour
1 teaspoon ground cinnamon
1 teaspoon grated nutmeg
1 teaspoon bicarbonate of soda
½ teaspoon salt
2 tablespoons desiccated coconut
12 walnut halves, chopped
250 g (9 oz) soft light brown
    sugar
125 ml (4 fl oz) sunflower oil
3 eggs, beaten
3 tablespoons milk
juice of 1 orange
300 g (10½ oz) carrots, grated
For the frosting:
125 g (4½ oz) low-fat soft cheese
100 g (3½ oz) very-low-fat
    plain fromage frais
1 tablespoon icing sugar, sifted
grated zest of 1 orange

1. Preheat the oven to Gas Mark 3/170°C/320°F. Line a 20 cm (8-inch), deep, loose-bottomed cake tin with baking parchment or greaseproof paper.
2. Sift together the flour, cinnamon, nutmeg, bicarbonate of soda and salt. Stir in the coconut and walnuts.
3. In another bowl, or large jug, whisk together the sugar, oil, eggs, milk and orange juice. Beat into the dry ingredients, with the carrots.
4. Spoon into the prepared tin and bake for 1½–1¾ hours, or until the cake is golden brown and has shrunk away from the tin slightly. Leave to cool in the tin for 10 minutes; then transfer to a wire rack to cool completely.
5. To make the frosting, beat together all the ingredients, until smooth. Chill well before frosting the cake. (You can split the cake in half and sandwich it with the frosting, or leave the cake whole and spread the frosting on top).
6. Store the cake in an airtight container in the refrigerator.

Cook's note
This carrot cake is delicious served warm as a pudding, with an orange-flavoured custard.

Ⓥ if using a free-range egg

Ⓥ

Strawberries and Cream Sponge

As light as a feather, this fatless sponge can also be adapted to a swiss roll (see Cook's note). Always serve them as freshly as possible.

3 eggs
100 g (3½ oz) caster sugar
100 g (3½ oz) plain flour
For the filling:
6 tablespoons Quark
6 tablespoons half-fat crème fraîche
artificial sweetener, to taste
1 tablespoon crème de cassis liqueur
250 g (9 oz) strawberries, hulled and sliced thinly

1. Preheat the oven to Gas Mark 5/190°C/375°F. Line the base of two 18 cm (7-inch) sandwich tins with a circle of baking parchment or greaseproof paper.
2. Bring a saucepan of water to the boil; then reduce the heat to a gentle simmer. Place the eggs and sugar in a large heatproof bowl and set this over the simmering water.
3. Using an electric whisk or hand-held rotary whisk, beat the mixture to a thick, pale cream foam. It should be thick enough to leave a trail for 2–3 seconds.
4. Remove the bowl from the heat and continue whisking for a couple of minutes. Sift in the flour and, using a metal spoon, lightly fold in the flour.
5. Pour the mixture into the prepared tins. Bake for 20 minutes or until the sponge is golden and just firm to the touch. Leave in the tin for 5 minutes before turning out on to a cooling rack to cool completely.
6. For the filling, mix together the Quark, crème fraîche and a little artificial sweetener, to taste. Fold in the cassis and strawberries. Sandwich the cakes with the filling. Dust the top with a little artificial sweetener. Serve as soon as possible.

Variation

Stir 1 tablespoon of brandy into the cream filling instead of crème de cassis.

Cook's note

If you prefer, bake the sponge in a 20 cm (8-inch), deep cake tin. Reduce the oven temperature to Gas Mark 3/170°C/320°F and extend the cooking time to 35 minutes.

Substitute cocoa powder for a tablespoon of the plain flour, to make a chocolate sponge.

For a swiss roll:

Proceed to step 4 and then pour the mixture into a 30 × 20 cm (12 × 8-inch), lined swiss roll tin. Bake for 8–10 minutes. When cooked, turn out on to a dampened tea-towel; carefully peel away the lining paper. Cover with a fresh sheet of baking parchment or greaseproof paper; then roll it up, using the tea-towel to lift and roll the sponge. Leave to cool, seam-down. Carefully, unroll and fill with 75 g (3 oz) low-fat plain fromage frais and 3 tablespoons low-calorie raspberry jam; or 300 ml (½ pint) whipped dessert topping and 2 tablespoons lemon curd; or 150 g tub of fruit-flavoured low-fat fromage frais. Remember to adjust the Points.

Strawberry Mousse Gâteau

A cross between an afternoon tea treat and an elegant dessert, this gâteau tastes as good as it looks.

20 cm (8-inch) fatless sponge cake (see Strawberries and Cream Sponge, page 198)
grated zest and juice of 1 orange
1 sachet of gelatine crystals
175 g (6 oz) strawberries
300 ml carton of low-fat ready-to-serve custard
150 g (5½ oz) very-low-fat plain fromage frais
1 teaspoon icing sugar, sifted

1. Split the sponge in half horizontally and lay one half in the base of the cake tin it was cooked in.
2. Place the orange zest and juice in a small basin. Sprinkle on the gelatine. Set the bowl in a pan of simmering water to dissolve. (Alternatively, heat it on a low setting in the microwave oven, until clear and liquid.)
3. Cut about 10 of the strawberries in half and arrange them around the edge of the cake tin, with their cut sides against the tin.
4. Purée the remaining strawberries in a liquidiser or food processor. Add the custard, fromage frais and gelatine and whisk to blend together for a few seconds.
5. Pour the mixture over the sponge base and cover with the second half-sponge. Chill until set.
6. Just before serving, remove the gâteau from the tin and decorate with a dusting of sieved icing sugar.

Variations

Replace the strawberries with 410 g (14 oz) canned apricot halves in natural juice, drained. Or try using a chocolate-flavoured sponge (see Cook's note, page 198) and replace the strawberries with 2 small bananas and replace the orange with a lemon. You may need to add a little sweetener, to taste.

Microwave Muesli Bars

Made in minutes, these nutritious bars are ideal for lunch boxes or as a satisfying snack at any time.

15 g (½ oz) butter
1 tablespoon honey
85 g (3 oz) muesli with no added sugar, e.g. Alpen
3 ready-to-eat dried apricots, chopped finely

1. Heat together the butter and honey in the microwave oven for 30–40 seconds or until melted. (Timings may vary according to the level of power selected.)
2. Stir in the muesli and apricots. Press the mixture evenly into a shallow, square microwaveable dish (about 15 × 10 cm/6 × 4 inches). Cook on full power for 1 minute.
3. Cut into four bars but leave the mixture to cool in the dish; then transfer to the refrigerator to firm up for 1 hour before removing from the dish.
4. Store in a cool place or the fridge in an airtight container.

Variation

Replace the apricots with 2 ready-to-eat prunes, chopped finely.

Cook's note

Individually wrap the bars and store in the freezer. They are then ideal to pop in the lunch box, thawing in time for 'elevenses'.

Weight Watchers note

Cut the bars in half again, to make 8 servings, reducing the Points per square to 1½.

Yuletide Mince Pies

Make up a batch of mince pies
well ahead of the Christmas
rush and freeze them in a rigid
plastic container at step 4. Just
take out the quantity you need
daily and bake them quickly, for
the freshest, tastiest mince pies.

225 g (8 oz) shortcrust pastry
    (see page 204)
225 g (8 oz) Yuletide
    Mincemeat (see opposite)
2 tablespoons skimmed milk
1 tablespoon icing sugar, sifted,
    to serve

1. Preheat the oven to Gas Mark
5/190°C/375°F. Roll half of the
pastry out thinly to about 3 mm
(¹/₈-inch) thick. Cut out 12 × 7.5 cm
(3-inch) rounds with a fluted
pastry cutter.
2. Gather up the scraps and
re-roll. Roll out the other half of
the pastry. Cut out 12 × 6 cm
(2¹/₂-inch) rounds with a fluted
pastry cutter.
3. Spray patty tins with some
canned spray cooking oil. Line
them with the larger circles of
pastry. Fill with the mincemeat.
Dampen the edges of the smaller
pastry circles and press into
position, to form lids.
4. Brush each pie with milk and
make a couple of snips in the
top, with scissors.
5. Bake for 20–25 minutes or
until golden brown. Transfer to a
wire tray to cool. Dust lightly with
icing sugar. Store the cooked
mince pies in an airtight container.

Yuletide Mincemeat

Commercially-bought mincemeat
has quite a high fat content, so
here is a fat-free version, which
will keep in jars for up to two
months. Perfect timing to use
up the glut of cooking apples.

225 g (8 oz) soft dark brown
    sugar
200 ml (7 fl oz) apple juice
900 g (2 lb) cooking apples,
    chopped
grated zest and juice of 1 lemon
¹/₂ teaspoon ground allspice
¹/₂ teaspoon ground cinnamon
¹/₂ teaspoon grated nutmeg
225 g (8 oz) currants
225 g (8 oz) raisins
55 g (2 oz) glacé cherries,
    halved
100 g (3¹/₂ oz) nibbed almonds
1 tablespoon calvados or brandy

1. In a large saucepan, dissolve
the sugar in the apple juice. Add
the apples and zest and juice of
the lemon. Bring to the boil; then
reduce the heat.
2. Add the remaining ingredients,
stir together thoroughly and then
cover tightly and simmer for 15
minutes. Turn off the heat and
leave for 15 minutes.
3. Give the mincemeat another
good stir and then pack into
sterilised, hot jars. Seal and label.

Cook's note
To sterilise the jars, first wash
them in very hot, soapy water and
rinse well. Dry carefully and then
put them upside-down in a low
oven to dry completely.

Strawberry Mousse Gâteau *(page 199)*
Chocolate Macaroons *(page 203)*

Almond Tuiles

Points per biscuit: 1
Total Points per recipe: 18

Makes: 18
Preparation time: 30 minutes
Cooking time: 5 minutes
Freezing: recommended
Calories per biscuit: 50

Tuile is the French word for 'tile' and these biscuits are, so called, because they resemble the shape of traditional French roof tiles – these lacy biscuits are delicious served with fresh fruit salads, or on their own.

50 g (1³/₄ oz) unsalted butter
finely grated zest of 1 lemon
  or orange
50 g (1³/₄ oz) icing sugar
1 tablespoon plain flour, sifted
50 g (1³/₄ oz) flaked almonds,
  roughly chopped

1. Preheat the oven to Gas Mark 7/220°C/425°F. In a mixing bowl, cream together the butter, orange or lemon zest and icing sugar, until pale and fluffy.
2. Mix in the flour and chopped almonds.
3. Line two large baking sheets with baking parchment or grease-proof paper. Place ¹/₂ tablespoons of the mixture, spaced well apart, on the sheets. Flatten each into a small disc.
4. Cook for 4–5 minutes, until they have spread and are golden. Remove from the oven. Cool for 1 minute then lift each biscuit off the tray, using a palette knife, and curl over a rolling pin to harden. Repeat until you have made 18 tuiles. Leave for a few minutes to become crisp; then slide off the rolling pin. Cool thoroughly. Store in an airtight container.

Cook's note

If the biscuits become too crisp to shape over the rolling pin, pop back in the oven for a few seconds, to soften.

Sticky Date and Oat Flapjacks

Points per flapjack: 2¹/₂
Total Points per recipe: 40

Makes: 16
Preparation time: 5 minutes
  + 15 minutes standing
Cooking time: 30 minutes
Freezing: recommended
Calories per flapjack: 135

These flapjack-style cakes are delicious served warm as a pudding, or cold as a tea-time or lunch-box treat.

225 g (8 oz) dried stoned dates,
  chopped
150 ml (¹/₄ pint) boiling water
1 teaspoon vanilla essence
150 g (5¹/₂ oz) low-fat spread
150 g (5¹/₂ oz) rolled oats
75 g (2³/₄ oz) soft brown sugar
6 tablespoons unsweetened
  apple juice
1 tablespoon sunflower seeds
1 tablespoon sesame seeds

1. Preheat the oven to Gas Mark 4/180°C/350°F. Line the base of a 20 cm (8-inch), square, shallow tin with greaseproof paper or baking parchment.
2. Place the dates in a heatproof bowl and pour on the boiling water. Leave to stand and soften for 15 minutes. Add the vanilla essence and beat to a smooth purée.
3. Gently melt the spread in a saucepan, or in a bowl in the microwave oven. Stir in the remaining ingredients. Mix well.
4. Spoon half of the oat mixture in the tin, pressing it down well with the back of a wooden spoon. Spread the date purée over the base and top with the remaining oat mixture.
5. Bake for 25–30 minutes or until the surface is golden. Allow the mixture to cool in the tin before cutting into 16 squares. Store in an airtight container.

Ⓥ if using vegetarian low-fat spread

Double Chocolate Chip Cookies

Points per biscuit: 1½
Total Points per recipe: 22½

Makes: 15

Preparation time: 10 minutes
+ 20 minutes standing

Cooking time: 12–15 minutes

Freezing: recommended

Calories per biscuit: 75

2 egg whites
175 g (6 oz) icing sugar
40 g (1½ oz) cocoa powder
2 teaspoons plain flour
a few drops of vanilla essence
55 g (2 oz) chocolate chips

1. Preheat the oven to Gas Mark 4/180°C/350°F. Line two baking sheets with baking parchment.
2. Whisk the egg whites in a large, grease-free bowl, until light and frothy, but not stiff. Gradually, sift in the icing sugar, cocoa powder and flour, whisking after each addition. Add a few drops of vanilla essence. Leave the mixture to stand for 20 minutes, to thicken.
3. Place 15 tablespoons of the mixture on the baking sheets. Dot with the chocolate chips.
4. Bake for 12–15 minutes until firm and cracked on the surface. Leave for 5 minutes before transferring to a wire rack to cool.

Variation
Use white chocolate chips.

Ⓥ if using free-range eggs

Cherry Coconut Chews

Points per biscuit: 1
Total Points per recipe: 20

Makes: 20

Preparation time: 10 minutes
+ 20 minutes standing

Cooking time: 10 minutes

Freezing: recommended

Calories per biscuit: 50

Chewy and delicious cookies – just enough to satisfy the sweet tooth without being too indulgent!

2 egg whites
125 g (4½ oz) caster sugar
4 teaspoons cornflour
55 g (2 oz) desiccated coconut
50 g (1¾ oz) glacé cherries, chopped finely

1. Preheat the oven to Gas Mark 4/180°C/350°F. Line two baking sheets with rice paper.
2. In a grease-free, clean bowl, whisk the egg whites until light and frothy. Stir in the sugar, cornflour and coconut. Leave the mixture to stand for 20 minutes.
3. Place 10 small desertspoon-fuls on each lined tray, allowing the mixture to spread slightly. Pop a cherry in the centre.
4. Bake for 10 minutes, until lightly browned. Leave to cool on the tray before breaking off the rice paper. Store in a airtight container.

Ⓥ if using free-range eggs

Melting Moments

Points per biscuit: 2
Total Points per recipe: 50

Makes: 25

Preparation time: 5 minutes

Cooking time: 15 minutes

Freezing: recommended

Calories per biscuit: 105

275 g (9½ oz) self-raising flour
75 g (2½ oz) butter
75 g (2¾ oz) low-fat spread
125 g (4½ oz) caster sugar
2 egg yolks
50 g (1¾ oz) cornflakes, crushed
7 glacé cherries, quartered

1. Preheat the oven to Gas Mark 4/180°C/350°F.
2. Place the flour, butter, low-fat spread, sugar and egg yolks in a bowl and mix to a soft dough.
3. Divide the dough into 25 portions. Form each into a ball and roll into the cornflakes, to coat lightly.
4. Line two baking sheets with baking parchment or greaseproof paper, space out the balls and press lightly with a damp fork. Top with a piece of cherry.
5. Bake for 15 minutes, until golden. Allow to cool slightly before lifting on to a cooling rack. Repeat with the remaining mixture. Store in an airtight container.

Ⓥ if using vegetarian low-fat spread and free-range eggs

Chocolate Macaroons

Points per macaroon: 1
Total Points per recipe: 16

Makes: 16

Preparation time: 10 minutes

Cooking time: 20 minutes

Freezing: not recommended

Calories per macaroon: 75

These make a lovely gift for a friend and, if she is on **1,2,3 Success Plus**, advise her of the Points per biscuit!

2 egg whites
50 g (1½ oz) ground almonds
175 g (6 oz) caster sugar
25 g (1 oz) ground rice or semolina
50 g (1½ oz) cocoa powder
a few drops of almond essence

1. Preheat the oven to Gas Mark 2/150°C/300°F. Line two baking trays with baking parchment or greasepoof paper.
2. Whisk the egg whites in a clean, grease-free bowl, until they are stiff and dry. Fold in the ground almonds, sugar, rice or semolina, cocoa powder and almond essence.
3. Spoon 8 teaspoonfuls of the mixture on to each lined tray. Smooth with the back of a spoon, to form circles.
4. Bake for 20 minutes. Leave to cool on the baking tray before lifting on to a wire rack.

Ⓥ if using free-range eggs

Melba Toast

Named after the famous Australian singer, Dame Nellie Melba, these crisp, thin toasts are delicious served very fresh, with pâtés, soups and first courses.

Simply toast 1 thin slice of white bread on both sides until golden. While hot, cut off the crusts. Lay your hand flat on top of the slice, cut through the toast horizontally to make 2 thinner slices, then pop the 2 slices back under the grill, to brown the freshly split sides.

Cook's note
Melba toast tends to curl whilst toasting. Take care if using a toaster – you may find a conventional grill easier.

Weight Watchers note
6 small, thin toasts = 1 Point.

Pancakes

> **Points per pancake: 1½**
> **Total Points per recipe: 12**
>
> Makes: 8
> Preparation time: 15 minutes
> Freezing: recommended
> Calories per pancake: 85

Why wait until Shrove Tuesday comes around to enjoy a pancake, with the endless choice of low-calorie savoury or sweet fillings?

125 g (4½ oz) plain flour
1 egg, beaten
300 ml (½ pint) skimmed milk
2 teaspoons sunflower oil
salt and freshly ground black
*   pepper (for savoury*
*   pancakes only)*

1. Sift the flour and seasoning into a bowl. Add the egg and half the milk. Whisk to a thick, smooth batter. Whisk in the remaining milk.
2. Place a small 20 cm (8-inch), non-stick frying-pan over a medium heat. When you can feel a steady heat rising, brush the surface of the pan with a little oil.
3. Pour one-eighth of the batter into the pan, whilst swirling the pan to distribute the batter evenly. Cook for about 30 seconds or until the surface has set and the underside is golden. Carefully flip over, with a fish slice or palette knife, and cook for a further 30 seconds. Remove.
4. To keep the pancakes warm and moist, stack between sheets of greaseproof paper and wrap in foil.

Variation
Fill savoury pancakes with cooked chicken or tuna in a tomato sauce, or try Bolognese sauce (see page 101) or Thai-Style Chicken and Potato Curry (see page 112). The fillings for Smoked Haddock and Mushroom Gougère (see page 129) or the Lentil and Carrot Cannelloni (see page 164) can also be easily adapted to savoury pancakes.

Cook's note
To freeze pancakes, first interleave each pancake with greaseproof paper and then wrap in freezer film. Pancakes will freeze successfully for three months.
Ⓥ if using free-range eggs

Shortcrust Pastry

> **Total Points per recipe: 16**
> **Makes: 115 g (4 oz)**
>
> Preparation time: 10 minutes
> + 30 minutes chilling
> Freezing: recommended
> Calories per batch: 830

115 g (4 oz) plain white flour
a pinch of salt
4 tablespoons hard margarine,
*   chilled*
4 teaspoons cold water

1. Sift the flour and salt together in a bowl. Add the margarine and rub in with your fingertips, until the mixture resembles fine breadcrumbs.
2. Mix in just enough water, to draw the mixture into a dough. Knead lightly, to form a smooth dough. Wrap and chill for 30 minutes before rolling out. (This helps to prevent shrinkage.)

Weight Watchers notes
Filo pastry is a low-fat alternative to shortcrust pastry. It is much more fragile when cooked, but lower in Points.

Rolling the pastry between two sheets of clingfilm will help prevent the dough from sticking to the board or rolling pin and help you to roll less pastry further!

Ⓥ if using vegetarian margarine

All-in-One White Sauce

300 ml (½ pint) skimmed milk, chilled
25 g (1 oz) low-fat spread
25 g (1 oz) plain flour
salt and freshly ground black pepper

1. Put the cold milk, low-fat spread and flour in a small saucepan and slowly bring to the boil, whisking all the time, until the sauce thickens and becomes smooth.
2. Simmer for a minute; then season to taste.

Variations

For a sweet sauce, replace the salt and pepper with artificial sweetener, to taste.

For a cheese sauce, add 50 g (1¾ oz) of grated Cheddar cheese. By choosing a mature or more strongly flavoured cheese, you can use even less. Add 5 Points.

For a mushroom sauce, add 115 g (4 oz) chopped button mushrooms at step 1.

For a herb sauce, stir in 4 tablespoons chopped fresh herbs, such as parsley, chives, and dill at step 2.

ⓥ if using vegetarian low-fat spread

Basic Chicken Stock

Home-made stock makes all the difference to the final flavour of casseroles, sauces and, in particular, soups. So, when you have the spare chicken carcass and time, reach for your largest saucepan and get simmering. It's easy!

1 chicken carcass
1 litre (1¾ pints) water
4 celery sticks, chopped
1 large onion, chopped
1 carrot, chopped
1 bay leaf
salt and freshly ground black pepper

1. Place all the ingredients in a large saucepan and bring to a steady simmer. Skim off any scum with a spoon.
2. Simmer very gently for 1½–2 hours. (Boiling will cause the stock to go cloudy.)
3. Strain the stock and allow to cool, then cover and refrigerate for 3 hours. During this time it will set slightly and fat will solidify on the surface. Remove the fat.

Variations

For beef or lamb stock, use the same method but substitute meat bones for the chicken carcass.

For fish stock, use the same method but simmer 450 g (1 lb) fish bones for 30 minutes.

For vegetable stock, use the same method, substituting a selection of vegetables of any kind (avoid very starchy ones, such as potatoes).

Cook's notes

Freeze stock in handy 300 ml (½ pint) portions or ice-cube trays.

If you have to rely on stock cubes, try to use the water in which you have cooked vegetables to dissolve the cubes. Go steady with added salt in the recipe. A tin of consommé is a good substitute for beef stock.

Index

208